POLITICA[L]
PHILOSOP[HY]
A complete introduction

Dr Phil Parvin & Dr Clare Chambers

'Phil Parvin and Clare Chambers have produced a state of the art textbook, which provides students with a comprehensive and bang up-to-date introduction to contemporary political philosophy. Topics are introduced in a clear and eminently readable fashion, using accessible real world examples whilst drawing on sophisticated scholarly literature. There is no comparable book which covers such a wide range of topics in such a student-friendly manner.'

Dr Daniel Butt, Lecturer in Political Theory, University of Bristol.

'A lively, accessible and engaging read. Comprehensive and well organized, it provides an updated account of key concepts in contemporary political philosophy, and highlights their relevance to political life in the 21st century. A valuable book for anyone taking their first steps in the world of political philosophy, or anyone who seeks to understand the normative challenges faced by our society today.'

Dr Avia Pasternak, Lecturer in Political Theory, University of Essex.

'Written in a clear and accessible style, it is an engaging introduction for those who are new to political philosophy and wish to think through some of its most important questions. In addition to offering outlines of key arguments, each chapter also contains a summary of main concepts, self-test questions, a wonderful selection of quotations and some attention-grabbing 'nuggets''

Dr Zosia Stemplowska, University Lecturer in Political Theory, University of Oxford.

First published in Great Britain in 2012 by Hodder & Stoughton. An Hachette UK company.

First published in US in 2012 by The McGraw-Hill Companies, Inc.

This edition published 2012

British Library Cataloguing in Publication Data: a catalogue record for this title is available from the British Library.

Library of Congress Catalog Card Number: on file.

10 9 8 7 6 5 4 3 2 1

Typeset by Cenveo Publisher Services.

Printed in Great Britain by CPI Group (UK) Ltd, Croydon, CR0 4YY.

Hodder & Stoughton policy is to use papers that are natural, renewable and recyclable products and made from wood grown in sustainable forests. The logging and manufacturing processes are expected to conform to the environmental regulations of the country of origin.

Hodder & Stoughton Ltd
338 Euston Road
London NW1 3BH
www.hodder.co.uk

Also available in ebook

For Harley and Caspar

Contents

Introduction: What is political philosophy?

Does the state have the right to tax its richer citizens in order to give to those who are worse off? How can we defend the idea that human beings have rights? How can we ensure equality between women and men? Do rich states have a moral obligation to give some of their wealth to poorer states? Should a democratic state follow the will of the majority, even if doing so would result in the persecution of minority groups?

Political philosophers ask questions like these – and attempt to answer them! Political philosophy interrogates our assumptions about politics, society and the relations between individuals. It is therefore different from other areas of political inquiry. Most political 'science' is *descriptive*: it seeks to describe and explain political phenomena through empirical data. Political philosophy, on the other hand, is primarily *prescriptive* rather than *descriptive*. Political philosophers may use the empirical evidence gathered by political scientists, but our aim is not to describe the world as it currently *is* but to determine how it *ought* to be. Political philosophy is *normative*: political philosophers are concerned not with what is efficient or economical, but with what would be morally right or wrong.

Political philosophy is *exciting* and *important*: as political philosophers we raise profound questions about the way we live our lives, the values that we hold, and the social and political institutions that regulate our lives. We ask *why* society is structured in the way that it is, and whether it should be structured differently; *why* we have the values that we do and whether they are the right ones; and *on what grounds* states, individuals and other organizations can justify their actions.

Political philosophy is also *challenging*. It requires us to think critically and deeply about issues that may seem settled or obvious or, alternatively, abstract and hard to grasp. In political philosophy we reason analytically about the nature of human beings, and about concepts such as freedom, equality, power, authority and justice. Members of liberal democratic states like Britain and the USA often take the meaning and value of these concepts for granted; political philosophy forces us to confront our assumptions.

Themes and structure

The book is split into two parts. In the first we discuss the meaning of some of the most fundamental concepts that we use to understand politics, the obligations individuals living in a society have toward one another, and the institutions that we create to regulate our public and private lives. The second part is devoted to a discussion of the different normative arguments which have divided Anglo-American political philosophers, and have served to shape the conduct of the discipline for the last half-century.

It is important to begin with conceptual analysis. It is too easy to assume that the meaning of fundamental concepts is settled simply because we are used to invoking them in a particular way. We are all used to appealing to ideas like freedom or equality or rights in political debate: such concepts provide the background context within which we debate more specific policies or government actions. But while we may be used to debating which policies are most in line with our most cherished ideals and values, it is not often that we go further and question these ideals and values themselves. What do we mean by freedom, or equality, or justice, or democracy? Why should we value these things? The fact that ideals like freedom and equality are widely supported in our public culture is not a good enough reason for valuing them: many practices and values, widely supported at one time or another by the citizens of liberal democratic states like Britain, have been subsequently rejected for being unjust; moreover, many just practices and values are not currently the subject of widespread agreement in liberal democratic states.

We need to know what ideas mean, and how they are justified, in order to know how important they are. This is crucial because we often have to choose between competing values. Should we prioritize freedom or equality, if they conflict? More fundamentally: how do we go about answering such a question? Similarly, how do we deal with the choice between security and civil liberties? And if we are forced to choose between respecting the rights of a child (for example, to receive an education which prepares them for an autonomous adult life) and the rights of parents (for example, to remove their children from formal education on the ground of religious beliefs), how are we to decide?

Some argue that the answers to these kinds of questions are provided by important documents or accepted practices: bills of rights, international agreements, constitutions and so on. But complex political questions cannot be resolved simply by recourse to legal precedents or constitutions.

Firstly, constitutions are particular to different nation-states and political regimes. The conceptual context set by the US constitution only holds for the US, and similarly the provisions embodied in the constitutions of Australia, Thailand, Iran, Britain and everywhere else only hold for those states.

Secondly, whether something is 'constitutional' and whether it is 'right' or 'just' are very different questions. Constitutions can be unjust, as can international agreements and other formalized political practices. Hence, we need deeper grounds than constitutions and international agreements if we are to know how to order our political lives. We need deeper grounds than constitutions and international agreements if we are to evaluate and (perhaps) criticize constitutions. We need normative debate about politics.

Thirdly, constitutions, international agreements and so on are themselves products of prior (and ongoing) philosophical, political and legal debate. True, we need a (conceptual, philosophical, moral) framework within which to undertake the difficult work of resolving complex questions about how to order our social and political lives, what institutions we need, why we need them, who should hold power, and what the limits of this power might be, and so on. We need a principled foundation of concepts and ideas that we can draw on in our discussions about specific questions. And, true, in the modern world these foundations tend to be provided by important documents like the Universal Declaration of Human Rights. But these documents are the distillation of years of philosophical debate about who we are and what kind of world we want to live in, and are themselves characterized by internal tensions and ambiguities. Constitutions, like international agreements, treaties and other formal documents which stipulate fundamental powers and responsibilities on the world stage, are works in progress.

While many people often use political concepts as if their meanings were settled, then, it is one of the duties of the political philosopher to explore the nature of political concepts and to challenge their validity. It is only having explored the nature of our basic political concepts, and the vocabulary that we use in our discussions about how to order our social and political lives, that we are able to move forward and form more concrete normative proposals about what politics should look like, what it should be about, and what we should expect from the institutions that we create.

We engage in this further normative debate in Part Two. We discuss the ways in which political philosophers have used normative concepts as the basis for arguments about the roles and responsibilities of social and political institutions, and the obligations that individuals have to one another.

Part Two begins by discussing utilitarianism (which was once the dominant approach to resolving normative questions about morality and politics) before introducing the canonical rejection of it provided by John Rawls in his ground-breaking work *A Theory of Justice* (1971), as well as his liberal alternative. Rawls's book remains the most important work in contemporary political philosophy. It effectively reinvented the Anglo-American tradition of political philosophy and showed that normative theorizing about politics was both possible and important. Rawls's work used the tools of analytic philosophy (its focus on clarity and logic) in order to present a ground-up defence of liberalism and the Enlightenment values of reason, individualism, freedom and equality on which it was based. In Part Two, we discuss in roughly thematic and chronological order some of the most important debates which emerged in the wake of Rawls's work and which continue to shape the discipline, from debates between libertarians and egalitarians about economic redistribution, inequality, and the role of luck, to issues concerning personal identity, community, the status of cultural and religious values in political life, the obligations that rich states may or may not be understood to have to poorer states, the obligations that currently living people may or may not have to those who lived before them or will live after them, and the very sources of morality and justice itself.

In doing so, we hope to encourage you to think more deeply, and in more detail, about the political world in which we find ourselves, about the values that we cherish, and the forms of behaviour that we take for granted as being right or appropriate. Philosophy is about the search for truth, and political philosophy is about the search for truth about the way we order our social and political lives: it is about subjecting accepted truths, and widely held assumptions, to rigorous examination in the interests of revealing new insights about them, including new strengths and weaknesses. It is about looking at the way we are governed, the institutions under which we live, the nature and distribution of power, wealth and status in a society, and the values which shape the political world, and asking: Is this how we should live? If so, why? And if not, how *should* we live?

Dig deeper

A.J. Ayer, *Language, Truth, and Logic* (London: Victor Gollancz, 1936).

Brian Barry, *Political Argument* (London: Routledge, 1965).

Isaiah Berlin, *The Proper Study of Mankind*, ed. Henry Hardy (London: Pimlico, 1998).

H.L.A. Hart, *The Concept of Law* (Oxford: Oxford University Press, 1961).

Robert Nozick, *Anarchy, State, and Utopia* (New York: Basic Books, 1974).

Phil Parvin, *Karl Popper* (London: Continuum Press, 2010).

Karl Popper, *Conjectures and Refutations* (London: Routledge & Kegan Paul, 1963).

John Rawls, *A Theory of Justice* (Cambridge, MA: Harvard University Press, 1971).

Bertrand Russell, *The History of Western Philosophy* (London: Routledge & Kegan Paul, 1946).

Quentin Skinner, *The Foundations of Modern Political Thought*, 2 vols, (Cambridge: Cambridge University Press, 1978).

Part One

Essential concepts

1

Freedom (1): Negative freedom

Freedom is one of the most important concepts in political philosophy. For many, the principal purpose of a legitimate political system is to protect the freedom of its citizens. Thus the majority of anglophone political philosophers agree that some form of *liberalism* is required. Liberalism seeks to maximize free choice for all individuals, but recognizes that freedom must have limits. As one of the founders of liberalism, John Locke, put it, *liberty* is distinct from *licence*: no one can do whatever they want all the time. The freedom of each individual must be balanced against the freedom of others. It also needs to be balanced against other values, such as equality, social stability and security. Thus liberty must be defended in the context of these other values.

The key is to work out which constraints on individual freedom are just. In other words, we need a normative theory about the requirements and limits of state action. But first we need to determine what freedom *is*. Is freedom merely the ability to make choices without external interference from the state or from other people? Or does freedom require particular circumstances: are things like poverty, lack of education, or social norms constraints on freedom?

In these first two chapters we discuss two ways of understanding freedom: negative freedom in this chapter and positive freedom in the next.

Isaiah Berlin's distinction between negative and positive liberty

Isaiah Berlin, in his famous lecture 'Two Concepts of Liberty' (1958), suggested that political philosophers throughout history have understood liberty in one of two ways: as a 'negative' or a 'positive' concept.

NEGATIVE LIBERTY

This is the idea that an individual is free in so far as they are able to act without interference from external bodies or forces. This, Berlin argued, was the idea of liberty shared by thinkers like Thomas Hobbes and John Locke, as well as by classical liberal thinkers like F.A. Hayek and Ludwig von Mises. It is 'negative' not in the sense that it is bad, but in the sense that it signifies the *absence* of restraints and tends to be defended by libertarians and classical liberals who argue for a minimal state and the protection of a private sphere of choice free from government intrusion. It is also associated with free markets, as free market thinking minimizes state intervention (for example, by minimizing the welfare state which requires coercive taxation).

> 'LIBERTY, or FREEDOME, signifieth (properly) the absence of Opposition; (by Opposition I mean externall Impediments of motion;) ... And according to this proper, and generally received meaning of the word, A FREE MAN, is he, that in those things, which by his strength and wit he is able to do, is not hindered to doe what he has a will to.'
> Thomas Hobbes, *Leviathan* (London: Penguin Classics, 1985 [1651]), pp. 261–2.

POSITIVE LIBERTY

According to this idea an individual is free if she is her own master, responsible for her own choices. She must be able to make those choices with reference to her own ideals and purposes, and to carry them out. This view of liberty is associated with thinkers like Jean Jacques Rousseau and emphasizes the communal nature of freedom: self-mastery requires, at least in part, membership of, and participation in, a political community. It is more wide-ranging in scope than negative freedom as it emphasizes not just the importance of *choice*, but also the *contexts* in which individuals make their choices. Not all choices are necessarily free choices; that is, social, economic and political factors can influence us and our choices in ways that may be fair or unfair. Consequently, to be free in a positive sense we might require that the state respect choices made in certain conditions and not others. For Berlin, this point meant that positive liberty was *dangerous*: it suggests that other people may be better placed to know when an individual is free than the individual herself. This, he thought, can justify coercion and lead to tyranny.

> *'Coercion is not [...] a term that covers every form of inability. If I say that I am unable to jump more than ten feet in the air, or cannot read because I am blind, or cannot understand the darker pages of Hegel, it would be eccentric to say that I am to that degree enslaved or coerced. Coercion implies the deliberate interference of other human beings within the area in which I would otherwise act.'*
>
> Isaiah Berlin, 'Two Concepts of Liberty' [1958], *The Proper Study of Mankind*, ed. H. Hardy (London: Pimlico, 1998), pp. 191–242, at p. 194.

Many political philosophers have criticized this distinction, but it has proven very influential. In this and the next chapter we will discuss *three* ways in which we might distinguish between negative and positive liberty. We will discuss the first distinction in this chapter and the other two in the next.

Spotlight: Isaiah Berlin

Berlin's personal history sheds some light on why he was so against positive liberty. Berlin was one of numerous émigré intellectuals who emigrated in order to escape political tyranny. Born in 1909 in Riga, which was then part of the Russian Empire, and living in Petrograd in 1917, Berlin witnessed the February and October revolutions in Russia, and the rise of the Bolsheviks. As a Jew, he and his family suffered anti-Semitism. Despite having moved to Britain in 1921, Berlin was acutely aware of the events unfolding in Russia, the centralization of power under Stalin, and the atrocities committed by the Party in the name of the greater good and freedom of the people. With the rise of fascism and Nazism in Europe in the 1930s and 1940s, and the terrible conflict of World War II, many liberals like Berlin sought to champion individualism and freedom over nationalism and oppression.

The distinction between *formal* and *effective* freedom

The first distinction between positive and negative liberty is the distinction between effective and formal freedom or, to put it a different way, the understanding of freedom as a *power* or *capacity* and freedom as the *absence of interference*. The distinction turns, therefore, on whether we should equate freedom with being *formally* permitted to do something, or with possessing the *capacity* to actually do that thing.

In most cases, having permission to do something, having no one stopping you from doing it, is very different from actually being able to do it. For example, we all have formal permission to break the 100-metre sprint world record. No one says we may not, or prevents us from making an attempt. We are, in that sense, free to break the world record. On the other hand, few of us are actually able to do so. We lack the strength, skill and training to run fast enough. In that sense, then, we are unable to break the record and so not free to do so.

Friedrich von Hayek defended a negative conception of liberty as a lack of interference in *The Constitution of Liberty* (Hayek 1960). For Hayek, the specific sort of interference that undermines freedom is *coercion*, which he defined as 'such control of the environment or circumstances of a person by another that, in order to avoid greater evil, he is forced to act not according to a coherent plan of his own but to serve the ends of another' (Hayek 1960: p. 71). Hayek therefore thinks that you can only be coerced by the *deliberate actions of other people*. Coercion is a political, interpersonal act: it is being subjected to the will of another.

This is crucial. It means that, firstly, you cannot be rendered unfree by mere physical objects or acts of nature. A rock climber who falls into a crevasse is not unfree, even though she has very limited options available to her. She would only be free if she were pushed into the crevasse, or held in it by another person, in which case her freedom would be constrained by that person and not by the crevasse itself. Freedom for Hayek is therefore not about having a range of available options or choices; it is about having no one prevent you from doing something that you want to do.

Secondly, Hayek's understanding of coercion means that you cannot be made unfree by accident. Coercion must be *willed*. So if you are locked in a room by someone who does not realize that you are inside, then you have not been coerced by that person and your freedom, on Hayek's account, is not limited.

Thirdly, for Hayek your freedom cannot be limited by factors that reside within *yourself*, such as certain physical or mental incapacities. So, if a person is unable to walk across the street because someone else is holding her back, then she is being coerced and is unfree. However, if she is unable to walk across the street because she cannot walk without crutches, which she does not have, then her freedom is unthreatened. She is *free* to walk across the street even though she is not *able* to do so.

> 'Above all [...] we must recognize that we may be free and yet miserable. Liberty does not mean all good things or the absence of all evils. It is true that to be free may mean freedom to starve, to make costly mistakes, or to run mortal risks. [...] But if liberty may therefore not always seem preferable to other goods, it is a distinctive good that needs a distinctive name.'
>
> Friedrich von Hayek, *The Constitution of Liberty* (Chicago, IL: University of Chicago Press, 1960), pp. 68–9.

Defenders of negative liberty thus understand liberty as a lack of deliberate interference in our choices. They therefore argue that a state protects individual freedom by keeping out of people's lives as much as possible, putting in place only those laws that are necessary to protect individuals from the relevant forms of interference.

In contrast, a positive conception of liberty (in which freedom is defined as the actual ability to act according to one's desires) would require much more wide-ranging intervention. Consider the disabled person who needs crutches to walk. From a Hayekian negative liberty perspective, she is free to walk. A policy of freedom-maximization will not mean that we should provide her with crutches. Providing her with crutches may well be a virtuous, charitable thing to do and, as such, may be morally required. However, provision of crutches will not be required in the name of freedom. On the other hand, if we take the view that freedom should be understood as the positive capacity to act, then a concern to maximize the disabled person's freedom *will* entail that we should provide her with crutches.

Consequently, the conception of freedom we hold will have *normative* implications: it will influence our thoughts on what the state should or should not do. In particular, it will influence our thoughts on the appropriate distribution of wealth and resources in a society. Hayek insists that freedom is about the formal absence of coercion and not about the actual capacity to act because the capacity to act requires, among other things, a certain amount of material resources. You may be allowed to buy a mansion but, without several million pounds to spare, you will lack the ability to do so. More mundanely, you may be allowed to have enough food to survive, but without money you will lack the means to acquire that food. If freedom is about the positive ability to act, then maximizing or ensuring your freedom may require giving you some money. In general, freedom will mean taxing the rich to provide money to give to the poor, thereby increasing their ability to act. On the other hand, if freedom is the negative absence of interference, then taxation limits the negative freedom of the rich but does not increase the negative freedom of the poor. This is because a compulsory system of state taxation is a form of coercion: other humans (the state officials) interfere with the plans of those who are taxed, forcing them to pay their taxes so as to avoid a greater evil, namely being sent to prison.

So, we could think of redistributive taxation as decreasing the negative freedom of the rich so as to increase the positive freedom of the poor. This means that, if you have an ideological aversion to redistributive taxation, it makes sense to claim that only negative freedom is real freedom. Redistribution then becomes a matter of decreasing the freedom of the rich without increasing the freedom of the poor. And, if freedom is a crucial value which should generally take priority over other considerations (as liberals and others tend to believe), then it follows that redistributive taxation is a bad policy. We have come full circle: if you do not like redistributive taxation, you will endorse a negative conception of liberty, which provides a justification for rejecting redistributive taxation.

Of course, we could accuse those in favour of redistributive taxation of circular reasoning in the other direction. If you are in favour of benefits for the poor, you define liberty as the capacity to act, which then justifies taxation in order to provide the benefits which are necessary for the poor to act. In fact, this reasoning might be even more problematic than the negative liberty approach. This is because taxation decreases the positive freedom of the rich at the same time as it increases the positive freedom of the poor. Taxation reduces the ability of those who are taxed to do whatever they want. Still, it may be reasonable to suppose that money gives diminishing marginal returns, so that £500 provides less additional positive freedom to a millionaire than it does to someone earning the minimum wage. If this is the case, a system of redistributive taxation will increase positive freedom overall, even though it will reduce the positive freedom of those who are taxed.

We can now see why negative liberty is often used by its defenders to justify a *minimal* state, while positive liberty is seen to justify a state which is more *extensive*. Defenders of negative liberty argue that states should not intervene in market transactions in order to redistribute wealth and resources to the poor in the name of freedom, because while the poor's capacity to *use* their freedom for particular ends may be constrained by their poverty, their freedom *itself* is not constrained by lack of wealth of resources. Such a view tends to be associated with the political Right, such as the Republican Party in the USA and the Conservative Party in Britain, and has been defended by libertarian political philosophers like Robert Nozick and David Gauthier. Indeed, Hayek himself was very influential among neoliberals like Margaret Thatcher who, during her time as British Prime Minister, explicitly sought to implement Hayekian policies. Defenders of positive liberty, however, emphasize the effective ability of all individuals to make choices from options which are not forced upon them by poverty or lack of resources. Such a view tends to be held by people on the traditional Left, and has been defended in different ways by socialists, Marxists and also liberal egalitarian philosophers like G.A. Cohen, John Rawls and Joseph Raz.

Spotlight: Thatcher and Hayek

Upon her election as leader of the UK Conservative Party in 1975, Margaret Thatcher quickly sought to galvanize the party around a new and dramatically reformist ideology. She was deeply impressed with Hayek's ideas. At a meeting early in her premiership, while listening to a speech advocating the adoption of a 'middle way' approach over radicalism, Thatcher 'reached into her briefcase and took out a book. It was Hayek's *The Constitution of Liberty*. Interrupting our pragmatist, she held the book up for all of us to see. "This", she said sternly, "is what we believe", and banged Hayek down on the table.' (John Ranelagh, *Thatcher's People: An Insider's Account of the Politics, the Power, and the Personalities* (London: Fontana, 1992), p. ix.)

Case study: Philip Pettit's 'third' conception of liberty

In his book *Republicanism* (1997), Philip Pettit presents a third conception of liberty which he thought improved upon both positive and negative liberty. Pettit points out that lack of interference is not enough to guarantee freedom. Imagine if you were a slave, but that your slave-owner were benevolent. Imagine that she were so benevolent that, for most of the time, she did not coerce you, or interfere in your plans, but allowed you to do whatever you liked. However, you would know that, at any moment, she could interfere in your life absolutely. She could control any aspect of your life: where you lived, what work you did, whether you were allowed to see other people and so on. In the normal course of things, she does not interfere at all, but the possibility and thus the threat of interference is always present.

Pettit's point is that, under the conception of freedom as non-interference, as a slave in such circumstances you will enjoy considerable freedom. But this seems wrong. A slave owned by a benevolent owner is still a slave and, hence, unfree. Pettit therefore argues that negative freedom, understood as freedom from interference, is inadequate. He proposes instead that we think of freedom as a lack of *domination*, where domination is understood as being subject to an individual, group or institution which has the *capacity* to interfere in our *choices* on an *arbitrary* basis. The slave is unfree because her owner could, at any time, choose to interfere in her life: they have the *capacity* to interfere, even if they choose not to do so.

G.A. Cohen on negative liberty

Let us now consider the critique of negative liberty provided by one of these thinkers: G.A. Cohen.

Spotlight: G.A. Cohen

G.A. Cohen (1941–2009) was not only a formidable and influential political philosopher, he was also a famously entertaining lecturer. In one book based on a collection of his lectures on political philosophy (provocatively entitled *If You're an Egalitarian, How Come You're So Rich?*) one chapter merely reads: 'Lecture 7 could not be reproduced here. That is because it was a multimedia exercise: the audience accepted the invitation to sing with me, to the accompaniment of tapes' (Cohen 2000: p. 116).

We have seen that Hayek appeals to the idea of negative liberty in order to avoid socialist systems of redistribution. But, according to Cohen, Hayek's argument is undermined by the fact that a lack of money threatens not only positive freedom, but also negative freedom (Cohen 2011). Cohen therefore argues that the libertarian/classical liberal argument fails on its own terms: free markets and minimal states violate, rather than protect, individual freedom.

To see why, imagine you want a pair of expensive jeans from Harrods. However, you lack the money to buy them. Undeterred, you go to Harrods, try the jeans on, find some that fit, and leave the shop with them. But as you are leaving the shop the alarm goes off and a security guard comes to investigate. The police are called, and they arrest you. You are charged with shoplifting, and tried, and ordered to pay a fine. But, as you have no money, you serve a short prison sentence instead.

At every stage of this story, you have suffered from human interference. More than that, you have suffered coercion. The security guard interfered with your plan to leave the shop. The police officer forced you to go to the police station. The judge coerced you into remaining in prison. As a direct result of your lack of money, you have suffered human interference. A lack of money has made you negatively unfree. Even if liberty is the absence of interference, then poverty entails a lack of freedom.

Notice that this argument does not apply to the disabled person who cannot walk without crutches. If she tries to cross the road without them, it is her legs and not other people which prevent her from doing so. For her, there is still a salient difference between freedom as non-interference and freedom as the capacity to act. A policy of negative freedom-maximization would not require that we, or the state, provide her with crutches. But such a policy would, on Cohen's argument, require that we redistribute wealth to the poor.

What would a defender of negative liberty like Hayek say in response to Cohen's argument? There are two main objections to Cohen's claim that poverty entails human interference, and that it therefore entails an infringement of negative freedom.

Firstly, they might say that the rules of private property are inevitable, and so enforcing them is not a form of interference.

It is simply the case that Harrods, and not the shoplifter, owns the jeans. The jeans do not belong to the shoplifter. So, the security guard et al. are not *interfering* with the shoplifter. They are simply maintaining the status quo, which is that Harrods owns the trousers. The interference comes not from them, but from the shoplifter, who tries to take something that she does not own. We should not look on the enforcement of Harrods's ownership rights as human interference, but rather as maintenance of the way things are.

However, the problem with this objection is it assumes that rules about private property are objective, inevitable rules, almost like the rules of physics. As a result, the constraints they place on people are seen as more like the presence of a mountain or river than as human interference. But this is clearly false. Rules of private property are not inevitable and objective. They are human creations and are enforced by humans. We, as a society, have decided to uphold a system of private property, and we have deliberately chosen to employ individuals such as security guards and judges to enforce it. We could do otherwise: Marx's theory of communism, for example, is a model of a society without private property. When capitalist societies uphold a system of private property they thereby uphold a particular system of interference.

Secondly, they might say that freedom is rights-based. While it is true that the shoplifter has suffered human interference, still that interference was justified, because she had no *right* to take the jeans. Furthermore, the fact that the shoplifter has no right to take the jeans means that it is no infringement on her freedom to prevent her from doing so. Freedom, on this view, applies only to those things which one has a right to do.

There are a number of problems with this objection. Cohen's own response is that freedom cannot apply only to those things that we have a right to do, because this argument leads to counter-intuitive conclusions. Cohen gives the example of a person who is accused of murder and, in a fair trial, is found guilty and sent to prison. Now, because the person has indeed committed murder, and has been found guilty in a fair trial, she is not entitled to be out of prison. By committing the murder, she has forfeited her right to live her life as she wants. On the rights-based definition of freedom, the imprisoned murderer has not had her freedom curtailed by being put in prison, because she has no right to be out of prison. And yet, is not imprisonment the paradigmatic example of an infringement of liberty? Indeed, the reason why imprisonment is a punishment is that it does curtail the freedom of criminals, even though they have no right to be free. Freedom cannot, then, be dependent on rights.

Conclusion

In this chapter, we introduced the distinction between positive and negative liberty.

We then considered the first distinction between positive and negative liberty and discussed some of the ways in which this distinction might be understood: as a distinction between formal and effective freedom. For negative liberty theorists, a constraint on freedom must be deliberately imposed by another human being. For positive liberty theorists, any constraint will count if it prevents the individual from acting as she chooses.

We saw how the motivating factor for those who insist on this kind of negative liberty is often a concern to reject arguments for redistributive taxation and the welfare state. Negative liberty theorists hope to show that taxation threatens negative liberty and increases only positive liberty. By refusing to recognize positive liberty as 'real' liberty, they therefore reject taxation on freedom-maximizing grounds.

In response to this argument, Cohen shows that a lack of money threatens even negative liberty. As a result, the question of redistributive taxation is open for debate again, even among those who prioritize negative liberty.

Key ideas

Negative liberty: The idea that the individual is free in so far as they are able to do as they please without interference from other people.

Positive liberty: The idea that the individual is free in so far as they are able to act upon their particular desires.

Coercion: A specific form of interference arising from the deliberate willed actions of other people.

Classical liberalism: A particular conception of liberalism rooted in a defence of negative liberty, individualism and free markets. Defended by thinkers like Hayek and von Mises, and often contrasted with the modern liberalism of thinkers like T.H. Green and L.T. Hobhouse, and the egalitarian liberalism of thinkers like John Rawls, who are more sympathetic to the idea of positive liberty.

Dig deeper

Isaiah Berlin, 'Two Concepts of Liberty' [1958], *The Proper Study of Mankind* (London: Pimlico, 1998), pp. 191–242.

G.A. Cohen, *If You're an Egalitarian, How Come You're So Rich?* (Cambridge, MA: Harvard University Press, 2000).

G.A. Cohen, *The Currency of Egalitarian Justice, and Other Essays in Political Philosophy*, ed. Michael Otsuka (Princeton, NJ: Princeton University Press, 2011).

F.A. Hayek, *The Constitution of Liberty* (Chicago, IL: University of Chicago Press, 1960).

F.A. Hayek, *The Road to Serfdom* [1944] (London: Routledge, 2001).

G.C. MacCallum, 'Negative and Positive Freedom', *Philosophical Review* 76/3 (1967), pp. 312–34.

Philip Pettit, *Republicanism: A Theory of Freedom and Government* (Oxford: Clarendon Press, 1997).

Adam J. Tebble, *Hayek* (London: Continuum Press, 2001).

Fact-check

1 Which of the following philosophers advocate negative liberty?
   A   Isaiah Berlin
   B   Friedrich von Hayek
   C   John Locke
   D   All of the above

2 Why is negative liberty so called?
   A   To signify that it is a bad thing
   B   To signify that it requires the absence of something
   C   To signify that its advocates are pessimistic
   D   To signify that it is the opposite of liberty

3 What sort of state is associated with a belief in negative liberty?
   A   The welfare state
   B   The nanny state
   C   The minimal state
   D   The totalitarian state

4 What sorts of policies are associated with a belief in negative liberty?
   A   A free market with minimal intervention
   B   Redistributive taxation
   C   The abolition of private property
   D   Extensive public services

5 According to Hayek, coercion is the opposite of freedom. What is coercion?
   A   Any interference
   B   Interference by another human being
   C   Deliberate interference by another human being
   D   Deliberate interference by an evil human being

6 According to Cohen, why does being poor limit your negative freedom?
   A   Because being poor makes you subject to deliberate interference
   B   Because the rules of private property are made by humans
   C   Because freedom cannot be based on rights
   D   All of the above

7 According to a rights-based conception of freedom, when is your freedom limited?

    A If you are prevented from doing something that you have a right to do

    B If you are prevented from doing something that you are right to want to do

    C If you are prevented from doing something that is the right thing to do

    D All of the above

8 Which of the following is the third concept of liberty, according to Pettit?

    A Freedom as non-interference

    B Freedom as non-coercion

    C Freedom as non-domination

    D Freedom as self-mastery

9 Why was Isaiah Berlin suspicious of positive liberty?

    A Because it can be used to justify totalitarianism

    B Because it can be used to justify libertarianism

    C Because it can be used to justify liberalism

    D All of the above

10 Which of the following would *not* usually be considered as a limit on negative freedom?

    A Being trapped in a room by accident

    B Being trapped in a room by a landslide

    C Being trapped in a room by one's fear of leaving

    D All of the above

2

Freedom (2): Positive freedom

In the previous chapter, we introduced the distinction between positive and negative liberty and discussed one way of understanding it: as a distinction between *formal* and *effective* freedom. In this chapter, we will discuss two further ways of distinguishing between positive and negative liberty.

Remember, Berlin distinguished between positive and negative liberty so as to *defend* negative liberty, and *reject* positive liberty. Berlin thought positive liberty was *dangerous*: it justified *coercion* and could lead to *totalitarianism*, the opposite of genuine (negative) liberty. We will evaluate this claim as we go along.

Freedom as doing whatever one wants vs. freedom as being in control of one's desires

In the previous chapter we characterized the distinction between positive and negative liberty as between formal and effective freedom. A second, related, characterization is of *negative* liberty as the freedom to do whatever one happens to want at any particular time, and *positive* liberty as being in control of one's desires.

On this understanding, negative liberty means that an individual is free if and only if she is doing what she actually wants to do at that time. It is negative in the sense that it retains the idea of an absence of interference in people's choices. It is not the business of the state or anyone else to second-guess the individual: it does not matter whether the thing she wants to do is good for her, or morally acceptable, or whether it is compatible with what she wanted to do yesterday. If she wants to do it, it is a constraint on her freedom to prevent her from doing so. This means, of course, that freedom may or may not be a good thing in its effects: people may make bad decisions, or decisions which they come to regret.

'The "positive" sense of the word "liberty" derives from the wish on the part of the individual to be his own master. I wish my life and decisions to depend on myself, not on external forces of whatever kind. I wish to be the instrument of my own, not of other men's, acts of will. I wish to be a subject, not an object; to be moved by reasons, by conscious purposes, which are my own, not by causes which affect me, as it were, from outside.'

Isaiah Berlin, 'Two Concepts of Liberty' [1958], *The Proper Study of Mankind*, ed. H. Hardy (London: Pimlico, 1998), pp. 191–242, at p. 203.

But is freedom simply about having the ability to do whatever you want to do? Many defenders of a more positive account of liberty do not think so. For example, we may at certain points make choices on the basis of weakness of will or irrational fears or whims. We might act out of anger, or our choices may be influenced by addiction or some other psychological compulsion. In all these cases, our 'choices' may be grounded in desires which are temporary or irrational.

Perhaps we are not acting freely when we act on the basis of such desires. Various thinkers have suggested that what matters from the point of view of freedom is not simply being able to do whatever we want, but rather being *in control of what we want*: being masters of our own lives. Thus liberals like John Stuart Mill, John Rawls and Joseph Raz share with many Marxists, socialists and feminists the idea that freedom is about possessing *autonomy*. Defenders of autonomy suggest that if we act in response to a momentary impulse or an addiction, we are unfree – even if we are not suffering from interference from another person. So, for example, if you want to give up smoking but have a cigarette, or if you are trying to eat healthily but eat too much chocolate cake, you are not acting freely. Your addiction and your appetite have constrained you.

One way of understanding this distinction, then, is as a disagreement about where a constraint must come from if it is to count as a constraint on liberty. Defenders of negative liberty argue that a constraint on liberty must be *external*: it must come from outside the person. In other words, someone else must be constraining you if your liberty is to be undermined. For defenders of positive liberty, however, the constraint can come from inside the person concerned. That is to say, freedom can be limited by your own desires, emotions, or physical or psychological state.

Another way of putting this (and the way that Berlin put it) is to think of the individual as constituted by two selves: a higher and a lower self. The lower self is the self that has base desires, whims and addictions and suffers from weakness of will. It is your lower self that wants the cigarette or the chocolate cake. The higher self is the self that forms long-term, considered plans, that considers the long-term benefits and harms of a particular course of action and, in evaluating them, decides which are more important. It is your higher self that wants to give up smoking and to eat healthily. If we are thinking in these terms, we will say that an individual lacks positive liberty, or autonomy, when her lower self rules her higher self: if, when the two disagree, the lower self wins.

Does this form of positive liberty justify coercion? Remember, even negative liberty requires some kind of coercion: each individual's freedom must be protected by a state capable of compelling all members of society to observe basic laws. But, Berlin argued, positive liberty goes further. Imagine that you are trying to give up smoking, and that you have told a friend that you have this firm desire. That friend might be justified in refusing to give you a cigarette when you want one, or throwing away any that you buy. She could justify this, moreover, in the name of your freedom. Because you have told her that you want to give up smoking, she may help you to be free when she forces you to carry out your wish: she ignores your fleeting need for a cigarette, putting it down to weakness of will, and respects instead your longer-term, autonomous, considered desire to give up. Your friend could – to use Rousseau's famous phrase – force you to be free.

> '[I]n order that the social pact not be an empty formula, it is tacitly implied in that commitment – which alone can give force to all others – that whoever refuses to obey the general will shall be constrained to do so by the whole body, which means nothing other than that he shall be forced to be free...'
> Jean-Jacques Rousseau, *The Social Contract* [1762], (London: Penguin Classics, 1968), p. 64.

Berlin thought that positive liberty could therefore be used to justify the notion that the individual may be less able to know what is in their interests than some other person or institution. At its most benign, this idea can justify *paternalism*: the idea that the state is sometimes justified in passing laws which force people to do things for their own good, such as wearing seatbelts in cars or motorcycle helmets.

At its most extreme, it can lead to *totalitarianism*: it can justify political rulers denouncing the expressed wishes of the people as irrational or ignorant, as merely the wishes of their lower selves. Hence, it is anti-democratic: it can justify the state ignoring the views of the people, oppressing them, and mistreating them, all the while claiming that they are doing so *in order to make them free*.

As we have suggested, many modern liberals like John Stuart Mill and John Rawls have defended a notion of freedom as autonomy. Some, indeed, have embraced an even more radical notion: that freedom is not just about satisfying the desires that people do in fact have, but is rather about satisfying the desires they *ought* to have. On this account of positive liberty, you are free only if you are acting in a particular sort of way, for example on the basis of true facts rather than ignorance or lies. Furthermore, we might sometimes 'choose' to do things which are contrary to our genuine best interests as a result of the fact that our choices are *socially constructed*: they may be influenced, or even determined, by society in ways that may or may not be explicit. The social construction of preferences is a particular concern for feminists, Marxists and other radical political thinkers. The basic idea is that in order for people to be free, they need to make their choices in a context in which principles of freedom and equality prevail. The man who 'chooses' to work two jobs in order to pay his rent is not free: his choice is forced upon him by his economic circumstances. Similarly, the woman who chooses to undergo cosmetic surgery, or to wear painful high heels, in order to comply with sexist beauty norms, is arguably not choosing freely at all: her choice to do these things is shaped by unjust social and cultural factors beyond her control. In these and many other cases, some argue, the fact that our choices are shaped by forces beyond our control means that we cannot act freely in circumstances which encourage us to make decisions which are harmful or demeaning or against our wider interests in some way. In other words, we cannot be said to have *autonomy* when our choices are shaped so profoundly by unjust circumstances beyond our control: we may choose to do what we want, but we are never really in charge of *what we want*.

It is *possible*, but not *necessary*, that such a view could justify the kind of coercion that Berlin was concerned about. For it suggests that freedom can only be exercised in a just society which works for the genuine best interests of its members. Many Marxists argue that people can only be free when they are able to make choices free from the dominating influence of the wider capitalist system. Hence, what is needed is not negative liberty embodied in constitutional rights and a minimal state, but genuine positive liberty brought about by radical social and political change. Similarly, many feminists argue that women can only be free in a society in which there is genuine equality between men and women. Consequently, feminism tends to call not for minimal states and negative liberty, but rather for the radical overhaul of sexist social norms and, hence, the unfair pressures experienced by women to 'choose' certain kinds of life over others (e.g. Radcliffe Richards 1980).

Freedom as a protected private sphere vs. freedom as political or community participation

The third and final distinction between positive and negative liberty understands negative liberty as dependent upon the individual having her own private sphere, protected from state (and other) interference, while positive liberty is dependent on the individual actively participating in community or political life.

This distinction associates negative liberty with what Benjamin Constant called the 'liberty of the moderns' and positive liberty with what he called the 'liberty of the ancients' (Constant 1819). The liberty of the moderns is the idea that freedom is about establishing a private sphere in which individuals are able to live their lives on the basis of their conscience, without interference from other people or the state. Liberalism, for example, is grounded in the claim that it is not the business of the state or anyone else to tell individuals how to live or what to believe. Thus John Locke argued that the liberal state should not seek to impose any particular way of life on its members, but should instead establish a regime of toleration, allowing all members of society to hold their own views on matters of conscience. Liberals thus want to protect a space in which individuals can live in their own way. This 'private' space might include religious and moral beliefs, and the family. Hence, liberals have traditionally advocated measures restricting the power of the state: constitutions, bills of rights, civil protections and so on.

This understanding of liberty is very different to that which Constant associated with pre-modern thinkers. Political philosophers writing before the Enlightenment, such as Plato and Aristotle in ancient Greece, and Cicero in ancient Rome, shared with more modern Romantic philosophers like Rousseau the idea that liberty was not a private condition enjoyed by individuals, but rather a public condition enjoyed by whole communities or peoples. These thinkers shared a *civic-republican* idea of freedom: freedom is about being a member of a self-governing political community. You are free in so far as you are able to participate in the collective life of your political community and, in association with your fellow citizens, shape that political community and decide its future. This view of liberty is 'positive' in its insistence that freedom is about being in control of one's life, not just in the sense that one is free from interference, but in the sense that one actively participates in the collective life of the polity.

Both approaches have their own strengths and weaknesses. Negative liberty, understood as the need to establish a private sphere free from interference, is perhaps more appealing as it is the view with which we are most familiar. However, it is not philosophically rigorous. People cannot be allowed to do whatever they want in their own homes, or to other members of their families. A liberal state needs to protect children from abuse and women from violent partners, for example. Similarly, while people are free to believe whatever they want, it is not clear that they should be free to *act* however they want, even if certain actions are required by their beliefs. The idea that the state should keep out of matters of religion and the family in the name of freedom seems to suggest that it has no legitimate interest in regulating harmful or unjust religious or cultural practices, like forced marriage. If the private sphere is defined as the area of one's life in which the state cannot intervene, then there is arguably no such sphere. States might operate on the presumption that they should avoid intervening as much as possible in matters of religion, culture, the family, and so on, but the idea that freedom requires a strict separation between public and private spheres is philosophically and politically untenable, a point made most convincingly by feminists (e.g. Okin 1989; Hirschmann 2003).

Spotlight: A private matter

Until 1991, there was no law in the UK against a husband raping his wife. Sexual relations between husbands and wives were seen as a 'private' matter and, hence, not something that should be regulated by the state.

The idea that liberty is about collective self-government seems to avoid this problem. It does not rely upon a distinction between public and private, and identifies freedom with the public pursuit of collective goals rather than the private pursuit of individual ones. However, in doing so it seems to collapse the interests of individuals into the interest of the community as a whole. That is, while there may be problems with the idea that liberty requires the establishment of a private sphere in which individuals can pursue their own self-interest, it at least takes seriously the idea that people have interests – goals, aspirations, ideals – and that this *matters*. The positive liberty view seems to suggest that each individual's interests can be appropriately subordinated to the common good of society as a whole.

It is this aspect of positive liberty which Berlin thought the most dangerous of all, as he believed that it had been used throughout history to justify totalitarianism. It subsumes the good of the individual into the good of the whole and thus violates not only individual freedom but also the moral status of individuals. Individuals are seen not as ends in themselves, but as the means by which the common good might be achieved. As we will see in Part Two of this book, a central theme of liberal thought has been to establish individuals as having a moral status that cannot be overridden even if doing so would promote the good of society as a whole. Indeed, liberals have specifically afforded individuals rights and legal provisions, enshrined in constitutional arrangements, which are seen as *protections* against the community at large.

Spotlight: New Labour and positive liberty

In 1997 the then Prime Minister, Tony Blair, wrote to Isaiah Berlin, saying 'The limitations of negative liberty are what have motivated generations of people to work for positive liberty, whatever its depradations [*sic*] in the Soviet model. That determination to go beyond laissez-faire continues to motivate people today. And it is in that context that I would be interested in your views on the future of the Left.' Berlin was too ill to reply.

Gordon Brown also defended positive liberty in his Hugo Young Memorial lecture, delivered in 2005 when he was Chancellor of the Exchequer. He argued: 'So in this century a consensus has evolved that liberty is not just passive, about restricting someone else's powers, but active, people empowered to participate. And I believe that when in our generation Robert F. Kennedy argued for citizen participation and community self-government, and gave us a modern idea of the empowered citizen, he echoed a strong British tradition of civic engagement I would like to recapture.'

The fact that this kind of positive liberty appears to reject the moral status of individuals and their interests is particularly problematic, Berlin believed, when we consider it in the context of the claim discussed above that positive liberty suggests that some people are better placed to know what is in an individual's interest than the individual themselves. Berlin believed that, taken together, these factors justified political leaders in doing whatever they want to do to the members of society in the interests of securing their wider freedom. When freedom is dependent upon the wellbeing of the collectivity (understood as the nation, for example, or the state), then protection of *freedom* and the protection of the wellbeing of the *collectivity* become synonymous. Berlin argued that Hitler, Mussolini and Stalin all used exactly this argument to justify brutal policies designed to rid the state of destabilizing forces, be they immigrants, Jews, homosexuals, the disabled, the rich or anyone else. Anyone who disagreed with the state's actions could be denounced as irrational, or not in possession of the requisite facts: their views could be rejected as merely the product of their lower selves. Several theorists have rejected this view as a caricature (e.g. Taylor 1979).

Case study: Republicanism – Skinner and Pettit on individual and collective freedom

In his article 'The Paradoxes of Political Liberty' (1984), Quentin Skinner defends a form of positive liberty as related to participation in political or communal life. Skinner argues that theorists of negative liberty have accused conceptions of positive liberty of being paradoxical in two ways: that it 'forces people to be free', and that it appears to require that the individual subordinates her desires to the needs of the group.

Skinner's argument is not that positive liberty does not entail these paradoxes. Instead, he argues that these paradoxes are not in fact paradoxical. Skinner, like Pettit, describes this conception of liberty as a *republican* one: one which draws its inspiration from thinkers like Cicero, Machiavelli and Montesquieu. The main feature of classical republicanism is its concern that individuals should live in a free state. A free state is defined, for republicans, in *negative* liberty terms. A state is free when it is not subject to external constraint, for example when it is not forced to follow another state's orders. If we think about what this means for the citizens of the state, it means that they (and not the citizens or government of another state) decide what the community should do. The citizens participate in forming a general will, in determining the aims and actions of their community and the state. Participation is therefore crucial to the protection of negative liberty.

This is a view shared by Philip Pettit, whose conception of liberty as 'non-domination' we discussed in the previous chapter. Pettit also argues that individual freedom requires public participation in collective political life. The reason for this is that it is the only way to ensure that individuals are not dominated. A republican state is required to act in the interests of its members. Pettit argues that the only way of finding out what is in the community interest is to engage in an ongoing process of consultation with the public. People must be able to participate in the decision-making process, to give their views on a matter, and to refute the decisions that the state makes. It follows, then, that people must actively participate in political life if they are to secure their freedom.

Conclusion

In this and the previous chapter we discussed the *concept* of freedom and the *normative* implications associated with different understandings of that concept. In this chapter, we discussed two further ways of understanding the distinction between positive and negative liberty. We discussed the idea that negative freedom might be understood as focused on protecting the individual's ability to pursue their own private self-interest, while positive liberty might be understood as the pursuit of collective, public goods within a particular kind of political community. Furthermore, we saw that the simple (some would say, simplistic) description of freedom provided by negative liberty thinkers like Hayek is complicated by the fact that, firstly, we may often make choices which are contrary to our real interests and desires and, secondly, that our desires are shaped by wider social, cultural, economic and political factors which lie beyond our control. While negative liberty theorists protect our ability to do *what we want*, positive liberty theorists seek to make sure that we have *control* over what we want by considering the ways in which things like social circumstances, income, and wider social norms influence our sense of who we are and what kind of lives we want to lead. Positive liberty theorists of this kind emphasize the importance of *autonomy*. We will discuss the role of autonomy in contemporary liberal theory in Part Two.

Key ideas

Autonomy: The idea that freedom is concerned with self-mastery, with being in control of one's desires.

Higher/lower self: The distinction between one's base desires and one's higher (rational) desires, used by some theorists of positive liberty to explain the idea of autonomy.

Paternalism: The idea that, in certain circumstances, the state is justified in passing laws forcing people to do certain things, or banning them from doing certain things, for their own good.

The private sphere: The notional space sought by defenders of negative liberty which is considered beyond the scope of the state or others to intervene in, covering areas of life such as religious and moral belief, opinion and the family.

Republicanism: A conception of politics and freedom, defended in different ways by Quentin Skinner, Philip Pettit, Michael Sandel and Charles Taylor, which links *individual* freedom with public participation in the *collective* life of the polity.

Social construction of choices: The idea, advanced by some defenders of positive liberty, that our choices (and our wider identities) are influenced by the social context in which we live and that this has direct implications for the idea of freedom.

Dig deeper

Ian Carter, Matthew H. Kramer and Hillel Steiner (eds), *Freedom: A Philosophical Anthology* (Oxford: Blackwell, 2007).

Clare Chambers, *Sex, Culture, and Justice: The Limits of Choice* (University Park, PA: The Pennsylvania State University Press, 2008).

Benjamin Constant, 'The Liberty of the Ancients Compared with that of the Moderns' [1819], in Biancamaria Fontana (ed.), *Constant: Political Writings* (Cambridge: Cambridge University Press, 1988), pp. 304–7.

Nancy Hirschmann, *The Subject of Liberty: Toward a Feminist Theory of Freedom* (Princeton, NJ: Princeton University Press, 2003).

Philip Pettit, *Republicanism: A Theory of Freedom and Government* (Oxford: Oxford University Press, 1997).

Janet Radcliffe Richards, *The Sceptical Feminist* (London: Routledge, 1980).

Quentin Skinner, *Liberty before Liberalism* (Cambridge: Cambridge University Press, 1998).

Quentin Skinner, 'The Paradoxes of Political Liberty' [1984], in S.M. McMurrin (ed.),*The Tanner Lectures on Human Values* VII (Salt Lake City: University of Utah Press, 1986).

Charles Taylor, 'What's Wrong with Negative Liberty?' [1979], *Philosophy and the Human Sciences*, vol. 2 (Cambridge University Press, 1985), pp. 211–29.

Iris Marion Young, *Justice and the Politics of Difference* (Princeton, NJ: Princeton University Press, 1990).

Fact-check

1 Why is positive liberty so called?
   A   To signify that it is a good thing
   B   To signify that it is optimistic
   C   To signify that it requires the presence of something
   D   All of the above

2 Why might you lack positive freedom even if you are doing what you want?
   A   Because you are acting out of weakness of will
   B   Because you are acting out of fear
   C   Because you are acting as the result of misinformation
   D   All of the above

3 Why, according to Berlin, does positive liberty lead to totalitarianism?
   A   Because only totalitarians endorse positive liberty
   B   Because there is a necessary connection between positive liberty and totalitarianism
   C   Because positive liberty means that the individual may not be the best judge of her own desires
   D   Because positive liberty is the same thing as coercion

4 How is positive liberty sometimes understood?
   A   As prioritizing the higher self over the lower self
   B   As prioritizing self-mastery over mere preferences
   C   As prioritizing the rational self over the irrational self
   D   All of the above

5 Which of the following are associated with positive liberty?
   A   Autonomy
   B   Autocracy
   C   Automata
   D   Automotives

6 Which of the following are associated with negative liberty?
   A   A protected private sphere
   B   An active political community
   C   Being in control of one's desires
   D   All of the above

7 Which of the following might undermine positive liberty?

    A Social welfare

    B Social life

    C Social conditioning

    D Socialism

8 Why is political participation important for positive liberty?

    A Because it enables individuals to resist totalitarianism

    B Because it enables individuals to affect the conditions of their lives

    C Because it limits domination

    D All of the above

9 One form of positive liberty is known as republicanism. What is meant by this term?

    A The views associated with the US Republican Party

    B The view that liberty requires the absence of domination

    C The view that liberty requires the availability of public houses

    D The views of Plato's *Republic*

10 Which of the following is the most accurate?

    A Feminists insist on the importance of the private sphere

    B Feminists criticize the public sphere

    C Feminists argue that the private sphere and the public sphere are the same thing

    D Feminists criticize the classical liberal view of the distinction between the private and public spheres.

3

Equality (1): The concept of equality

Equality is a difficult concept: What does it mean to say that all people are equal? Indeed, the idea that all human beings are in some sense equal is relatively new and controversial, and was rejected by Plato, Aristotle, Kant, Hegel, Rousseau, Nietzsche and the American Founding Fathers, to name but a few. People are straightforwardly unequal in all kinds of ways: in their talents, physical characteristics, ambitions and desires. People are also unequal in their social endowments: their wealth, class and status. Nevertheless, we (including contemporary political philosophers) now hold that people are all *equal* in some sense – but what do we mean by this?

In this chapter and the next we discuss a range of issues concerning the idea of equality. We begin by discussing the idea that equality means treating people with equal respect, or as having equal worth. We then introduce the distinction between *equality of outcome* and *equality of opportunity*, both of which are discussed in greater detail in later chapters.

Defining equality

One suggested answer to the question 'What is equality?' is that people are equal in that they all possess *rights*. But this is a circular argument: rights need to be justified, and they are often justified by an appeal to equality. Furthermore, if equality is understood in terms of equal rights, then even the most egalitarian societies in the world violate equality: all societies think it appropriate to deny some members of society (e.g. criminals) the kind of basic rights that others enjoy.

Another suggestion might be that we can ground equality in the idea that we are all rational, reasoning beings. But again, not everyone straightforwardly fits this description: young children, those with learning difficulties, the psychologically ill, and addicts are just some examples of people who may not count as fully rational. Does this mean that they are unequal to those who can reason more clearly? And if so, what normative implications follow? Should people with learning difficulties be denied the right to vote? Do they have different rights and claims on resources? If not, why not?

'The doctrine of equality! There exists no more poisonous poison: for it seems to be preached by justice itself but is the end of justice [...] "Equality for equals, inequality for unequals" – that would be the true voice of justice: and, what follows from it, "Never make equal what is unequal."'

Friedrich Nietzsche, *The Twilight of the Idols* [1889] (Harmondsworth: Penguin, 1968), p. 102.

Treating people as equals

The first way of thinking about equality is via the notion of equal treatment. On this understanding, equality entails treating people *as though* they are equals. This might entail treating them with equal respect, treating them as having equal status, or appealing to the idea of equal humanity. The idea is that, while we may have unequal talents or resources, still there is something about our common humanity that requires some sort of equality. No one, on this understanding, should be considered as more important than anyone else, as having more status, or more moral worth.

Bernard Williams has suggested that equality understood in terms of common humanity is either *false* or *trivial* (Williams 1985). The statement 'all people are equal' is clearly false, if it is supposed to mean that all people are the same, or that they have the same levels of skill or intelligence. On the other hand, if the statement 'all people are equal' is merely supposed to mean something like 'all people are people, and thus share a common humanity', it is not saying very much. We know that all people are people. We want to know what, if anything, follows from that.

Case study: Telic and deontic egalitarianism

In 'Equality and Priority' (Parfit 1997), Derek Parfit distinguishes two different kinds of egalitarianism: telic egalitarianism and deontic egalitarianism.

Telic egalitarians, he suggests, are those who believe that equality is a good thing in and of itself. The more a policy, decision, or distributional scheme equalizes the positions of each and every individual in society (in some important sense), the better. The term 'telic' comes from the word *telos*, meaning 'end point' or 'goal': telic egalitarians thus believe that equality is the end point or goal to which egalitarian justice should be aimed.

Deontic egalitarianism takes its name from the idea of deontology. This is an idea that we will discuss in more detail in Part Two. For now, it is enough to say that deontology is a moral position which holds that actions or decisions should be judged right or wrong according to independently derived principles of justice, rather than, say, the consequences that these actions have or the extent to which they contribute to some overarching *telos*, or goal, for society as a whole. Deontology is thus closely associated with the idea of justice, as defended by liberal thinkers like Rawls and Dworkin. For Parfit, therefore, a deontic egalitarian is someone who believes that inequality is wrong if and only if it is unjust. That is, some forms of inequality are wrong and others are not, and we distinguish between the two by appealing to principles of justice. In other words, we value equality only because equality is a way of achieving some other desirable value, like justice.

Telic and deontic egalitarianism have very different normative implications, as we can see. Telic egalitarians hold equality to be the supreme value, and thus subordinate other values to it. It is possible that such an approach might lead to unjust consequences: consequences which reduce the general welfare of society or some individuals within it, for example. Deontic egalitarians, on the other hand, might be said to have a more *instrumental* understanding of equality: equality is important because it brings about the satisfaction of other, wider, more important goals like justice. Therefore, on this view, it may sometimes be appropriate to violate equality if doing so brings about a more just outcome. Liberal egalitarians like John Rawls, Ronald Dworkin, Richard Arneson and Brian Barry tend to value justice over other values such as equality, social stability or community, as we will see. Hence, they tend to argue for fair (or just) inequality over strict equality. On Parfit's terms, they are deontic egalitarians, not telic egalitarians.

Nevertheless, Williams argues, it is sometimes important to remind ourselves that all people are people, and therefore to remind ourselves that all people have similar capacities to feel pain, suffering and need. This statement is egalitarian because it reminds us that we need to find reasons to justify treating people differently, given these similarities. If it is bad for us to be poor, then it will be bad for others, too. If it is bad or disrespectful for a white person to be denied access to a restaurant, then it will be bad and disrespectful for a black person, too. The statement that we are all equally human is egalitarian, Williams argues, because it requires that we take account of the needs and capacities of all people, and do not fail to consider particular people or groups of people on grounds that ignore their common humanity.

Equality and difference: Does equality mean treating people the same?

Even if we share a common humanity, there are numerous ways in which we are different. Does equality mean that we should treat people in ways that ignore the differences between them, or that we should act in ways which take account of them?

Consider equality between the sexes. Nancy Fraser argues that there are two possible approaches to sex equality: one based on *sameness* and the other on *difference*. Equality which focuses on *sameness* argues that treating women equally means treating them the same as men. In other words, if we are trying to pursue gender equality, we need to allow women to do the same jobs as men, to enjoy the same rewards as men, and to compete on the same basis as men. If a man and a woman apply for the same job, they should be judged on the same criteria. If a male candidate should be able to show that he responds well under pressure, then the same criterion should apply to a female candidate. The aim of this approach is to eradicate unfair discrimination.

There are two problems with the sameness approach, Fraser and others have argued. The first is that it takes men as the norm, and implies that women can only be equal if they are like men. The second is that it fails to take adequate account of the ways in which men and women are different. It is all very well requiring men and women to meet the same criteria, but some criteria might be inherently biased toward either men or women. For example, treating women the same as men would mean denying them maternity leave, for men do not have babies. Or, if a job had minimum height requirements, then treating women the same as men would mean that women would have to meet the same requirement. As women are, on average, shorter than men, such a policy would mean that many women would not meet the height requirements. The effect would be the same as discriminating against women.

A possible response to this argument is that these differences between men and women – such as childbearing and average height – mean that women simply cannot be equal to men because they are naturally different. It is appropriate to insist that women meet the same criteria as men because those are the criteria which are necessary to the job. If women tend to be shorter than the minimum requirements for becoming a firefighter, for example, then that means that women are not qualified to be firefighters. Male standards should be the universal standards because they are the objectively required standards. The problem, though, is that setting *male* standards as the *universal* standards does not treat women equally because it fails to recognize the ways in which their differences might be valuable. It may be true that you need to be a certain height in order to operate firefighting machinery. But why is machinery not designed with women as well as men in mind? And the fact that many professional careers require employees to work for very long hours during the first half of their careers, in their twenties and early thirties, while they become established, will disproportionately disadvantage women as these just happen to be their key childbearing years. Adopting universal male standards fails to question whether those standards are really necessary, or whether the conditions of the job could be altered so as to allow for more equal access to it. Universal male standards also affect women unequally because women face different pressures from men outside of work.

On the other hand, equality based on difference would mean that differences between men and women should be taken into account when designing policies, so that equality might require different treatment. So, biological mothers might be offered more parental leave than biological fathers or non-biological mothers, to take account of the particular demands of pregnancy, childbirth and breastfeeding. Such a policy might be extended to mothers and fathers more generally, this time to take account not of biological parenthood but of the different roles usually ascribed to male and female parents.

This last example demonstrates one problem with the difference approach: it risks entrenching difference and inequality. It may be that the different social roles ascribed to mothers and fathers are themselves the result, and the cause, of inequality. If this is the case, then taking them into account may not be an egalitarian thing to do after all.

> 'I have a dream that one day this nation will rise up and live out the true meaning of its creed: "We hold these truths to be self-evident, that all men are created equal."
>
> 'I have a dream that one day on the red hills of Georgia, the sons of former slaves and the sons of former slave owners will be able to sit down together at the table of brotherhood.
>
> 'I have a dream that one day even the state of Mississippi, a state sweltering with the heat of injustice, sweltering with the heat of oppression, will be transformed into an oasis of freedom and justice.
>
> 'I have a dream that my four little children will one day live in a nation where they will not be judged by the color of their skin but by the content of their character.
>
> I have a dream today!'
>
> Martin Luther King, 'I Have a Dream' speech, delivered 28 August 1963 at the Lincoln Memorial, Washington, DC.

Equality of outcome

Rather than focusing on the idea of equal treatment we might instead focus on the idea of equality of outcome. Equality of *outcome* is the idea that equality is about distributing some sort of good like wealth, income or welfare, and that what matters is not the amount each person is given but the amount each person ends up with. According to equality of outcome, it makes sense to give a rich person less than a poor person because what matters is the amount that each person has at the end of the process. Similarly, it might make sense to treat women and men differently, if doing so means they end up in comparable positions.

Equality of outcome has come to occupy a central place in contemporary debates about social justice, with different thinkers clashing over what the appropriate equalization should be. We will therefore put off our detailed discussion of equality of outcome until Part 2. For now it is sufficient to mention that the implications of equality of outcome vary, depending on what it is that is being equalized. A commitment to the equalization of wealth will have very different implications to the equalization of welfare, for example: ensuring equality of welfare may well require giving especially needy people more money than less needy people, or giving people with expensive tastes more money than people with simpler tastes. Similarly, ensuring equality of *resources* will often produce quite significant inequalities in wealth and income as a result of what different people choose to do with the resources they have.

Spotlight: The impact of inequality

Richard Wilkinson and Kate Pickett have argued that inequality has a dramatic negative effect on almost every area of our lives (Wilkinson and Pickett 2010). Their research suggests that people living in societies characterized by low levels of inequality between rich and poor live longer, are less likely to experience mental illness, to use illegal drugs, to be obese, to be murdered, or to experience social mobility, and are more likely to trust one another, to do better at school, and to live in a cohesive community. Child wellbeing is higher in equal societies, too, as is general health.

Equality of outcome can be more or less desirable, then, depending on what the relevant good is and how it deals with important differences between luck and choice. We will discuss this tension between luck, choice and equality in Part Two. For now, let us discuss in more *general* terms reasons why we should value the idea of equality of outcome.

'No government is legitimate that does not show equal concern for the fate of all those citizens over whom it claims dominion and from whom it claims allegiance. Equal concern is the sovereign virtue of political community – without it government is only tyranny – and when a nation's wealth is very unequally distributed, as the wealth of even very prosperous nations now is, then its equal concern is suspect.'
Ronald Dworkin, *Sovereign Virtue: The Theory and Practice of Equality* (Cambridge, MA: Harvard University Press, 2000), p. 1.

Why should we value equality?

Equality of outcome looks intuitively desirable because it seems to identify what really matters to people: having valuable resources. It also seems to be in line with the common-sense idea that it is better to devote resources to those who have the least. And yet several philosophers have suggested that equality is undesirable, unimportant or positively harmful. The most obvious criticism is that it removes any incentive for ambition or hard work. However, there are two further objections worth mentioning.

THE LEVELLING-DOWN OBJECTION

Perhaps the best-known objection to the ideal of equality is the levelling-down objection. Imagine that there are five people and seven five-pound notes. There is no change, and so none of the notes can be split. If we believe that equality is valuable in and of itself, we will think that everyone should get one five-pound note and that the final two notes should be thrown away. Equality would bring everyone down to the lowest level, rather than allowing two people to have ten pounds.

Or, imagine a society in which the principle of equality is taken to apply to all areas of life. Some parents are very devoted to their children, and spend a lot of time with them, reading stories, playing games and so on. Other parents are too busy to do so, or lack the necessary motivation or skills to read to their children or play sports with them. If we think that equality is valuable in and of itself, we will think that it is a good idea to prevent all parents from reading to their children and playing games with them. In that way, we ensure that all children receive equal amounts of parenting, and that no child has more than another.

Intuitively, many people feel it would be a bad thing to throw away the extra money, and to prevent parents from doing the best they can for their children. This intuition is the basis of the levelling-down objection: equality is undesirable because it requires making people worse off than they could otherwise be.

The levelling-down objection is powerful, but egalitarians can escape it. This is because it relies on the idea that in order to be committed to equality we must believe it to be the only value that is important. But few if any egalitarians believe that equality is the only, or the most important, value. After all, if equality were the only thing that mattered, then an egalitarian would see no difference between a society where people were equally well-off, happy and healthy, and one in which they were equally badly-off, miserable and ill. But of course such indifference would be perverse, and so egalitarians must value other things, such as utility, alongside equality.

The problem, though, is that equality and utility can conflict. In the case of the five-pound notes, we cannot increase utility without compromising equality. In the case of the parents, we cannot allow some parents to give their children a better upbringing without at the same time allowing inequality between children. In such cases, we will have to decide whether we value equality or utility more highly. If we value equality as an end in itself, it might seem that we will have to argue in favour of levelling down.

SUFFICIENCY OR PRIORITY ARE MORE IMPORTANT

Derek Parfit and Harry Frankfurt have suggested that many egalitarians who claim to be committed to equality are not committed to equality at all, but to the idea that the conditions of the worst-off should be improved. That is, they argue that the reason why egalitarians tend to reject the levelling-down objection is because it violates the central egalitarian idea that what matters, in the end, is not that everyone has the same amount of money or income, or that everyone is understood to be the same in terms of their talents, intelligence, etc., but that those who have the least in society are provided with enough resources to lead a life that is worthwhile. Parfit, in 'Equality or Priority?' (1997), advocates the *priority* view, the idea that the worst-off should have priority when allocating new resources. Many liberal egalitarians, such as John Rawls, accept some version of this argument. Thus Rawls argues for *fair inequality* over *equality*, which amounts to a version of prioritarianism. However, the view that the worst-off should be given priority is not necessarily a view about *equality*. It would be quite possible to maximize the position of the worst-off but then disregard all inequalities above that position. So many egalitarians agree with prioritarianism but do not wish to stop there.

An alternative approach is Frankfurt's sufficiency approach – outlined in 'Equality as a Moral Ideal' (1987) – according to which egalitarians should focus on everyone having enough, or sufficient, resources. Frankfurt gives many reasons for preferring sufficiency to equality. His general claim is that usually, when we think that an inequality is morally wrong, we are actually reacting to the wrongness of the position of the worst-off. More specifically, we think it is wrong for some people not to have *enough* of a particular resource. So, when we say that global inequality is wrong, we mean that poverty and famine are wrong. When we say that it is wrong for some people to be able to afford a great deal of leisure time when others must work extremely long hours to earn enough money to support themselves, we are actually saying that it is morally wrong that some people do not have sufficient leisure time.

Often, then, when we complain about inequality we are actually complaining about insufficiency. But Frankfurt goes further. He argues that it is morally *undesirable* to care about equality rather than sufficiency. Caring about equality, Frankfurt argues, means caring about how you are doing in relation to others, and ignoring the more important question of whether you yourself have enough to meet your own goals. What is important in life, he maintains, is considering your own preferences and your own welfare, not jealously comparing yourself to others and meanly complaining that they have more than you, regardless of the fact that you have enough.

The sufficiency view raises two important questions.

▶ 1 How should we define sufficiency?

If egalitarianism is about making sure that everyone has sufficient resources to live a worthwhile life, we need to know at what level they can be said to have enough to do this, and what a 'worthwhile' life consists in. These questions are at the heart of contemporary debates about justice, as we will see in Part Two. Frankfurt defines sufficiency as the condition where having more, though it might be nice, has no effect on one's *happiness*.

Frankfurt maintains that one can be perfectly happy even in a situation where more resources would be desirable. This leaves many questions unanswered, in particular:

▶ 2 How likely is it that everyone can have sufficient resources?

We live in a world of scarce resources. Not everyone can have everything they want because there is only so much of everything to go around. Therefore, one of the principal challenges facing a theory of justice is to manage conflicts which arise out of differing claims on available resources. The sufficiency approach suggests that we should distribute resources in such a way as to allow people to pursue a life that makes them happy. But this may not always be possible, given scarcity of resources. In other words: in a world in which not everyone is able to have enough resources to be happy, how should we determine who gets what, and why? Equality (as opposed to sufficiency) is one response to this kind of conflict.

Spotlight: Happiness

In his *Happiness: Lessons from a New Science*, the economist Richard Layard suggests an interesting link between happiness and equality (Layard, 2005). According to empirical studies, he says, one of the most important factors in how happy we are is our *perception* of our *relative* wealth. What really matters to us is not how much money we have, or even how much money we have relative to others, but how much money we *think* we have relative to others. Layard uses these findings to subvert the dominant economists' view that economic policy should be geared toward creating growth, arguing instead that it should be aimed at increasing overall happiness, through higher taxes and egalitarian redistribution.

Conclusion

In this first chapter on equality we introduced various ways in which the concept of equality might be understood: equality of status (as human beings), equality of treatment (as either sameness or difference), equality of opportunity, and equality of outcome. We focused on the first two, putting off a detailed discussion of equality of outcome until Part Two, and equality of opportunity until the next chapter. We then discussed several criticisms of the idea of equality.

There is a lot more to be said, as we will see throughout the rest of this book. Is equality valuable as an end in itself or as a means to other ends such as justice? Does the idea of equality ignore the ways in which people are not, and should not be considered, equal? Or is the point of equality to ensure that all people have a fair opportunity to succeed, and to live a life that they value, despite the many inequalities of talent, intelligence, ambition and so on which distinguish them? We will look at this final question in more detail in the next chapter.

Key ideas

Equality of opportunity: The idea that equality is about ensuring that no one is unfairly excluded from the same opportunity to succeed, or to live the life that they want, as a result of some arbitrary fact about them, such as the colour of their skin, their religion, their sex, or their social status.

Equality of outcome: The idea that the aim of equality is to ensure that all individuals end up with an equal amount of some set of goods.

Prioritarianism: The idea that egalitarian redistribution should be concerned not with ensuring strict equality, but rather, improving the condition of the worst-off. Defended by, among others, Derek Parfit and Richard Arneson.

Sameness/Difference: The idea that treating people equally requires treating them the same, or treating them differently (for example, by recognizing their unique perspectives or rectifying past injustices through affirmative action).

Sufficiency: The idea that egalitarian redistribution should be concerned with ensuring that everyone has sufficient resources to live a life that they believe is worthwhile. Similar to *prioritarianism*. Defended by Harry Frankfurt.

Dig deeper

Harry Frankfurt, 'Equality as a Moral Ideal', *Ethics* 98 (1987), pp. 21–42.

Nancy Fraser, *Unruly Practices: Power, Discourse, and Gender in Contemporary Social Theory* (Cambridge: Polity, 1990).

Nancy Fraser, *Justice Interruptus: Critical Reflections on the 'Post Socialist' Condition* (London: Routledge, 1997).

Richard Layard, *Happiness: Lessons from a New Science* (London: Penguin, 2005).

Thomas Nagel, 'Equality', *Mortal Questions* (Cambridge: Cambridge University Press, 1979), pp.106–27.

Derek Parfit, 'Equality or Priority?', *Ratio* 10 (1997), pp. 202–21.

Samuel Scheffler, 'What is Egalitarianism?', *Philosophy and Public Affairs* 31 (2003), pp. 5–31.

Larry Temkin, *Inequality* (Oxford: Oxford University Press, 1993).

Stuart White, *Equality* (Oxford: Blackwell, 2006).

Richard Wilkinson and Kate Pickett, *The Spirit Level: Why More Equal Societies Almost Always Do Better* (London: Penguin, 2010).

Bernard Williams, *Ethics and the Limits of Philosophy* (London: Fontana, 1985).

Fact-check

1 What is the priority view?
   A The view that what matters is giving priority to the worst-off
   B The view that what matters is giving priority to equality
   C The view that what matters is giving priority to the best-off
   D The view that what matters is giving priority to treating people the same

2 What is the sufficiency view?
   A The view that equality is sufficient for justice
   B The view that what matters is that everyone has enough
   C The view that everyone should be self-sufficient
   D The view that what matters is maximizing resources

3 'Equality says that it would be better if everyone were blind than if some people were blind and some people were sighted. Therefore, equality is not a good goal.' Which objection to equality is being expressed in this quote?
   A The prioritarian objection
   B The sufficientarian objection
   C The incentives objection
   D The levelling-down objection

4 'Equality would encourage everyone to be lazy. We need inequality to make people work hard.' Which objection to equality is being expressed in this quote?
   A The prioritarian objection
   B The sufficientarian objection
   C The incentives objection
   D The levelling-down objection

5 'If a person has enough to live a decent and worthwhile life it is petty and undesirable for her to care that some people have more than her.' Which objection to equality is being expressed in this quote?
   A The prioritarian objection
   B The sufficientarian objection
   C The incentives objection
   D The levelling-down objection

6 Which of the following policies could be justified by appealing to equality based on sameness?

   A Laws against sex discrimination in the workplace

   B Equal pay for equal work

   C Unified standards of work for all employees

   D All of the above

7 Which of the following policies could be justified by appealing to equality based on difference?

   A Different retirement ages for men and women

   B Unequal pay for equal work

   C Allowing employers to promote men before women

   D All of the above

8 Which of the following policies could be justified by appealing to equality of outcome?

   A Redistributive taxation

   B Special benefits for the disabled

   C Help for housewives to return to the workplace

   D All of the above

9 Which of the following policies could be justified by appealing to the idea that people have equal moral worth?

   A Paying people according to how moral they are

   B Ending racial discrimination

   C Not imprisoning criminals

   D All of the above

10 Which of the following weakens the force of the levelling-down objection?

   A The fact that egalitarians do not believe that equality is the only value

   B The fact that we prefer no athletes to take steroids rather than have some take steroids and perform better as a result

   C The fact that levelling-down would have some good effects

   D All of the above

4

Equality (2): Equality of opportunity

In the previous chapter we looked at the concept of equality, including the idea that equality requires equal treatment and the idea of equality of outcome. In this chapter, we consider the idea of equality of opportunity. Most contemporary political theorists, and most people in contemporary liberal societies, endorse equality of opportunity. However, there is disagreement over what such a commitment entails. In this chapter, we analyse two versions of equality of opportunity: non-discrimination and meritocracy.

Equality of opportunity as non-discrimination

Equality of opportunity differs from equality of outcome. Defenders of equality of opportunity do not tend to argue that it is the responsibility of a just state to ensure that everyone has an equal share of society's resources and wealth. Rather, they seek appropriate criteria by which it is possible to distinguish between *fair* and *unfair* inequalities in outcome. There may be good reasons why some people should have more money than others; what is important is that the inequality is fair. Defenders of equality of opportunity generally argue that it is a responsibility of the state to ensure that all individuals have an equal opportunity to succeed, and to live a worthwhile life, on a level playing field with everyone else.

Securing a level playing field means that the state must remove any unfair influence of arbitrary, unchosen social and economic circumstances and personal characteristics. It must ensure that people are not held back by factors over which they have no control. In particular, equality of opportunity means that no one's life-chances should be influenced by factors like race, sex, sexuality or religion. These ascriptive characteristics are, to use John Rawls's phrase, 'arbitrary from a moral point of view': they are distributed according to luck rather than choice, and so it would be unfair to distribute public goods like jobs, places at university, and so on, on the basis of these characteristics. Defenders of equality of opportunity therefore generally agree that jobs and positions should be allocated on the basis of *relevant* characteristics rather than *irrelevant* ones, and that things like race, sex, sexuality, and religion are irrelevant.

This idea of equality of opportunity is sometimes called a principle of *non-discrimination*, but is perhaps more accurately called a principle of *fair discrimination*. After all, employers have to be able to discriminate between candidates for jobs on some grounds, just as university admissions offices need to discriminate between applicants for places on popular degree programmes: not everyone can be offered a place, or a particular job, and so we need to work out the criteria on which it is appropriate to discriminate between candidates.

Although it is popular to do so, it is not good enough to simply state that race and sex are not relevant to the process of allocating jobs or university places. Discrimination on grounds of sex and race does sometimes seem to be justified. Imagine, for example, that a gym is hiring somebody to work in the men's changing rooms, someone who will be required to enter the changing rooms when customers are undressed. Surely it is reasonable to insist on hiring a man, or at least to give preference to a man? Or imagine if a university wishes to show that it is welcoming to black people even though it is currently disproportionately white. To achieve this aim, it hires someone to go to schools which have mainly black pupils and talk to the pupils about the university and encourage them to apply. Might it not be reasonable for the university to give preference to a black applicant for the job?

One response to these kinds of cases is to say that race and sex are *sometimes* relevant to the job in question and that they can be considered in such (and only such) cases. That is to say, it is justifiable to hire only men or black people in those cases where men or black people will be *better* at the job than women or white people. On this view, equality of opportunity means hiring people according to their ability to do the job, not according to some other extraneous characteristic.

The issue of relevance still does not solve the problem, however. Imagine if a shopkeeper is hiring shop assistants, and that most customers of the shop are white and racist. As such, the customers will not buy from the shop if it hires non-white assistants. As a result, then, a non-white assistant will be worse at the job than a white assistant, because a non-white assistant will reduce, not increase, sales. Given that the point of a shop is to sell as much as possible, race is surely relevant to the job of shop assistant. So, is the shopkeeper entitled to hire only white people?

The problem here is that characteristics like race and sex become relevant to successful performance of a job in precisely those cases in which there is widespread discrimination concerning a particular job. In other words, the more entrenched is the discrimination, the more it actually is the case that being a member of the discriminated-against group really does make one less able to do the job in question.

Positive discrimination (or affirmative action)

The conception of equality of opportunity as non-discrimination is further complicated when we consider arguments in favour of positive discrimination, sometimes called affirmative action. Unfair discrimination tends to be *historically entrenched*: part of a long pattern of treating people differently. Consequently, we might allow race and sex to count as appropriate grounds for discrimination in certain circumstances, in order to undermine entrenched systems of oppression. Actively discriminating *in favour* of historically disadvantaged groups might be part of remedying that disadvantage.

Thus affirmative action has become popular among many defenders of equality in liberal democratic states such as Britain and the USA. Defenders of positive discrimination like Iris Marion Young and Anne Phillips argue that it is only fair that those who have suffered from an unjust disadvantage in the past should benefit from advantage now, so as to make up for their bad treatment (Young 1990; Phillips 1999). If black people have been denied access to a university for years, it is only fair that they get most of the places now. If women have been denied senior management positions for years, then it is right that they should now be given a higher priority for promotion. A policy of positive discrimination therefore represents a short-term, temporary corrective to entrenched patterns of unfair discrimination: once the composition of the universities, political institutions, the labour market and so on are made more equal as a result of favouring historically excluded people, then the policy of favouring these groups above others in the distribution of positions and opportunities will be redundant.

Positive discrimination is controversial. It requires us to think of people as fundamentally members of *groups*, rather than as distinct *individuals*. If we think of people individually, then past discrimination is no justification for current positive discrimination unless the same people are involved. Some have argued that this view is at odds with the wider liberal concern for individuals, over groups or communities. Others, however, have argued that liberalism *requires* positive discrimination.

One reason that liberals have given in defence of positive discrimination is that it is important to have more people from disadvantaged groups in certain positions, regardless of whether those particular individuals have faced past discrimination. This is the kind of argument that is often used in favour of women-only shortlists for candidates for the UK Parliament. It is important to give women priority, one could argue, because it is important to have more women in Parliament in order that it be more representative of society as a whole.

A second sort of reason why we might think of people as members of groups and not as individuals is if, as we have said, we are taking account of the fact that a particular group has suffered from oppression in the past. Past oppression or discrimination may still have an effect in the present. Even if a group is not currently being discriminated against, it may be the case that past discrimination disadvantages current members of the group.

For example, imagine if black people have been discriminated against in the past, as they were openly and explicitly under segregated schooling in the USA which persisted in many states until the 1960s. Imagine that, for the sake of argument, there is currently no racial discrimination in schooling. It might still follow that this generation is disadvantaged by the past discrimination. If the parents of the current generation of schoolchildren received relatively poor schooling, they may be less able to help the current generation with homework, for example, and this might have a knock-on effect for the achievements of the current generation. Or, parents who had a very negative experience of schooling under segregation might be disinclined to encourage their children to continue with schooling, or might show their children by example that their lives have not been based on school success. If this is the case, it seems that children of the current generation are suffering from the discrimination suffered by their parents, even if that discrimination no longer persists. So, we might think that positive discrimination is justified in order to break the generational cycle of disadvantage. Perhaps we need to provide extra resources to encourage black children to continue with their education if their parents are not doing so, or perhaps we need to make allowances if black children do less well than white children because their parents are less able to help with homework and so on.

Of course, the fact that the parents in our example suffered from discrimination in their schooling does not *necessarily* mean that they will be less able to help their children with homework, or will be less inclined to encourage their children to continue with their schooling. Individuals *can* overcome discrimination, and people whose schooling was relatively poor can still achieve extremely high levels of academic and career success. This fact leads some opponents of positive discrimination to argue that it treats people unequally by, ironically, failing to respect those whom it is trying to help. Opponents often argue that positive discrimination is harmful because it implies that individuals only received their job, or place in university, or whatever, because they are members of a particular group. Hence you hear people arguing that women-only shortlists actually harm women because they imply that women are not good enough to be selected as MPs without help, or that positive discrimination for ethnic minorities implies that someone only got a place at university because they are black. If we really want to treat people equally and have true equality of opportunity, such philosophers argue, we must apply the same standards to all and allow women and black people to succeed on their own merits. Positive discrimination and equality, this objection goes, are incompatible.

Equality of opportunity as a meritocracy

Another way of understanding equality of opportunity is as *meritocracy*. This is the idea that positions of advantage such as jobs should be allocated on the basis of relevant competences and, importantly, that all individuals should have an equal opportunity to develop those competences. Meritocracy thus balances a concern for a fair society (defined as one in which no one is held back by factors over which they had no control) and individual responsibility: if the state implements public policies which genuinely succeed in giving everyone a fair and equal start in life, then any disadvantages will be a result of choices that individuals have made.

Meritocracy thus rewards talent and effort, while removing the barriers to success over which individuals have no control. If people do not succeed in a meritocracy, its advocates argue, it is because they chose not to, or did not try hard enough, rather than because they came from a poor family, or from a low socio-economic position. The point of equality of opportunity understood in terms of meritocracy is to eliminate those arbitrary factors which hold people back and to reward those who work hard and develop their talents.

> 'As a nation we are wasting too much of the talents of too many of the people. Our mission [...] must be this: to break down the barriers that hold people back, to create real upward mobility, a society that is open and genuinely based on merit and the equal worth of all.'
> Tony Blair, *The Sunday Times*, 7 April 2002

Meritocracy has become very popular across the political spectrum. Its defenders (which include Tony Blair, Bill Clinton and David Cameron) argue that it aids social mobility. All individuals are given the resources they need to transcend the socio-economic conditions into which they were born. In a meritocratic society, you will not be hampered by the kind of generationally or historically entrenched structures of disadvantage that we mentioned earlier (in cases like that of black people's exclusion from public education, for example). The fact that your parents were poor, for example, or that you were born into a low socio-economic status will not, in a meritocratic society, negatively constrain your life-chances.

This is because public policy in such a society will be focused on negating the importance of these factors: a programme of state-funded education, training initiatives, progressive employment rules and similar measures will remove those entrenched and generational forms of disadvantage which can deny the worst-off the opportunities to succeed on a level playing field with those who have been born into more favourable circumstances. Furthermore, as jobs are allocated on the basis of merit rather than the benefits derived from social class and privilege (such as family contacts, friendships and so on), meritocracy requires that everyone spend time and effort developing their skills. This, defenders argue, is good for the individual, and for society.

Spotlight: Inequality and the UK political elite

To date, there have been 52 UK Prime Ministers: 38 of these studied at either Oxford or Cambridge (not including Nick Clegg, who also studied at Cambridge). 51 were men. Of those 51 men, 40 attended private school. Half of those (19) attended the *same* private school (Eton). Eton's annual fee for the year 2010–2011 was just under £30,000. The average annual salary in the UK, before tax, that same year was just under £26,000.

Meritocracy is thus an alternative solution to the entrenched forms of disadvantage addressed by positive discrimination. However, opponents have raised a number of concerns.

1 It forces people to develop certain kinds of skills at the expense of others

2 It is epistemologically incoherent and, consequently, politically dangerous

3 It wrongly assumes that people deserve the fruits of their talents.

Iris Marion Young's idea of the 'myth of merit' is discussed in a separate section. Here we will look at each of the above objections to meritocracy in turn.

> '*I have been sadly disappointed by my 1958 book,* The Rise of the Meritocracy. *I coined a word which has gone into general circulation, especially in the United States, and most recently found a prominent place in the speeches of Mr Blair.*
>
> *The book was a satire meant to be a warning (which needless to say has not been heeded) against what might happen to Britain between 1958 and the imagined final revolt against the meritocracy in 2033. Much that was predicted has already come about. It is highly unlikely the prime minister has read the book, but he has caught on to the word without realizing the dangers of what he is advocating.*'
>
> Michael Young, 'Down with Meritocracy', *The Guardian*, Friday, 29 June 2001

IT FORCES PEOPLE TO DEVELOP CERTAIN KINDS OF SKILLS AT THE EXPENSE OF OTHERS

Equality of opportunity as meritocracy encourages people to develop their skills *unequally*. It will be more efficient for an individual to develop only those skills which she is best at, or only those skills which are required for and recognized in the job market. This means that some skills (especially those not highly valued by a capitalist economy) might go undeveloped, and individuals may not develop a wide range of skills. In particular, there may be some skills which are valuable to society but which the job market gives individuals little incentive to develop, such as empathy or kindness (see, for example, Barry 2005).

IT IS EPISTEMOLOGICALLY INCOHERENT AND, CONSEQUENTLY, POLITICALLY DANGEROUS

A government committed to establishing a meritocracy is concerned to establish a level playing field among all members of society by sweeping away those arbitrary and unfair sources of disadvantage which hold people back in their pursuit of success. But how do we know, with certainty, when this level playing field has been achieved? How are we to know when we have established a meritocracy? How many

years need to have gone by before we can say with certainty
that the current generation of black children are free from
the debilitating effects of segregation in public schooling?
And what needs to have happened during those years? How
can we state with certainty that society is no longer sexist or
homophobic?

Philosophically, it is not clear that a precise answer to these
questions is possible. Politically, it is just as unlikely that
any stable consensus will prevail, given the often intense
disagreement that exists regarding these matters among
those on the Right, Left and Centre of the political spectrum.
Many libertarians, for example, would describe themselves as
defenders of meritocracy and would base their defence of the
free market on exactly this principle. Only the free market,
they might say, frees people up from state oppression and
gives them the freedom and the space that they need to be
all that they can be. A free market economy rewards talent,
ambition and hard work, and punishes laziness. Everyone
has an 'equal opportunity' to succeed in the sense that everyone
is given the freedom to do whatever they want with the skills
that they have, and to develop new skills if they wish. Such a
view was championed by neoliberals like Margaret Thatcher
and Ronald Reagan in the 1980s and is at the heart of the
'American Dream': the idea that even the poorest in society can
nevertheless achieve great things if they work hard and develop
their talents.

Egalitarians and others from the political Left, on the other
hand, argue that such a view is naive and creates (rather than
resolves) inequality. For them, the level playing field is not
established by the free market. Rather, it is established by
intervention in free markets aimed at removing those obstacles
which stand in the way of individual achievement.

The fact is that it is very difficult to measure the extent to
which particular social and economic policies have succeeded
in removing sources of unfair disadvantage, especially when
the forms of disadvantage that we are dealing with have been
entrenched and strengthened over generations. Yet meritocracy
requires that we are able to do so with a high degree of certainty.

After all, we need to know at what point (from what date) we can confidently assert that someone's failure to succeed was their own fault rather than the fault of structural disadvantage. We need to know when we can stop blaming the system, and start blaming the individual. The concern among opponents of meritocracy, then, is that the principle of meritocracy is epistemologically compromised: it requires us to know something that it is not possible to know and, hence, that it does not provide us with sufficient guidance as to what should be done to resolve inequalities.

IT WRONGLY ASSUMES THAT PEOPLE DESERVE THE FRUITS OF THEIR TALENTS

Meritocracy is based on desert: if you work hard and develop your talents then you *deserve* to have your hard work and talent rewarded. The driving idea behind this view is that you do *not* deserve to be penalized for things that you cannot do anything about, and which are purely a matter of luck (like the kind of family you were born into, how much money your parents had, etc.), but that you *do* deserve to be rewarded for things that are in your control, and that you yourself have chosen to do (like develop your talents, study hard at school, take evening classes, etc.).

But this, too, is problematic. We might concede, for example, that *effort* is in the control of the individual, and that, therefore, an individual who works hard deserves greater rewards than someone who is lazy and does not work at all. However, the question of *talent* is less clear-cut. Several philosophers have pointed out that, just as it is pure luck to be born into a rich or poor family, so it is sheer luck to be born clever or stupid, good at maths or bad at maths, good at sport or bad at sport. Of course, people can affect their skills – with practice, most people can improve at most things. But people start with different levels of talent, and may have natural limits on their ability to develop their talents as well. Even practice will not make everyone equally good at maths or sport. But, if natural endowments are just a matter of luck, how can individuals *deserve* them, or deserve to profit from them?

This kind of argument has led some contemporary political philosophers to advance a theory known as 'luck egalitarianism'. According to this theory, equality of opportunity means that people should have equal chances of success regardless of their natural endowments, as well as regardless of their race, sex, social class and so on. We discuss this view in Part Two.

Case study: Iris Marion Young and the 'Myth of Merit'

In her book *Justice and the Politics of Difference* (1990), Iris Marion Young offers a far-reaching critique of the idea of meritocracy. Her central claim is that there are no objective standards of merit that can be used to measure people's relative desert. As a result, judgements of merit are simply subjective judgements which often reflect the prejudiced interests and goals of dominant groups. The idea of merit should therefore not be used as a basis for allocating jobs in society, for four reasons.

1 Most jobs and skills are too complex to be easily observed and measured. It may be possible to measure how many products an assembly-line factory worker can process per hour, but it is much more difficult to measure how good a teacher is, or how efficient a secretary is. Most jobs require a complex mix of skills which cannot easily be measured, and so the individuals who do those jobs cannot easily be compared.

2 It is often not possible to measure the contribution of any particular individual. If a shop meets its sales targets, how can we tell what extent of sales are down to the sales skills of each individual assistant, and how many are down to other factors such as advertising and competitive prices? Again, this problem makes it difficult to measure an individual's merit.

3 Most jobs entail a considerable amount of discretion, in that they can be performed in a number of different ways. A doctor, for example, might be exceedingly technically competent and knowledgeable about disease but very poor at communicating with patients and making them feel at ease. It is not clear how we would compare that sort of doctor with another who has an excellent bedside manner and is well-liked by patients,

but who is marginally less technically expert. Communication and technical competence are both part of being a doctor, and different doctors will excel in different aspects of the job.

4 Those who are supposedly evaluating an individual's merit will often not be familiar with their work. This is clearly the case when an individual goes for interview for a new job – the interviewers must rely on the applicants' CV, references and interview skills, and may not get a full picture of the relative merits of the candidates. Even within an organization, Young suggests that decisions about pay and promotion are often made by those without direct experience of the employee's work, and are therefore not perfectly accurate.

Consequently, Young argues, the idea of merit actually strengthens entrenched inequalities and hierarchies rather than negating them.

Conclusion

Equality of opportunity is widely supported. However, it is philosophically ambiguous and politically controversial. The commitment to establishing a level playing field among all members of society can be interpreted very differently. Depending on what one thinks one needs in order to have an 'equal opportunity' to succeed, equality of opportunity can be invoked to justify anything from very extensive state intervention to completely free markets. It can be used to justify positive discrimination and to criticize it.

Nevertheless, the central insight – that all individuals should be enabled to live lives that they believe are worthwhile, and to succeed on an equal playing field with others, without having their efforts (and their future success) thwarted by arbitrary factors over which they had no control – remains a core commitment of the majority of Anglo-American political philosophers, and egalitarians more generally. Indeed, the majority of those philosophers, politicians and others who describe themselves as being committed to equality hold to some notion of equality of opportunity rather than equality of outcome. This is not universally true, of course, as we will see in Part Two. In particular, the idea of equality of opportunity has formed a key component of the kind of liberal egalitarianism defended by thinkers like John Rawls and Ronald Dworkin, whose work continues to shape the discipline of political philosophy.

Key ideas

Desert: The idea (supported by meritocrats and others) that people deserve to benefit from their talents and their hard work.

Meritocracy: A conception of equality of opportunity premised on the idea that jobs and positions should be allocated on the basis of talent and effort, once the state has removed unfair barriers to success.

Non-discrimination: A conception of equality of opportunity which emphasizes the need to exclude irrelevant characteristics (such as race, sex, sexuality, disability, etc.) from decisions concerning the appropriate allocation of jobs and positions in a society.

Positive discrimination / affirmative action: The idea that certain historically disadvantaged groups should be favoured for certain positions or jobs in order that this historical disadvantage be ended.

Dig deeper

Brian Barry, *Why Social Justice Matters* (Cambridge: Polity, 2005).

Matt Cavanagh, *Against Equality of Opportunity* (Oxford: Oxford University Press, 2002).

Ronald Dworkin, *Sovereign Virtue: The Theory and Practice of Equality* (Cambridge, MA: Harvard University Press, 2002).

Anne Phillips, *Which Equalities Matter?* (Cambridge: Polity, 1998).

John Roemer, *Equality of Opportunity* (Cambridge, MA: Harvard University Press, 1998).

Iris Marion Young, *Justice and the Politics of Difference* (Princeton, NJ: Princeton University Press, 1990).

Fact-check

1 An employer only hires people who attended the same expensive boys' private school as he did. What sort of equality of opportunity is this?
- **A** Non-discrimination
- **B** Meritocracy
- **C** Affirmative action
- **D** None of the above

2 An employer disregards race, sex and disability when hiring. What sort of equality of opportunity is this?
- **A** Non-discrimination
- **B** Meritocracy
- **C** Affirmative action
- **D** None of the above

3 An employer prefers to hire people from disadvantaged backgrounds. What sort of equality of opportunity is this?
- **A** Non-discrimination
- **B** Meritocracy
- **C** Affirmative action
- **D** None of the above

4 An employer chooses her employees by using an aptitude test. What sort of equality of opportunity is this?
- **A** Non-discrimination
- **B** Meritocracy
- **C** Affirmative action
- **D** None of the above

5 Which of the following are ascriptive characteristics?
- **A** Preferences and tastes
- **B** Talent and effort
- **C** Sex and race
- **D** Religion and lifestyle

6 Which of the following criticisms best applies to equality of opportunity as non-discrimination?
- **A** It is not easy to identify someone's ascriptive characteristics

    B   Ascriptive characteristics are sometimes relevant to the job

    C   Some people like to discriminate

    D   Some members of disadvantaged groups have not themselves suffered disadvantage

7 Which of the following criticisms best applies to affirmative action?

    A   It is not easy to identify someone's ascriptive characteristics

    B   Ascriptive characteristics are sometimes relevant to the job

    C   Some people like to discriminate

    D   Some members of disadvantaged groups have not themselves suffered disadvantage

8 What should be taken into account when hiring people, according to meritocrats?

    A   Their sex and race

    B   Their talent and effort

    C   Their religion and lifestyle

    D   Their tastes and preferences

9 Which of the following criticisms best applies to meritocracy?

    A   It is not easy to identify someone's merit

    B   Merit is sometimes relevant to the job

    C   Some people like to discriminate on merit

    D   Some people with merit have not themselves suffered disadvantage

10 Why is merit a myth, according to Young?

    A   Because everyone has equal merit

    B   Because merit is inefficient

    C   Because judgements of merit are often biased or inaccurate

    D   Because merit violates liberty

5

Power

Politics, it is sometimes said, is all about power. Hence, the study of politics is the study of power.

Political philosophers throughout history have sought to determine *who* should wield ultimate political, coercive power in a society, *why* they should hold it and not others, and what *limits* it is appropriate to place upon this power. But there is more to power than that held by rulers and states. Many contemporary political philosophers, informed by insights provided by social theorists, have suggested that power does not just reside in the hands of those who occupy formal positions of power or even in the observable behaviour of those people, but can be seen, too, in the many relationships that we have in our public and private lives, and in the very language that we use to describe the world around us and make sense of our own identities and desires. Power, that is, is often invisible, pervasive and experienced in ways that we may not easily measure or comprehend. This approach to the study of power is primarily associated with approaches such as post-structuralism, feminism, critical theory and Continental philosophy, but can also inform analytic philosophy.

We will discuss the normative question of who should rule in the chapter on democracy. In this chapter, we discuss the *concept* of power.

Some initial thoughts

We can identify two understandings of power in everyday language:

1 Power may be interpersonal: it may be something that one individual (or group) has over another individual (or group). This understanding of power leads to statements like 'the Prime Minister has power over the Cabinet' or 'the employer has power over the employee'.

2 If a person is able to do something, we may say that they have power. Thus we might say 'I have the power to lift this box' or 'the Prime Minister has the power to make policy decisions'.

What these two uses of the term 'power' have in common is that they both demonstrate that the powerful person can achieve certain goals, that she can act so as to make something happen. So, a first attempt at a general definition of power might be 'one is powerful when one makes things happen'.

However, not all cases where a person makes something happen will count as power. For the first part of our investigation into power, we need to consider three elements of powerful action: intentions, counterfactuals and capacities.

INTENTIONS

People can make things happen in all sorts of ways, many of which do not seem to show that they have power. Imagine that you are playing a game of hide-and-seek, and that it is your turn to hide. You are therefore trying to be very quiet. But, as bad luck would have it, your nose tickles and you are unable to suppress a sneeze. Hearing the sneeze, the seeker opens the wardrobe door and finds you. Now, in sneezing you have made something happen. But you don't have power. You have made something happen that you neither wanted nor intended. In fact, it looks as though you are powerless: you were unable to suppress the sneeze.

As our first qualification of the concept of power, then, we could say that a person is powerful if she makes something happen that she wants to happen. She is powerful if she gets what she wants.

If we look at this definition a little closer, however, we can see that it too has problems. Imagine that you enter the lottery. It just so happens that your numbers come up. In winning the lottery, you have got what you want. But it does not seem right to say that you are powerful. This is because it was pure chance that you won, and that chance had nothing to do with any action of yours. It was not in your control to determine whether or not you won. You have got what you want, but you have not exercised power.

It seems, then, that power must be about actively exercising some sort of control to bring about what you want. In order to be powerful, you must get what you want not as a matter of chance, but as the result of some definite action.

COUNTERFACTUALS

This brings us to the second element of power. One way of capturing this idea of power as involving some form of control is to say that, if a person is to be powerful, she must cause something to happen that would not have happened otherwise. It cannot just be a matter of simply getting what you want. Instead, you must bring it about in some way, and one way of measuring this is to consider what would have happened if you had not acted in the way that you did. Only if getting what you want depends on you doing something can we think of you as powerful.

But this cannot be a sufficient criterion for power either. We could say that winning the lottery depended on an action by you. If you had not bought the lottery ticket, and if you had not chosen those particular numbers, then you would not have won the lottery. In this sense, winning the lottery *was* crucially dependent on your actions. As we have seen, it also meant that you got something that you wanted. So why doesn't it count as an instance of power?

CAPACITY AND CONTROL

The third element of power alerts us to the fact that the powerful person must have some sort of control. If one is to be powerful in relation to something, one must have the capacity to control that thing. So, if winning the lottery is supposed to demonstrate your power, then you must be able to *ensure* that you win the lottery. It cannot just have been a lucky occurrence, a matter of chance. One way of determining whether you have the capacity to control the outcome might be to see whether you are able to bring about the same outcome again, and whether you are able to predict accurately what will happen when you are supposedly exercising power. If you are unable to repeat or predict your powerful action, we might suspect that it was not really powerful at all.

'The essence of Government is power; and power, lodged as it must be in human hands, will ever be liable to abuse.'
James Madison, Speech in the Virginia Convention, Richmond, Virginia, 2 December 1829.

The issue of capacity also alerts us to another factor of power. If power is a capacity to act, the ability to control or at least affect an outcome, then one could be powerful without actually doing anything or making anything happen. That is because one can have a capacity without actually exercising it. So, for example, the employer might have power over the employee in the sense that the employer has the capacity to sack the employee. The employer has this power whether or not she actually exercises it. Even when the employer is not sacking anyone, she is still able to do so, and is thus powerful.

These three elements, very briefly described, form part of the concept of power. Different thinkers disagree about the relative importance of each element, and therefore about what should truly count as an instance of power. Let us now consider what a number of different philosophers have said about power, and how they have weighed these three elements.

'Every communist must grasp the truth; "Political power grows out of the barrel of a gun."'
Mao Tse Tung, 'Problems of War and Strategy' [1938], *Selected Works*, vol. 2, p. 224.

Lukes and the three dimensions of power

We have seen that power, in its most general sense, might be defined as the ability of a group or individual to deliberately *cause* something else to happen, or to *influence* a particular course of events. A person might be said to have power if she is able to bring about certain events, or cause others to make certain decisions, as a result of her interventions.

However, this definition only gets us so far. Events or decisions may be influenced in all kinds of different ways, only some of which are obvious and measurable. In fact, the more we examine any particular event or decision, the more difficult it may become to establish causal links between actors in a social or political context. Furthermore, decisions can be influenced by social forces or structures. Social theorists from Durkheim, Weber and Comte to Marx and Bourdieu have emphasized that power can reside in social norms and structural factors like class, socio-economic status and education: factors that shape our decisions, preferences and actions.

Thus we might think of power not as a single phenomenon but as one which can be defined and exercised in different ways in different contexts. This is the approach taken by Steven Lukes in his book *Power: A Radical View* (1994). Lukes outlines three conceptions (or 'dimensions') of power. Let us look at each in turn.

ONE-DIMENSIONAL POWER

One-dimensional power describes those most straightforward cases of influence: cases where we would easily recognize that an actor had affected an outcome. Examples might include a pupil following the instructions of a teacher, or a soldier following orders given by an officer. In Robert Dahl's words: '*A* has power over *B* to the extent that he can get *B* to do something that *B* would not otherwise do' (Dahl 1957: pp. 202–3). Importantly, the actors involved are people and the exercise of power is observable in the behaviour of those involved. In particular, it is observable in the context of decision-making. By observing the outcome of the decision-making process, we can gain some insight into forms of influence. Where actors have expressed disagreement on their preferred courses of action, and where one actor's preference prevails, we can infer the existence of one-dimensional power. Thus, as Lukes puts it, 'this first, one-dimensional view of power involves a focus on *behaviour* in the making of *decisions* on *issues* over which there is observable *conflict* of (subjective) *interests*, seen as express policy preferences, revealed by political participation' (Lukes 1994: p. 15).

A paradigmatic example of one-dimensional power relates to government. If we were trying to work out who had one-dimensional power in the process of government, we would see who wins in cases of policy disagreement. So, our method would be to compare the policy preferences of different groups with the outcomes of the policy-making process. The group whose preferences most coincide with outcomes is deemed to be most powerful.

The one-dimensional view has the benefit of being clear and measurable. But there are three main problems with this concept of one-dimensional power, all of which will be discussed in more detail. The first problem is that it ignores the question of why and how it is that some issues become relevant and others do not: it ignores questions of which issues are introduced into the decision-making process and which are not. The second problem is that it falls foul of what Keith Dowding called the 'blame fallacy'. The third problem is that it does not deal with the question of why certain decisions are reached, or what incentives the decision-makers face. Why is it that some groups want certain things, and other groups want other things?

The first and third problems can be understood more clearly in relation to the two- and three-dimensional views of power.

Case study: The 'blame fallacy' and systematic luck

One way of understanding power is as the capacity to intentionally control events in order to make something happen. One way in which political scientists have measured power, therefore, has been to identify who benefits from particular outcomes and generalize trends from their findings. If it can be shown that public policies tend to favour the interests of big business over local communities, for example, then we might feel it reasonable to conclude that big business exerts greater power in the policy-making process than local community groups.

However, Keith Dowding points out that such a conclusion is too hasty (Dowding 1991a). While it may be true that looking at who benefits from a particular outcome, or who wanted the outcome, gives us some guidance as to who is powerful, it does not tell us anything definitive about power. For the people who benefit from a policy or decision may not actually be very powerful. They may be very lucky instead – their desired outcome may have come about without them actually doing anything. In general, Dowding warns us that we must avoid committing the *blame fallacy*. The blame fallacy occurs when we ask the question 'who benefits from a (supposed) power structure?' and conclude that the beneficiary must be the one exercising power.

While some people are lucky rather than powerful, other people or groups are what Dowding calls 'systematically lucky'. Dowding defines systematic luck as getting what you want without having to act *because of the way that society is structured*. The example that he gives is capitalists in a democratic society with regular elections. Politicians in such societies have to seek regular re-election. In general, politicians' and governments' chances of re-election depend on the state of the economy. If the economy is strong, the government is likely to be re-elected, but if it is weak, the government will probably fail. As a result, Dowding argues, all governments will try to ensure that the economy is strong, and this means that capitalists are thriving. Simply because it is in their own personal interests, politicians will work in the interests of capitalists. Capitalists in this situation do not have to do anything to persuade the government to act in their interests. In this sense, capitalists are just lucky. However, they are lucky as a result of the way that society is structured. A system of regular re-elections in an existing capitalist society will always mean that politicians have an incentive to act in the interests of capitalists. This organization of society means that capitalists will always be lucky. As Dowding puts it, they are *systematically* lucky.

TWO-DIMENSIONAL POWER

Two-dimensional power is an attempt to take into account the fact that not all issues are aired in the policy-making procedure and, as such, not all issues are decided upon. It is the power that some individuals or groups have to set the political agenda: to decide which issues are discussed and which are not. To illustrate this idea, Lukes cites Matthew Crenson's work on air pollution (Crenson 1971). Crenson's claim is that, given that all citizens have an equal interest in breathing non-polluted air, one would assume that cities with comparable levels of air pollution would spend comparable levels of legislative and executive time debating the issue. However, Crenson shows that this is not the case and that in some cities the issue is hardly discussed at all. From a one-dimensional viewpoint, this means that no one has power as regards air pollution. As no decisions are made concerning it, we cannot tell which group is more powerful. Indeed, as there are no debates on the issue, a one-dimensional theory might assume that there is no conflict of interest on air pollution, that everyone is happy with the status quo.

However, Crenson argues that the issue of air pollution is kept off the political agenda in those cities in which industry is prominent. Dominant industrial companies are able to use their reputation for power – that is, their reputation for employing large numbers of people and making large contributions to the local economy – to prevent the issue of air pollution from being raised at the explicitly political level. Lukes suggests that industry is exercising two-dimensional power: the power to influence the decision-making *process*. One way of putting this is that two-dimensional power is the power of non-decision-making. If you can prevent a decision from being made, that is a form of power – even though, by one-dimensional power standards, nothing has happened and so no power can be observed.

THREE-DIMENSIONAL POWER

The third dimension of power goes still further, and interrogates the question of what it is that people want. Lukes argues we should understand power three-dimensionally: the most effective use of power does not force people to do things that they do not want to do but rather affects what they want to do in the first place. A person who has three-dimensional power is able to affect people's desires and goals, so that what those people want corresponds to the interests of the powerful. Advertising is a good example. The point of an advert is to adjust the desires of consumers, so that they begin to want things which they did not previously want. Moreover, it is not just *people* who can be said to hold power in this sense but also social forces, institutions and norms. As we will see, many feminists have argued that gender inequality is perpetuated by prevailing sexist attitudes toward gender roles which in turn influence the choices that men and women make in their daily lives. Social norms are an example of three-dimensional power, therefore, in that they shape preferences. Marxists, too, have argued that capitalism has a similar power to shape our desires and our understanding of ourselves in ways which strengthen the dominance of entrenched elite interests. Consequently, thinkers who draw on the Marxist tradition (for example, the critical theorists of the Frankfurt School) investigate the various ways in which power is exerted by and through social norms, extinguishing political radicalism and encouraging people to embrace the capitalist system even while it undermines their genuine interests.

Three-dimensional power is therefore an extremely effective form of power because it prevents conflict before it has started. If you can organize things so that people want the same thing that you want, then you will not have to expend effort in fighting with them to achieve your goals. The fight is won before it has even begun.

The problem with this notion of power, however, is that it is difficult to identify, and difficult to distinguish cases where an individual's desires are the result of power from cases where the individual's desires are in some sense genuine, or independent of power.

Michel Foucault and self-policing citizens

Let us now discuss this radical view of power in more detail through the work of Michel Foucault. Foucault argues that power is everywhere, that we cannot escape it, and that we can never, therefore, be autonomous or free from its grasp in the way that liberalism suggests (Foucault 1975 and 1976).

Foucault argues that modern society can be compared to the Panopticon: a sort of prison in which the inmates cannot tell when they are being watched by the guards and so must assume that they are *always* under surveillance. Initially, the inmates obey the rules for fear of punishment from the ever-watchful guards, but over time this obedience becomes habitual and even desired by the prisoners. Similarly, members of modern societies may initially obey social norms for fear of punishment from fellow citizens, but much obedience is secured by habit and the *desire* to conform. Although social rules and norms are sometimes enforced explicitly, for the most part people obey without the need for constant surveillance and sanctions. We do not need to be forced to obey most laws. For the most part, most people do not kill, steal or engage in fraud even when there is no police officer standing over them. Usually, we obey the law without thinking. Similarly with social norms. A social norm is an uncodified, implicit rule about how people in society ought to behave. Norms are implicit in that we obey them without thinking, even when they are really quite odd.

Spotlight: The Panopticon

The idea of the Panopticon is not just a theoretical abstraction used by the likes of Michel Foucault to understand the nature of power. It has actually been used as the basis of the design of several prisons built around the world, such as the Presidio Modelo in Cuba, in which prisoners are kept under continual surveillance in open cells arranged in a circle around a central watchtower.

For example, it is a social norm that women but not men in Western societies can wear skirts. Most men do not have to think about not wearing a skirt. Moreover, we not only understand social norms, we often internalize them. Thus we might agree that skirts make men look silly but women look attractive. So, most men wear trousers not because they have to, but because they want to. At the same time, however, we are aware that there would be sanctions if rules of gendered dress were flaunted. If a man were to consider wearing a skirt in a public place, he would think (probably correctly) that people would condemn his choice, by staring at him, laughing at him or even explicitly expressing their disgust.

In this way, for Foucault, we are all under the influence of power all the time. Indeed, our very identity is the result of power. The fact that we like certain forms of dress, or practise certain forms of social interaction, or have certain beliefs about how people should behave, is the result of the internalization of norms, a process which constitutes power. From a Foucauldian standpoint, getting people to want to obey the rules is a form of power.

> *Power is omnipresent 'not because it has the privilege of consolidating everything under its invincible unity, but because it is produced from one moment to the next, at every point, or rather in every relation from one point to another. Power is everywhere; not because it embraces everything, but because it comes from everywhere.'*
> Michel Foucault, *The History of Sexuality, Vol. 1: An Introduction* [1976] (New York: Vintage, 1978), p. 93.

Foucault's conception of power is thus very radical. It rejects the behavioural focus of Lukes's one- and two-dimensional power, and suggests that power is exerted all the time in many ways which we cannot measure. Power is not exercised by one particular conscious individual, or by the state (as liberals tend to emphasize), but rather by all of us all the time. Any time you tell a woman that she looks nice in a skirt or tell a man that he looks too girly, you are contributing to the social norm of gendered dressing and in some way transmitting power, even if you have no intention or even awareness of doing so. Indeed, whenever you adhere to social norms your conformity contributes to their status. Power occurs whenever people interact.

Conclusion

If the study of politics is the study of power, as many believe it is, then its subject matter is as broad or as narrow as our definition of power. Liberal political theorists have tended to view power as something that is primarily found in the public sphere. Hence, liberal theorists have defended constitutional checks on state power such as the separation of powers, elections and constitutional rights. Many political scientists have equated the study of power with the study of governments and the state.

A Foucauldian understanding of power undermines this definition. If power accompanies all social interaction and does not require coercive state action, then the study of politics is much broader. Politics becomes a matter of the sorts of norms that a society upholds, and the sorts of influence which people exert on each other. Feminists, postmodernists, critical theorists and others have, in exploring the subjective, social nature of power, challenged traditional liberal assumptions.

And these conceptual discussions have normative implications. The assumption implicit in much liberal thought is that power is a dangerous thing from which individuals need protection. Although power can be used to benefit others, powerful people may often further their own interests at the expense of others. It is partly this concern that drives the argument for democracy: power is dangerous if it is in the hands of the few, and so it must be distributed equally among as many people as possible.

Again, however, if we adopt a more radical, Foucauldian conception of power, the focus will shift. While it clearly is the case that governments exercise certain forms of power, a more radical conception of power suggests that there are other hidden forms of power which go unchecked by liberal constitutional safeguards. The dominance of particular social norms, for example, is not something that we can easily undermine with traditional checks on government. If power is more than mere government activity, then it will not be so easy to ensure that it is distributed evenly, or that it does not benefit some groups more than others.

Key ideas

One-dimensional power: Lukes's term for the most straightforward and obvious manifestation of power, whereby one individual or group behaves in a way that directly influences the behaviour of another.

Two-dimensional power: Lukes's term for the power embodied in the ability of a group or individual to set the political agenda and, hence, to ensure that certain issues are not discussed.

Three-dimensional power: Lukes's radical definition of power as the ability of social forces, groups, individuals, institutions and structures to alter the preferences of individuals and, hence, to control what they want, the lives they choose, and the decisions they make in many (or all) aspects of their lives.

Social norms: The implicit social understandings and attitudes held by members of a society which determine appropriate behaviour, social roles and many other aspects of our lives. Seen by Marxists, critical theorists and feminists, as well as thinkers like Foucault and Lukes, to be important sources of power.

Dig deeper

Hannah Arendt, *On Violence* (New York: Harcourt, 1970).

Brian Barry, *Democracy, Power, and Justice: Essays in Political Theory*, vol. 1. (Oxford: Clarendon Press, 1991).

Matthew Crenson, *The Un-Politics of Air Pollution: A Study of Non-Decision Making in the Cities* (Baltimore: Johns Hopkins Press, 1971).

Robert Dahl, 'The Concept of Power', *Behavioural Science* 2 (1957), pp. 201–15.

Keith Dowding, *Rational Choice and Political Power* (Aldershot: Edward Elgar 1991a).

Keith Dowding, *Power (Concepts in Social Thought)* (Minnesota: University of Minnesota Press, 1991b).

Michel Foucault, *Discipline and Punish* [1975] (London: Penguin, 1991).

Michel Foucault, *The History of Sexuality, Volume 1: The Will to Knowledge* [1976] (New York: Vintage, 1978).

Steven Lukes, *Power: A Radical View* (Basingstoke: Palgrave Macmillan, 2004).

Fact-check

1 When your friends start getting married, you feel that you would like to get married, too. Which dimension of power might this be an example of?

    A One-dimensional power

    B Two-dimensional power

    C Three-dimensional power

2 You hand in your essay on time because your lecturer has told you that late submissions will have points deducted. Which dimension of power might this be an example of?

    A One-dimensional power

    B Two-dimensional power

    C Three-dimensional power

3 No mainstream political party in the USA advocates instituting a National Health Service (such as is found in the UK). Which dimension of power might this be an example of?

    A One-dimensional power

    B Two-dimensional power

    C Three-dimensional power

4 Which dimension of power could you study by analysing the outcome of parliamentary debates?

    A One-dimensional power

    B Two-dimensional power

    C Three-dimensional power

5 Which dimension of power could you study by analysing social norms?

    A One-dimensional power

    B Two-dimensional power

    C Three-dimensional power

6 Which dimension of power could you study by analysing dominant interests and organizations?

    A One-dimensional power

    B Two-dimensional power

    C Three-dimensional power

7 Which of the following best describes Foucault's conception of power?

A Power exists in all social interactions

B Power is concentrated in the ruling class

C Power is mainly held by the rich

D Power can be overthrown

8 According to Foucault, why is modern society like a Panopticon?

A Because we are unable to leave society

B Because compliance becomes habitual

C Because we are dominated by guards

D All of the above

9 What is systematic luck?

A Always winning the lottery

B Always winning the lottery because you control it

C Benefitting without having to act

D Benefitting without having to act because of the way society is organized

10 Which of the following best characterizes a liberal perspective on power?

A Governmental power should be kept in check by constitutional safeguards

B Governmental power should be kept in check by violence

C Power should be kept in check by critical analysis of social norms

D Power is less important than luck

6

Democracy

From ancient thinkers like Socrates, Plato and Aristotle, to modern thinkers like Locke, Hobbes, Rousseau and Kant, political philosophy has been dominated by the question of who should rule. In particular, political philosophers have asked: Where in a polity should ultimate decision-making power lie? What are the appropriate limits to this power? And who or what is responsible for policing these limits?

It has become almost universally accepted in Western liberal democratic discourse that democracy is the answer: that ultimate power should lie with the people and the political institutions which govern in their name. The authority of these institutions arises from their accountability to the citizens. Like rights, freedom and equality, democracy is often seen as self-evidently normatively justified. The assumption that those in charge should exercise the will of the people and be held to account by the citizen body is now so commonplace that it is sometimes easy to think that we no longer need to defend this idea, or that it does not give rise to profound philosophical and political problems. But we do, and it does. Although the philosophical roots of democracy can be traced back to ancient Greece, its widespread appeal is relatively new and many political philosophers have rejected it.

From direct to representative democracy

The term 'democracy' originates in the Greek word *demokratia*: *demos* (meaning 'the people'), and *kratos* (meaning rule). So in democratic systems of government (as opposed to aristocratic, monarchical, elitist or theistic ones) power is held by 'the people' rather than 'some people'. Democracy is based on *political equality*: the idea that no individual or group is inherently more worthy of holding power. Power is spread among all members of the polity equally. Decisions about the fate of the political community are made by the people of that community either directly (in direct democracy) or indirectly through elected representatives (in representative democracy). Democracy thus embodies the liberal value of *equality*, and it also protects liberal *freedom*: citizens cannot be tyrannized by their rulers because these rulers, and the laws that they enact, are extensions of the will of the people themselves.

Spotlight: Women's suffrage

The first country to grant the right to vote to all adult women was New Zealand, in 1893. In the UK some women gained the vote in 1918, with suffrage being extended to women on the same terms as men in 1928. In the USA the Nineteenth Amendment to the US Constitution, prohibiting sex-based voting restrictions, was ratified in 1920.

Democracy is therefore the ideal of *self-government*. Rather than be forced to accede to the will of a leader who is assumed to have an unquestionable right to hold power (e.g. kings, or priests, or the rich) individuals rule themselves. Democracy thus embodies the general spirit of the Enlightenment. Previous thinkers who had rejected the idea of democracy, such as Plato, Aristotle and Nietzsche, generally did so because they rejected the notion of equality: anti-democrats tend to argue that people are inherently either fit or unfit for office. But as the authority of faith and tradition declined and were replaced by the idea that authority should be based on *reason*, which is possessed by all, power became something that needed to be endorsed by all.

This vision of a self-governing population of moral and political equals has come to justify a set of institutional arrangements designed to protect individuals from tyranny. The original vision of the democratic society described by the ancient Greeks (like Aristotle), Romans (like Cicero) and later Italian republicans like Machiavelli was of a small, self-contained sovereign polity such as a city in which the citizens actively decide their fate. This ideal of direct democracy is the purest and most straightforward conception of what a democratic state should look like. However, the rise of the modern state posed a serious challenge to this view of democracy. As societies grew larger and more diverse many came to see the pure model as too idealistic. The decline of the city-state and the rise of the modern nation-state made the collective face-to-face decision-making required by direct democracy too difficult. It also made consensus difficult to achieve. Furthermore, the increased size and complexity of the modern state meant that the business of government became much more complex and beyond the reach of simple democratic decision-making. If democracy requires direct participation in the process of decision-making by the entire citizen body, then modern-day citizens would have little time for anything other than engaging in it.

So the rise of the modern state prompted the development of indirect, or *representative* democracy, in which members of society elect representatives to govern on their behalf. Representative democracy is now the dominant form of democracy in polities around the world. The representative model retains the idea of popular sovereignty (that sovereignty should lie with the citizen body) without requiring every individual citizen to engage in the affairs of state. The business of government is handled by representatives who are charged with the responsibility of legislating in accordance with the will of the people. On such a model citizen participation is limited to certain key activities, such as voting, by which political power is transferred to the representatives.

'Certainly, Gentlemen, it ought to be the happiness and glory of a representative to live in the strictest union, the closest correspondence, and the most unreserved communication with his constituents [. . .] But his unbiased opinion, his mature judgment, his enlightened conscience, he ought not to sacrifice to you, to any man, or any set of men living. These he does not derive from your pleasure, – no, nor from the law or the Constitution. They are a trust from Providence, for the abuse of which he is deeply answerable. Your representative owes you, not his industry only, but his judgment; and he betrays, instead of serving you, if he sacrifices it to your opinion.'

Edmund Burke, 'Speech to the Electors of Bristol' [1774], in
The Works of the Right Honourable Edmund Burke, vol. 1
(London: Henry G. Bone, 1854), p. 446

Three problems with democracy

The idea of democracy, in both its direct and representative forms, has been criticized by numerous thinkers throughout history. We will concentrate on three main criticisms.

THE TYRANNY OF THE MAJORITY

Democracy is a method for making decisions when people disagree. Given the diversity of modern liberal democratic states, it is unrealistic to expect consensus on most political issues. Indeed, populations of democratic states like Britain or the USA rarely, if ever, reach unanimous consensus. People disagree about almost everything: state provision of healthcare, immigration, state funding of the arts, sentencing of criminals, religion and so on. Consequently, the best that democratic states can do is enact the will of the *majority* of the people. But this means that there will be winners and losers: some people get the leaders and the laws that they want, and others do not. The losers must accede to laws and leaders with which they may profoundly disagree.

> '[T]he democratic movement is not only a form of the decay of political organization, but a form of the decay, namely the diminution, of man, making him mediocre and lowering his value.'
>
> Friedrich Nietzsche, *Twilight of the Idols* [1989] (London: Penguin Classics, 2003), p. 117.

On one level, this is not too problematic: the fact of inevitable disagreement simply underlines the fact that politics is a messy business. The role of democratic institutions is precisely to take difficult decisions in circumstances of deep disagreement. The real problem, however, is when one group or individual systematically loses out because it is permanently in a minority. The needs of homosexuals, Muslims or ethnic minorities, for example, are systematically marginalized in democratic societies with homophobic, Islamophobic or racist majorities. Such systematic marginalization seems to violate democratic principles: it violates equality *in practice*, by denying some individuals the ability to influence the political system. It denies freedom too, by repeatedly forcing some individuals to submit to the will of others.

THE TENSION BETWEEN JUSTICE AND DEMOCRACY

What happens when a majority wants to do something unjust? In a democracy, one measure of the rightness or wrongness of a policy is whether it is endorsed by the majority. When considering questions such as 'Should black children receive the same education as white children?' or 'Should the state punish homosexuality?', democratic institutions are required to take account of the will of the majority. If the majority believes that black children should receive a worse education than white children, or that homosexuality merits imprisonment, then the most democratic response to these questions seems to be that the state should legislate accordingly.

This conclusion is obviously problematic and has worried many liberals. As will become clearer in Part Two of the book, liberals have generally held that political and moral decisions must conform to principles of justice which are independent of public opinion. Such principles act as constraints on what can be done in the name of public opinion: for liberals, states cannot violate principles of justice even if the overwhelming majority of the citizen body would like them to.

Contemporary liberals seek not to *replace* democracy with justice but rather to determine constitutional safeguards to protect justice. On this approach, public opinion dictates decision-making except where stipulated by the justice-protecting liberal constitution. Nevertheless, there is a tension between justice and democracy. The more we emphasize *democracy*, the more we will have to reconcile ourselves to the possibility of states acting unjustly. The more we constrain decision making with liberal principles of *justice*, on the other hand, the less *democratic* the system becomes.

Spotlight: Freedom Day

In 1992 white South Africans voted overwhelmingly to end the system of apartheid, under which black South Africans had been denied the vote. On 27 April 1994 the first election under the new system was held, with Nelson Mandela becoming President. His party, the African National Congress, had been banned at the previous election and Mandela himself had spent 27 years in prison for his anti-apartheid activities. Millions of South Africans queued for hours to cast their votes over a three-day election period, which resulted in just under 20 million votes being counted. 27 April is now celebrated as a public holiday in South Africa, under the name 'Freedom Day'.

THE ROLE OF EXPERTISE

The third criticism of democracy can be traced back as far as the work of Plato and Aristotle, and is found most obviously in conservative critiques of democracy made by Edmund Burke and Joseph de Maistre. The criticism is that the idea that all people are equally able to govern is false. So democracy, which is based on this supposed falsehood, leads to injustice, instability and bad decision-making. The democratic claim that all individual citizens should possess equal power and that, therefore, the opinions of each and every individual in society should count equally in collective deliberations about political decisions, is intended as a safeguard against tyranny. But why shouldn't the opinions of certain people carry more weight than others in such deliberations? In virtually any realm of life outside of politics we are happy to entrust decision-making power to those who have expertise. We want brain surgery to be carried out only by people who have been trained in it, and medical research to be conducted by scientists, and children to be taught by qualified and skilled teachers.

When it comes to the business of politics, however, democracy requires the opposite. In democratic societies we think that *everyone* should have an *equal* right to influence decisions about state action. Why? It is not as if political matters are straightforward or easy. On the contrary, states require incredibly complicated and difficult decisions on a range of complex topics which have national and international implications. Democracy seems to hold that there is no role for expertise in the realm of politics, but this seems implausible. Who is best placed to decide whether, for example, Britain should sign up to an EU constitution: a team of professional politicians who have the time to develop a considered position on the matter, drawing upon the advice of experts from law, economics, business and so on, or the general public, many of whom will not have any knowledge of the issues at hand, or any appreciation of the complexities involved? Similarly, whose views should carry more weight in deliberations about environmental policy, or education policy, or policing, or the provision of healthcare, or the content of international trade agreements, or defence spending, or counterterrorism: people who, over the course of their lives, have developed specialized knowledge in these areas, or people who have not?

Representative democracy offers a solution. In placing a tier of professional decision makers above citizens, each of whom is accountable to, but not entirely controlled by, the people who elected them, the representative model puts decision-making power in the hands of people who are charged with thinking about these issues on a full-time basis, without abandoning the idea that ultimate power lies in the hands of the citizen body at large. But still, politicians in a representative system are broadly required to act in accordance with the will of their constituents, even if only out of a desire to get re-elected. And at the normative level, the fact still remains that a central pillar of democracy is that political decisions are best taken collectively, with each and every individual's opinions counting the same. Consequently, democracy necessarily embodies the claim that governing, unlike virtually anything else, is something that everyone is equally able to do, not something best conducted by experts.

Two alternative conceptions of democracy: deliberative and radical democracy

A number of contemporary political theorists have developed alternative versions of democracy. Some, including Amy Gutmann, Dennis Thompson, Joshua Cohen and James Bohman, have suggested that we should understand democracy as a process of collective deliberation about policies and laws rather than as a particular set of institutions. Democracy, they argue, describes not an *end-state* but rather an ongoing *process* of dialogue among free and equal individuals. Its aim should be to identify and prioritize social and political problems, and to seek collective agreement on how to resolve these problems. While a traditional, representative conception of democracy focuses on establishing institutional and constitutional structures necessary to hold the power of legislators in check (e.g. regular free and fair elections, constitutional checks and balances, bills of rights, etc.), deliberative democrats emphasize the process of deliberation about policy.

Deliberative democracy has become very popular among liberal political philosophers. The reason for this popularity is that it appears to resolve the tension between justice and democracy and the problem of the tyranny of the majority. Deliberative democracy is not simply about translating the will of the majority into action; it is about bringing diverse people together in active dialogue so they can find genuine agreement on controversial matters. Citizens meet as moral and political equals and reason collectively with one another about political questions. The answers and agreements they come up with are not set in stone but can be revisited in the light of new developments.

Despite its popularity among liberals, deliberative democracy has been fiercely criticized by radical democrats like Chantal Mouffe and Ernesto Laclau (Mouffe and Laclau 2001). Radical or 'agonistic' democracy retains the notion of active deliberation but rejects the idea that it is possible, or even desirable, for diverse groups and individuals to reach agreement on political and moral questions. Radical democrats reject the optimism that liberals have about the ability of reason to generate consensus. From Mill to Rawls, liberals have emphasized the role of reasoned argument and deliberation as a means of revealing the truth or falsity of claims about the world, which is why they defend free speech: public deliberation on moral, ethical, political and other matters can be the basis for unity between diverse groups. It is not surprising, therefore, that many liberals have sought to reconceive democracy as a deliberative process grounded in liberal principles of freedom, equality and reason: such a model brings democracy within liberal theory, and (they argue) resolves the tensions between justice and democracy, and the problem of the tyranny of the majority, that we described earlier.

The problem with deliberative democracy, however, is that it simply asserts the good of liberal values at the outset. That is, deliberative democrats simply reconceive the democratic process as necessarily characterized by liberal principles such as individualism, freedom and equality. They also hold that free and equal individuals can and should seek agreements among one another about political and ethical matters via reasoned public deliberations which are themselves constrained by the norms of liberal deliberation. That is, deliberative democracy resolves the tension between liberal justice and democracy by simply ruling out forms of deliberation which would produce outcomes inconsistent with liberal justice.

Radical democrats like Mouffe and Laclau are more pessimistic about the capacity of reasoned debate to produce agreement, and are fiercely critical of both liberalism and liberal democracy. Drawing on a more radical, Marxist, literature, Laclau and Mouffe criticize liberalism for its inability to take moral diversity seriously, since it requires divergent groups to put aside their differences and adopt the values of liberalism in order to come up with collective decisions about institutions, policies and political principles. But, they suggest, you are not taking diversity seriously if you require, for the purposes of resolving political questions, everyone to adopt the same values, understand themselves in the same way, and deliberate according to the same norms.

Liberals and deliberative democrats do not see this as a problem because they believe that liberal principles are neutral. But, Laclau and Mouffe argue, liberal values are neither: they embody a substantive moral and political world view which is controversial and which will be incompatible with the world views held by many groups and individuals in diverse states. Consequently, if a democratic system is to take diversity seriously, and is to avoid oppressing non-liberal members of states into adopting a perspective on the world that they find alien or mistaken, then it needs to make room for the very real possibility that disagreement on fundamental matters of politics and morality is inevitable. Reason may not provide the common ground that liberals and many democrats need it to, because different groups and individuals will 'reason' in different ways.

Thus radical democracy emphasizes the inevitability of disagreement. Democracies should establish institutional frameworks in which different groups can express their disagreements, but they should not necessarily seek to resolve these disagreements. Agonistic democracy is thus more unstable than deliberative or more traditional conceptions of democracy, and insists that politics is inherently unstable. Deliberative and traditional democrats try to ensure stability by misrepresenting the nature of politics and downplaying the divisions which will inevitably exist in society. Consequently, democracy may be a less stable form of politics than many would like it to be, but that is simply unavoidable in a world characterized by fundamental disagreement over moral, political and ethical matters.

Case study: The problem of political disengagement

Liberal democratic states across the world are suffering from declining levels of political engagement among their citizens (Parvin and McHugh 2005; Putnam and Feldstein 2003; Stoker 2006). In Britain, for example, only just over half of those eligible to vote in general elections choose to do so, and even fewer choose to vote in local or European elections, in which turnout stands at around 35 per cent. Turnout is especially low among the young, with only 44 per cent of 18- to 24-year-olds choosing to cast a ballot in the 2010 general election. Furthermore, membership of political parties is currently at its lowest point in the post-war era, party allegiance has eroded, and trade union membership has fallen in recent years.

This general story is replicated in other countries, too, with levels of political engagement and trust in politicians declining in many advanced Western democracies. The fact of increased political disengagement among citizens of liberal democratic states raises serious concerns about the enduring strength and legitimacy of the democratic system. Democratic institutions rely on participation by the citizen body for their legitimacy. Governments need a democratic mandate acquired through an electoral majority among a broad cross section of the population. Political parties need members, and activists, if they are to survive, as do the pressure groups and lobby organizations which represent particular interests in the policy-making process. If citizens turn away from the political process, then they become estranged from the institutions and organizations which are assumed to be working in their name. Representative democracy is more able to cope with the decline in participation than direct democracy, of course, as it does not rely on active participation among the public in the business of decision-making. However, as levels of participation continue to fall, it becomes increasingly difficult to see elected representatives as embodying the will of the people.

The concern, therefore, is that declining participation in liberal democratic states robs the political system of its legitimacy and its ability to make good on democratic ideals. Laws and decisions become external impositions rather than extensions of the will of the people, thus undermining individual *freedom*. And declining engagement places disproportionate power in the hands of those who *do* choose to engage in political activity, thus threatening political *equality* and the idea of equal *representation*.

Conclusion

Democracy has widespread appeal. It places power in the hands of the people, enshrines individual freedom and equality, and protects citizens from tyranny by making political institutions, and the people who work in them, accountable to each and every member of society. In an era in which democratic ideals have spread around the world, and are used as a benchmark against which regimes are evaluated, it seems odd to suggest that it is not clear what democracy actually is, or whether it can hope to live up to its high ideals. But as political philosophers we are required to look beyond popular assumptions, and evaluate the coherence and persuasiveness of the evidence before us. The fact that there are so many different definitions of democracy suggests that there is a problem somewhere: different thinkers have understood democracy in so many different ways that, upon close inspection, the idea begins to become ambiguous and unclear. Does democracy require active participation from citizens? Who should be granted the status of a citizen? What is the appropriate relationship between citizens and their representatives? Does democracy describe a particular set of institutional and constitutional structures? Or is it best understood as a process of deliberation among free and equal individuals? Should states ultimately be guided by the will of the people, or justice, or something else? Should democratic decisions be grounded in collective agreement? Or is this utopian and oppressive? What is the relationship between democracy and rights? And is it true that all individuals are equally deserving of power, or have an equal right to influence political decisions?

'It has been said that democracy is the worst form of government
except all the others that have been tried.'
Winston Churchill, British Prime Minister (1940–45 and 1951–55)

It is inevitable that a chapter this length will raise more questions
than it answers. What is certain, however, is that the nature
and persuasiveness of democracy is not as self-evident as many
academics, politicians and political activists may initially believe.

Key ideas

Democracy: A contested term, defined in many different ways,
broadly understood as a system of politics in which ultimate power
(or 'sovereignty') lies with each and every individual citizen equally,
and that political institutions and the people who work in them are
accountable to the people.

Deliberative democracy: A relatively recent re-conception of
democracy, particularly popular among contemporary liberals,
which understands democracy as describing a process of
collective deliberation among free and equal individuals rather
than a particular set of institutional or constitutional structures.

Radical – or 'agonistic' – democracy: A conception of democracy,
associated with the work of Chantal Mouffe, Ernesto Laclau and
Bonnie Honig, which rejects the idea (found in deliberative democracy)
that reason can transcend or resolve deep disagreements about
moral, political and ethical matters in order to provide grounds for
substantive agreement on decisions about politics.

Direct democracy: The idea that democracy requires the active
participation of citizens in decision-making, unmediated as far as
possible by external organizations, institutions or representatives.
Draws on ideas associated with civic republicanism.

Representative democracy: The most widespread conception of
democracy, arising as a consequence of the growth and increased
diversity of political communities as they moved from cities to
nations, in which the citizen body elect a body of professional
representatives tasked with engaging in the business of
government on their behalf.

Dig deeper

David Beetham, *Democracy* (Oxford: One World, 2005).

Robert A. Dahl, *Democracy and its Critics* (New Haven, CT: Yale University Press, 1991).

Amy Gutmann and Dennis Thompson, *Why Deliberative Democracy?* (Princeton, NJ: Princeton University Press, 2004).

Chantal Mouffe and Ernesto Laclau, *Hegemony and Socialist Strategy: Towards a Radical Democratic Politics* (London: Verso, 2001).

Phil Parvin and Declan McHugh, 'Defending Representative Democracy: Political Parties and the Future of Political Engagement in the UK', *Parliamentary Affairs* 58 (2005), pp. 632–65.

Robert Putnam and Lewis Feldstein, *Better Together: Restoring the American Community* (New York: Simon & Schuster, 2003).

Gerry Stoker, *Why Politics Matters: Making Democracy Work* (Basingstoke: Palgrave Macmillan, 2006).

Iris Marion Young, *Inclusion and Democracy* (Oxford: Oxford University Press, 2000).

Fact-check

1 What is the literal meaning of 'democracy'?
   A   Rule by the people
   B   Rule for the people
   C   Rule by the best
   D   Rule by the monarchy

2 What is direct democracy?
   A   The idea that decision-making should be directed at the most pressing problems
   B   The idea that decision-making should provide direction to the state
   C   The idea that all people should be directly involved in decision-making
   D   The idea that decisions should be unanimous

3 What is representative democracy?
   A   The idea that democracy best represents how people actually make decisions
   B   The idea that democracy is representative of political processes around the world
   C   The idea that decisions should be made by the best-qualified people
   D   The idea that decisions should be made by representatives of the people

4 What is the 'tyranny of the majority'?
   A   The problem that, in a democracy, only the majority's view counts
   B   The problem that, in a democracy, the majority can act unjustly
   C   The problem that, in a democracy, minority groups can find themselves unable to influence policy
   D   All of the above

5 How have liberals tried to resolve the tension between democracy and justice?
   A   By rejecting democracy
   B   By rejecting justice
   C   By introducing constitutional safeguards to prevent unjust decision-making
   D   All of the above

6 What sort of democracy do Britain and the USA have?
   A Direct democracy
   B Representative democracy
   C Deliberative democracy
   D Agonistic democracy

7 What is the difference between deliberative and agonistic democracy?
   A Agonistic democracy rejects deliberation
   B Agonistic democracy rejects the rule of the people
   C Agonistic democracy rejects the need to reach consensus
   D All of the above

8 What is the difference between deliberative democracy and representative democracy?
   A Deliberative democracy focuses on process rather than on institutions
   B Deliberative democracy requires people to try to reach consensus
   C Deliberative democracy encourages compromise
   D All of the above

9 What is wrong with democracy, according to thinkers such as Plato and Aristotle?
   A It is based on the false notion that people are equally fit to rule
   B It is based on the false notion that freedom is important
   C It is based on the false notion that people enjoy politics
   D It is based on the false notion that politics is about power

10 Which of the following are required for a polity to be a democracy?
   A Elections
   B Written constitution
   C High levels of political engagement
   D None of the above

7

Rights

Most readers of this book will support the idea of rights, particularly human rights. The idea that there are certain things that people may not do to one another, and that these limits should be expressed in the language of rights, has become deeply engrained in the political culture of Western liberal democratic states. Moreover, *human* rights have been adopted by the United Nations and other bodies as providing the basis for standards of international justice. Documents such as the Universal Declaration of Human Rights stipulate the limits of what can be done by individuals to other individuals in the name of faith, or community values or traditions, but they also impose constraints on what *states* can do to their own people. *Human* rights are therefore different to *legal* rights: they are not derived from laws but are held by all individuals regardless of the laws which happen to exist in any country and regardless of the particular traditions or values which shape the public culture of those countries. Rights are therefore controversial.

What implications do rights have for our theorizing about politics? What are their strengths and weaknesses? It is not possible to offer a ground-up defence of rights here. Such a defence can be pieced together throughout this book, in particular the chapter on global justice, in which we discuss the idea of liberal universalism in some detail. In this chapter, we focus on the role rights have played in contemporary debates about justice, and in the doctrine of liberalism more generally.

Two liberal arguments in defence of rights

DWORKIN'S 'RIGHTS AS TRUMPS'

Liberalism is committed to protecting the individual from tyranny. It does so by establishing constitutional checks on the power of the *state* and on the power of the *community* at large. In doing so, liberalism holds the interests of the individual as sacrosanct, and rejects the idea that the interests of the individual can be overridden by the interests of the state or the community as a whole. These constitutional checks are often (but not always) framed in terms of rights: things which all human beings hold on account of their basic humanity which cannot be denied or overridden by other considerations. This general approach is most obviously embodied in Rawls's liberal egalitarianism (which we will discuss later).

However, perhaps the most influential liberal account of *rights* was presented by Ronald Dworkin in his 'Rights as Trumps' (Dworkin 1984). Dworkin's basic assertion is that rights act as trumps over any justification for communal decisions. A trump is something that beats, or overrides, other considerations. So, by calling rights trumps, Dworkin is saying that a right overrides other considerations or interests. Imagine, for example, that a government wants to prevent its citizens from expressing opposing political views. We might respond that to do so would violate the *right* of free expression. The effect of our response would be to assert that free expression must override the will of the government. The *right* to free expression *trumps* the government's desire. Or, imagine if a society democratically agreed to execute all members of a minority group. We could appeal to that minority's right to life as a tool to defend their interests from the interests of the society as a whole. By saying that the minority has a right, we are saying that it must trump, or override, the community decision.

For Dworkin, this feature is true of rights by definition. His claim is that it is part of what we mean by a right that it must have overriding importance. Indeed, this often is the common usage of the concept of rights. A bill of rights is a statement of the fundamental interests of citizens which the state may not infringe. The United Nations Declaration of Human Rights is intended to *limit* the powers of states, to set out what they may not do to their citizens and what they must provide for them. The idea here, then, is that human rights trump other interests or wishes of states. Human rights override state sovereignty.

> 'Rights [...] are best understood as trumps over some background justification for political decisions that states a goal for the community as a whole. If someone has a right to moral independence, this means that it is for some reason wrong for officials to act in violation of that right, even if they (correctly) believe that the community as a whole would be better off if they did...'
>
> Ronald Dworkin, 'Do We Have a Right to Pornography?', *A Matter of Principle* (Cambridge, MA: Harvard University Press, 1985), p. 359.

Importantly, for Dworkin, rights override even other moral considerations. If a proposed system or principle of morality tells us or allows us to do something that violates someone's rights, then the rights must take precedence. As an example, Dworkin considers the moral theory of utilitarianism. Utilitarianism, as we see in Chapter 9, is the theory that morality or justice depends on maximizing happiness, or utility. For a utilitarian, the right thing to do is the thing that maximizes overall utility. Dworkin, like Rawls and other liberals, argues against utilitarianism, claiming that individual rights stipulate things that we cannot do to people even in the name of increasing general utility.

The obvious question is how to justify this idea that rights override other moral principles. Logically speaking, there are two possible answers. First, we could say that rights override other moral principles or theories because they are justified by a different, more important principle. So, if our moral theory is based on the principle of maximizing overall utility, we could say that rights are based on a different principle which is actually more important than utility – perhaps the principle of respect for individuals and their interests. Alternatively, we could say that rights override other moral principles because rights are actually implied by those other moral principles. In other words, if we understood our moral principles properly, we would see that they require us to respect individual rights. Dworkin proposes this second approach, arguing that rights should trump even utilitarian conclusions, because utilitarian theories in fact presuppose a prior commitment to rights.

The reason for this, he argues, is that utilitarianism embodies the idea that the preferences of each and every individual should count equally, and that no individual's preferences should be considered more or less important in decisions about how the state or individuals should or should not act. To stop the interests of some receiving unequal consideration, Dworkin argues, it is necessary to assert the *right* of each and every individual to have their preferences considered on an equal basis with others.

NUSSBAUM, RELIGION AND CONFLICTING RIGHTS

Dworkin argues for a liberal, rights-based morality so as to protect individuals from injustices arising from prevailing opinions. Rights therefore protect against the tyranny of the majority. This majority may be society as a whole, or it may be the majority in some particular cultural group. Martha Nussbaum argues, in *Sex and Social Justice* (Nussbaum 1999), that rights should protect individuals from injustice perpetrated in the name of religion or culture.

Nussbaum argues that the fact that a particular religion sanctions certain acts does not serve to excuse those acts, if they contravene liberal rights. Broadly speaking, religious communities living within liberal democratic states must constrain the pursuit of their religious beliefs and not violate anyone's individual rights. For example, religious groups which hold that women are inferior to men, or which seek to enforce strict gender roles which entrench sexist attitudes, or which hold illiberal views regarding homosexuals, are nevertheless required to conform to laws ensuring equality. So the liberal state would protect the right of Orthodox Jewish women to seek legal divorce and equitable reparations even though Orthodox Judaism bans women from seeking divorce. Similarly, the liberal state would not uphold claims by Muslim groups which hold that homosexuals should be punished on account of their sexuality.

> 'I understand a human right to be a claim of an especially urgent and powerful sort, one that can be justified by an ethical argument that can command a broad cross-cultural consensus, and one that does not cease to be morally salient when other circumstances render its recognition inefficient. A human right, unlike many other rights people may have, derives not from a person's particular situation of privilege or power or skill but, instead, just from the fact of being human.'
>
> Martha Nussbaum, *Sex and Social Justice* (Oxford: Oxford University Press, 1999), p. 87.

But there is a tension here. Liberal rights are supposed to enshrine the basic liberal claim that the state should, as far as possible, allow individuals to decide for themselves what kind of life they want to lead. And so rights have been invoked by many liberals as a protection against religious persecution. That is, liberal rights specifically protect the right of all individuals to practise their religion, and to live their lives according to traditional religious teachings. But what happens when the right to practise religion conflicts with other rights? The issue of conflicting rights is an important one. Often an appeal to individual rights will not solve acute moral dilemmas so much as open other complex issues. How should states adjudicate conflicts between the rights of children and their parents, for example, or the clash between the right to free speech and the right to be protected from slander or hate speech? The idea that normative questions can be resolved by an appeal to individual rights ignores the fact that many rights conflict.

This is a real problem with rights-based moralities. On the specific case of religion, however, Nussbaum is clear in her defence of what is a dominant (but not unanimous) view among liberals: if a religion conflicts with other human rights then, she states, the other human rights should take precedence. This is because the bearers of rights are *individuals* not *groups*: the right to freedom of religious exercise should be taken to apply to each individual person, not to a religious group and, hence, religious groups do not have the 'right' to force their members to adopt certain values or engage in practices with which those individual members disagree.

Are rights too individualistic?

Dworkin and Nussbaum both use rights to distinguish between the interests of 'the individual' and the interests of 'the group', giving priority to the former. For liberals like them, therefore, rights are necessarily *individualistic*. But many critics of liberalism have rejected rights as too individualistic.

There are two main ways in which theories of rights have been criticized for being overly individualistic. First, rights-based moralities might be wrong in emphasizing the good of the individual over the good of the community. Second, rights-based moralities might be wrong in assuming that individuals themselves do not value community.

THE GOOD OF THE INDIVIDUAL VS. THE GOOD OF THE COMMUNITY

Rights ensure that the interests of the individual can override the interests of the community. However, although there are cases where we might think that this prioritization of the individual is correct, there may be other cases in which we think that the greater good should prevail. Indeed, there are many cases in which we might think that it is right to put the good of the community above the good of a particular individual or group of individuals.

> '[T]here are no... rights, and belief in them is one with belief in witches and in unicorns. The best reason for asserting so bluntly that there are no such rights is indeed of precisely the same type as the best reason which we possess for asserting that there are no witches and the best reason which we possess for asserting that there are no unicorns: every attempt to give good reasons for believing that there are such rights has failed.'
>
> Alasdair MacIntyre, *After Virtue: A Study in Moral Theory* (London: Duckworth, 1981), p. 69.

For example, consider the philosophical example of the ticking time bomb scenario. You are the chief of police of a major American city, and you have apprehended and detained a known terrorist. Imagine, further, that this terrorist has informed you that he has hidden a time bomb that will explode in one hour in a highly populated area of the city. Given the size of the city, it is all but impossible to find the bomb, or to evacuate the city. The question is: Are you, as chief of police, justified in authorizing the torture of the terrorist in order to find out the location of the bomb and, hence, save many innocent people?

Your answer will largely depend on your approach to moral theory and how committed you are (if at all) to the idea of individual rights. The liberal approach, as exemplified in the work of Dworkin and Nussbaum, implies that you should not torture the terrorist. The terrorist, like any other individual, possesses rights which cannot be trumped by the general good of the community as a whole, such as the right not to be tortured. However, this seems like a very demanding principle. It would not matter if, in our example, the bomb would kill five or one hundred or 20 million people. The wrongness of torture is not affected by the number of casualties. It comes from the fact that it violates fundamental rights that all people, including terrorists, have and so it is just as wrong to torture a terrorist in order to save 20 million lives as it is to save a single life.

You may well find this conclusion unpalatable. Of course, you might want to say, there should be a presumption against torture, because it is awful. You might even agree that torture represents a violation of individual rights. However, you might nevertheless envisage a set of circumstances in which it would be morally appropriate to violate the terrorist's rights. This requires you to weigh the rights of some people against others, and to evaluate the good of respecting the terrorist's right not to be tortured against the rights of others not to be killed. It also makes the specific consequences of the specific action morally relevant in a way that it is not for the liberal: it makes a difference (morally) whether we are talking about saving one or 20 or 20 million lives. The nature and extent of the good that our actions will bring about needs to be weighed against the bad that would be brought about by our not acting. While presumably no one would argue that torture should be considered anything other than terrible, some may wish to argue that there may nevertheless be circumstances in which we, with heavy heart, are morally required to do whatever is necessary in the interests of the greater good, even if this means violating the rights of one or more individuals. That is, to put it in more formal philosophical language, we may adopt a *consequentialist* approach to moral reasoning rather than a liberal *deontological* one (see Chapter 9).

Spotlight: 'Want to Torture? Get a Warrant'

In 2002 Alan Dershowitz – a highly respected legal theorist, lawyer, and Harvard professor – wrote a very controversial article for the *San Francisco Chronicle* in which he argued that, under certain circumstances, the state should be legally permitted to torture terror suspects. In the article, entitled 'Want to Torture? Get a Warrant', Dershowitz argued that authorities could apply for, and be granted, warrants allowing the use of 'non-lethal' torture techniques on suspected terrorists if there were an 'absolute need to obtain immediate information in order to save lives coupled with probable cause that the suspect had such information and is unwilling to reveal it'. (Alan Dershowitz, 'Want to Torture? Get a Warrant', *San Francisco Chronicle*, 22 January 2002.)

This is an extreme case, and many people think that torture is so morally repulsive that the right not to be tortured *should* always be a trump. Still, we can imagine less extreme examples. Think of the right to free speech, including the right of the media to speak freely. Imagine that a newspaper journalist learns that the police are planning a dawn raid on the houses of a ring of child pornographers. The journalist plans to publish the story in her newspaper the day before the raid, and thus to exercise her right of free speech. However, if she does so, the child pornographers will read that they are to be arrested the next day, and will immediately destroy any evidence of wrongdoing, or will go on the run so that the police can't catch them. If this happens, they will not be arrested and will continue to abuse children. If we endorse Dworkin's rights as trumps, we will have to uphold the journalist's right to free speech even if that results in the pornographers going free. This result, we could say, is an unacceptable prioritization of the individual against the overwhelming interest of the community.

Case study: Civil liberties

The issue of individual rights vs. community safety has become much more central to public political discourse in the past decade. Following 9/11 and the 7/7 terrorist bombings in London, the USA and Britain introduced anti-terror legislation which dramatically strengthened the powers of the police to search and detain suspected terrorists. The USA introduced the Patriot Act which made it legal, among other things, to record the private phone calls of suspected terrorists and Britain introduced a raft of controversial measures including greater police powers to stop and search people and to detain suspected terrorists for long periods of time without charge. Furthermore, in Britain and the USA the police were authorized to make greater use of CCTV cameras and other forms of surveillance in the interests of defending society against the perceived terrorist threat.

Many human rights organizations including Amnesty International and Liberty have pointed out that the anti-terror legislation introduced in Britain and the USA represents a straightforward erosion of individual rights: it places further constraints on what people can and cannot do; it strengthens the powers of the police relative to individuals; it makes it possible (in Britain, at least) for the police to detain suspects for extended periods of time without charge, and it violates citizens' right to privacy by allowing the state to monitor, and video, our everyday lives. The controversy is not whether these and other measures lead to a weakening of our individual rights, then, but whether or not it is defensible to weaken our individual rights in the name of some other good like national security.

George W. Bush and Tony Blair, among others, argued that while the constraint of individual rights was regrettable, it was nevertheless a necessary price to pay to ensure public safety from terrorists. Handing the police greater powers to question and detain citizens, and allowing the police to record our actions on film, made us safer, they argued, and as such, it was the morally right thing to do. It placed justifiable constraints on *individual* rights in the interests of the wider, *public* good. As with the ticking time bomb scenario, your own position on this question will depend on how committed you are to the inviolability of individual rights and whether you think that it is ever justifiable to trade rights off against other goods.

RIGHTS-BASED MORALITIES IGNORE CITIZENS' COMMUNITY SPIRIT

Rights formally attribute entitlements and duties to individuals, implying that people are not naturally inclined to assist each other. Rights-based moralities thus imply that there will be conflict between individuals, rather than mutual co-operation. Some critics thus argue that rights might encourage individuals to do only what is absolutely required of them. People will jealously guard their rights and insist that others perform their duties. Rather than treating each other with compassion and generosity, rights as trumps encourage people to insist on their entitlements and perform only those kindnesses which are absolutely required as duties.

Some political philosophers and political scientists suggest that one only need look at contemporary US society to see the problems associated with a preoccupation with individual rights. Robert Putnam argues that there has been a decline in 'social capital' in America and elsewhere: a decline in the social and communal bonds which stop liberal societies becoming merely a collection of abstract individuals (Putnam 2000). The rise of the free market reinforces the idea that people are *individuals* who possess *rights*, rather than *citizens* who co-operate for *collective* ends.

These changes, along with other cultural, economic and legal shifts toward an individualist, rights-based moral and legal culture, have had a number of profound consequences for liberal democratic societies. First, they have created an explosion in litigation, in which public life is characterized by conflicts between rights-bearing individuals played out in courtrooms, adjudicated by judges who do their best to interpret the implications of the liberal rights-based constitution. And, secondly, they have encouraged an expansion of the realm of rights into areas in which many believe to be inappropriate. The more comfortable we become with invoking our individual rights as a way of getting what we want, the more we do so. Consequently, while citizens of liberal democratic states used to think of themselves as having rights to things like free speech and religion, now an increasing number think they have 'rights' to do things like use the Internet or to keep pets.

Communitarian critics of liberalism like Michael Sandel, Alasdair MacIntyre and Charles Taylor (discussed in detail in Chapter 13) see these problems as consequences of the rise of liberal individualism and rights-based morality. Our moral ties with our fellow citizens wane and we try to replace them with liberal rights, which are not suited to do the job. What we end up with, therefore, is a decline in community and the moral ideas that we drew from it. Consequently, they argue, we need to rescue modern morality and politics from liberal individualism by reclaiming the idea of community, and emphasizing the common bonds which all members of a particular community share (and which can therefore provide the basis for a common morality based on a particular conception of the good life) rather than those things (like individual rights) which emphasize the distinctiveness of each and every individual, and put them in competition with one another.

Liberals reject this claim, arguing that a focus on community may lead to injustice and oppression of minorities and, furthermore, that just because a constitution stipulates that all people hold rights, it nevertheless does not mean that everyone need always invoke them (e.g. Tomasi 1991).

Conclusion

Some of the most enduring social and political reforms of the past century have been in the name of rights. The suffragettes and, later, the activists of the women's movement who campaigned for political equality for women in Britain and the USA, the civil rights activists who campaigned for equality for black people, and the NGOs, organizations and individuals who have worked, often in frightening and difficult circumstances, to establish equal rights around the world, have all fought to realize a political and moral vision in which all people are considered free and equal, and no one suffers exploitation or oppression on account of their race or religion or sex or anything else.

But, as we have seen in this chapter and will continue to see throughout this book, rights are complicated and sometimes problematic. Rights establish conflicts: between the individual and the community, or between different rights, or between states which respect rights and those which do not. Rights must be traded off against one another: How important is the right to free speech compared to the right not to be libelled, for example, or the right to practise one's religion compared to the right not to be subjected to unfair religious traditions? What aspects of our lives are appropriately understood as within the realm of rights, and which fall outside it? And on what *exactly* are rights based? – If in our basic humanity, then what is it about being human which leads to rights? If in legal statutes, then how can rights be used to criticize unfair laws?

Once we get beyond idealistic generalities, we soon realize that the appeal to rights raises as many questions as it answers. This is not to say that we should reject rights, for a framework of rights is the cornerstone of liberal democracy. However, it is to say that our commitment to rights needs to be evaluated in the context of other fundamental principles, and that the consequences of a thoroughgoing commitment to rights are perhaps unclear and, often, problematic.

> **Spotlight:** The European Convention on Human Rights

The UK incorporated the European Convention on Human Rights into British law in 1998. It protects rights such as the right to life, the prohibition of torture, the right to freedom of expression and the right to respect for private and family life.

Key ideas

Communitarianism: Discussed in detail in Chapter 13. Broadly speaking, the view, exemplified in the work of thinkers like Michael Sandel and Alasdair MacIntyre, that the liberal emphasis on rights is philosophically mistaken and politically dangerous.

Rights as trumps: A definition of rights, defended by Ronald Dworkin, whereby rights are understood to 'trump' other moral and political considerations.

Tyranny of the majority: Initially explained in the work of Tocqueville, but later taken up by Mill and other liberals. The idea that individuals can have their interests or opinions unjustly overridden by majorities. Represents a key concern for liberals and a principal justification for the establishment of civil rights to act as protections against the will of the majority.

Dig deeper

Ronald Dworkin, *Taking Rights Seriously* (London: Duckworth, 1978).

Ronald Dworkin, 'Rights as Trumps', in Jeremy Waldron (ed.), *Theories of Rights* (Oxford: Oxford University Press, 1984).

Ronald Dworkin, *A Matter of Principle* (Cambridge, MA: Harvard University Press, 1985).

Joel Feinberg, *Rights, Justice, and the Bounds of Liberty* (Princeton, NJ: Princeton University Press, 1980).

Alasdair MacIntyre, *After Virtue: A Study in Moral Theory* (London: Duckworth, 1981).

Martha C. Nussbaum, *Sex and Social Justice* (Oxford: Oxford University Press, 1999).

Robert Putnam, *Bowling Alone: The Collapse and Revival of American Community* (New York: Simon & Schuster, 2000).

Joseph Raz, *The Morality of Freedom* (Oxford: Oxford University Press, 1986).

Hillel Steiner, *An Essay on Rights* (Oxford: Blackwell, 1994).

John Tomasi, 'Individual Rights and Community Virtues', *Ethics* 101 (1991), pp. 521–36.

Fact-check

1 Who argues that rights are trumps?
   A Gerald Dworkin
   B Andrea Dworkin
   C Ronald Dworkin
   D John Tomasi

2 What does it mean to say that rights are trumps?
   A Rights are more important than anything else
   B Rights are more important than the interests of the community
   C Rights are more important than justice
   D All of the above

3 Why might the ticking time bomb scenario challenge the idea that rights are trumps?
   A Because it suggests that terrorists do not value rights
   B Because it suggests that we should sometimes condone rights-violations
   C Because it suggests that there is no right not to be tortured
   D Because it suggests that torture is good

4 Why is liberalism sometimes described as a rights-based morality?
   A Because it focuses on the individual
   B Because it is associated with the historical struggle for individual and civil rights
   C Because it rejects community-based conceptions of justice such as utilitarianism and communitarianism
   D All of the above

5 What is 'social capital', according to Robert Putnam?
   A The sense of community existing in a society
   B The amount of money in a society
   C The main city in a society
   D The rights that are recognized in a society

6 Why might rights-based moralities undermine the value of community?

    A Because they prioritize the individual

    B Because they encourage people to focus on their self-interest

    C Because they assume conflict rather than co-operation

    D All of the above

7 How could liberals respond to the challenge of Question 6?

    A By pointing out that individuals can voluntarily choose not to use their rights

    B By arguing that individuals should be subordinate to the community

    C By arguing that rights are unimportant

    D All of the above

8 Which of the following might conflict with the right to free speech?

    A The right to privacy

    B The interests of the community

    C A right not to experience hate speech

    D All of the above

9 Which of the following is most likely to be a rights-based morality?

    A Liberalism

    B Communitarianism

    C Utilitarianism

    D Totalitarianism

10 Which of the following is least likely to be a rights-based morality?

    A Liberalism

    B Feminism

    C Utilitarianism

    D Anarchism

Political obligation

There are many reasons why we might obey the law. We might do it out of fear of punishment, for example, or habit. But why *should* we obey the law? What normative reasons are there for obeying the state and the laws that it passes? This is the question of political obligation: why are we obligated to obey the law, to obey our political rulers? Neither fear nor habit, though they may explain our obedience in practice, are sufficient to entail an *obligation* to obey.

In this chapter, we discuss three arguments that have been offered as answers to this conundrum: consent, fair play and natural duties. For each, we consider how well they meet the three requirements of obligating everyone, even if they do not like the law, while preserving freedom and equality.

A successful theory of political obligation

A law is a coercive rule, enacted by a government and enforced by a state, that applies to everyone in the relevant territory. A theory of political obligation is a theory of how and why laws can be legitimate. To be successful, a theory of political obligation must explain three things:

1 It must explain why *everyone* in a given territory is obligated to obey. Without universal obligation the law would be unworkable. Laws of taxation, traffic and property only work if everyone has to obey them; if there is only partial obligation then the benefits that the laws are designed to protect will be undermined or destroyed.

2 Related to the above, a successful theory of political obligation must explain why we are obligated to obey laws that we do not like. We might not like a law simply because it restricts our freedom (such as a law that imposes speed limits or requires us to pay taxes). More seriously, we might not like a law because we disagree with it on principled grounds (such as a law that we would not have voted for even for others).

3 A successful theory must account for obligation while preserving freedom and equality. In pre-modern political theory, the authority of political institutions was often rooted in appeals to divine right or traditional hierarchies or the natural order. Enlightenment liberalism undermined these justifications, insisting that individuals should be conceived of as equals and that their freedom should be protected. Political obligation becomes problematic for liberalism because laws just are restrictions of freedom, and because the fact that only some people are lawmakers seems to undermine equality. If freedom and equality are important, what justifies some people telling other people what to do?

Social contract theories: obligation based on consent

The dominant liberal response to the problem of political
obligation turns to *consent*. If citizens consent to a government,
or to a system of laws, we can derive obligation without
undermining freedom and equality. This is because consent
can be undertaken freely, and between equals, and yet still be
binding on the consenting parties. A promise is the paradigmatic
example of the fact that consent implies obligation but preserves
freedom and equality. If you voluntarily promise your friend
that you will help her to paint her flat, then you are morally
obligated to paint her flat. The fact that your promise was
voluntary means that your freedom is preserved. The fact that
you are friends, and not employer and employee, or monarch
and subject, means that you are in a relationship of equals
and that your obligation does not result from inequality.
Nevertheless, once you have made the promise you are under
an obligation.

It is relatively easy to see how consent theory preserves freedom
and equality, then. What is more difficult to see is how it does so
while obligating everyone to obey even those laws that they do
not like, for why would anyone consent to a law they disagreed
with? Different answers to this question give different versions
of consent theory.

HYPOTHETICAL RATIONAL CONSENT

One response is to say that consent should not be considered on a law-by-law basis. Instead, the question is whether we consent to a system of laws in general. If it benefits us to have a system of laws in general then it is rational for us to consent to living under the authority of the state.

Thomas Hobbes makes such an argument (Hobbes [1651] 1985). According to Hobbes, life without laws – in what he calls the 'state of nature' – would be so insecure and uncertain that it would be better for everyone to live under the authority of a state, or leviathan. Hobbes asks us to imagine a state of nature in which we are all at risk of being murdered, injured or stolen from at any time. Life in such a state, he writes, would be 'solitary, poor, nasty, brutish, and short' (Hobbes [1651] 1985: p. 186). Hobbes concludes that it would be rational for everyone to consent to a state. The job of the state is to pass laws that protect people's lives by preventing them from killing each other, and to ensure compliance the state must be more powerful than any individual. Hobbes does not claim that everyone has in fact consented, merely that it would be rational for everyone to do so, and so his theory is based on *hypothetical rational consent*. After all, refusing to consent to the state is to say one is happy to remain in the state of nature, and in the state of nature there is nothing to prevent anyone else, including the representatives of the state, from killing you!

'The finall Cause, End, or Designe of Men (who naturally love Liberty and Dominion over others,) in the introduction of that restraint upon themselves, (in which we see them live in Common-wealths,) is the foresight of their own preservation, and of a more contented life thereby; that is to say, of getting themselves out of that miserable condition of Warre, which is necessarily consequent (as hath been shewn) to the naturall Passions of men, when there is no visible Power to keep them in awe, and tye them by feare of punishment to the performance of their Covenants.'

Thomas Hobbes, *Leviathan* [1651] (London: Penguin, 1985), p. 223.

Hobbes's theory therefore obligates everyone because anyone who has not consented can be coerced or even killed, since they would be subject to coercion and murder in the state of nature. And people are obligated to obey even laws that they do not like because Hobbes asks us to consider consent as being to the state as a whole, not to individual laws. This is because any set of laws that meet the minimal requirement of ensuring our physical safety will be preferable to the state of nature, and so any set of laws can be justified by hypothetical rational consent.

Ronald Dworkin argues that a 'hypothetical contract is not simply a pale form of an actual contract; it is no contract at all' (Dworkin 1975: p. 18). The problem is whether a theory like Hobbes's really can preserve individual freedom and equality. If the consent is only hypothetical, it is difficult to see how freedom is preserved. In Hobbes's state of nature there is no real freedom: we are all effectively forced to agree because the alternative is so dreadful.

TACIT CONSENT

Theories of tacit consent attempt to connect all existing individuals with the state, by providing a way in which we all can consent in our everyday life. If everyone can *actually* consent, then the political obligation ought to be stronger than if we rely on *hypothetical* consent.

'[E]very man, consenting with others to make one body politics under one government, puts himself under an obligation, to every one of that society, to submit to the determination of the majority, and to be concluded by it; or else this original compact, whereby he with others incorporate into one society, would signify nothing, and be no compact, if he be left free, and under no other ties than he was in the state of nature.'

John Locke, *Second Treatise of Government* [1690], ed. C.B. McPherson (Indianapolis, IN: Hackett), p. 52.

This is the approach of another social contract thinker, John Locke (Locke, [1690] 1988). While Hobbes characterized life without a state as thoroughly unpleasant and brutal,

Locke characterizes it as a situation of perfect freedom and equality. Because there is no formal government, no individual has more power than other, and equality is preserved. Because there is no law, everyone has perfect freedom, constrained only by the limitations of nature. Locke therefore concludes that the state of nature is not the worst sort of situation to be in.

Because, for Locke, the state of nature is not intolerable, it follows that the requirements of consent are much more strident. That is, a state is legitimate only if people actually do consent to it. We cannot infer rational hypothetical consent, because it might sometimes be rational to prefer the state of nature. This means that, for Locke, we must find a way for each individual *actively* to consent.

How, then, do we give our consent? Locke argues that people give *tacit* consent when they use or enjoy what he calls 'any part of the dominions of any government'. *Tacit* consent means unstated, implied consent. So, the idea is that people do not have to sign a formal document in order to be politically obligated. Instead, consent is given tacitly: it is implied by the performance of some other action. For Locke, we tacitly consent to the state when we enjoy or use anything that the state provides. So, tacit consent could occur when we walk down the street, for then we use the roads that the state has provided.

Does this mean that we could live in society without consenting to obey the state? If we could avoid things such as using public highways, we would not tacitly consent. If this were the case, then we would face one of the problems of political obligation, that of ensuring universal obligation. Locke's theory of tacit consent gets round this problem rather well. It would obviously be very difficult to avoid walking down any public roads – though not impossible. It would be impossible, however, to live within the territory of a state and not enjoy or benefit from any of its provisions. Even if you never left your house, you would still benefit from the system of law and order that the state enforced. If your house were burgled, or if you were assaulted, the state would prosecute the perpetrators. Indeed, the fact that the state punishes criminals makes it much less likely that you will be burgled or attacked. So, even if you remain within your house, you are still enjoying the benefits of the state. Tacit consent, in the end, is given by everyone.

This notion of tacit consent is useful because it solves the problem of ensuring that political obligation is universal. However, there are problems with it. The most obvious, of course, is that the fact that it is not really possible to withhold consent undermines the consent. How genuine can consent really be if it cannot be withheld?

The second problem is, as with hypothetical consent, determining the extent of our obligation. It seems fairly clear that we are obligated to support those services which we use, those services which show our tacit consent. So, if you visit a GP, it seems reasonable to suppose that you have consented to pay taxes in support of the NHS, and if you complain to the police that you have been assaulted, it seems reasonable to suppose that, at the same time, you are obliged not to assault anyone yourself. It is less clear, however, whether and why going to the GP should signal that you also consent to the public education system, or to the existence of regulations on drug-taking, or to contributing to public subsidy of the arts. Rather than provide a general justification for the state, tacit consent theory only seems to create obligations to obey laws one by one.

Spotlight: Voting and tacit consent

It is sometimes suggested that voting can be a form of tacit consent. The problem with this suggestion is that the number of people voting is often inadequate to obligate even the majority of citizens, let alone everyone. Average turnout for British general elections is around 60 per cent; for local and European elections it is more like 35 per cent!

Fair play

The second approach to political obligation is based on the principle of fair play. The idea here is that, if you receive some benefit from the state, you have a duty to reciprocate, to contribute your fair share of resources or effort into maintaining that benefit. It is only fair, so this theory goes, if you contribute toward that which you have benefited from. It would be unfair for you to visit the GP but then refuse to pay taxes toward the NHS, or for you to enjoy the protection of the law as regards your personal property but then to steal from others. Political obligation is derived from the principle of fairness.

This approach was defended by H.L.A. Hart (Hart 1955). Hart argued that 'when a number of persons conduct any joint enterprise according to rules and thus restrict their liberty, those who have submitted to these restrictions when required have a right to a similar submission from those who have benefited by their submission' (Hart 1955: p. 185). Hart's idea, then, is that if others restrict their liberty so as to provide something that benefits you, it is right that you ought to restrict your liberty when necessary, so as to continue to provide the benefit: if others are providing a benefit for you, you must make your fair share of contributions. An example of a restriction of liberty would be taxation. Being forced to pay taxes is a restriction on liberty: the compulsion involved means that you cannot do whatever you like with your money but must donate some of it to the government. So, to continue with the example of the NHS, if other people are restricting their liberty by paying taxes to the NHS, you are obliged to restrict your liberty by doing the same.

Fair play theory preserves freedom and equality in two ways. Firstly, by referring to occasions when others restrict their liberty, Hart shows that restrictions on liberty are costly and must be recompensed in some way. If other people are restricting their liberty for your benefit, their sacrifice requires that you do something significant in return. Secondly, equality is maintained in Hart's insistence that *everyone* must contribute to public goods. It is precisely because people are equal that it would be wrong for only some to restrict their liberty so as to secure a benefit for everyone. Equality applies not just to entitlements but also to duties. If people are equal, then they must all have a duty to contribute to public goods.

One implication of this approach is that you are obligated to contribute to benefits that you have not consented to. Even if you do benefit from some public service, it may be that you would rather not have the service and avoid the contribution. Still, according to fair play theory, you are obligated nonetheless.

Libertarian philosopher Robert Nozick criticizes this implication of fair play theory (Nozick 1974). He argues that if a person would prefer not to receive a benefit so as to avoid paying the costs, it is unreasonable to suppose that she is obligated to pay. In effect, Nozick returns the issue to one of consent. If you have explicitly consented to a particular practice or act because it benefits you, then it seems reasonable to say that you are obligated to contribute. But, if you haven't consented, it seems unreasonable to require you to contribute to something just because it is a benefit. After all, there might be no end to the things that people could do for you and then demand a contribution. What if you come back to your house one day to find that your neighbour has mown your lawn, another one has painted your house and another has washed your car? Surely you are not *obliged* to pay them, or even to return the favour.

'Individuals have rights, and there are things that no person or group may do to them (without violating their rights). So strong and far-reaching are these rights that they raise the question of what, if anything, the state and its officials may do... [A] minimal state, limited to the narrow functions of protection against force, theft, fraud, enforcement of contracts, and so on, is justified;... any more extensive state will violate persons' rights not to be forced to do certain things, and is unjustified.'
Robert Nozick, *Anarchy, State, and Utopia* (Oxford: Blackwell, 1974), p. xi.

Nozick's example also suggests another problem with the theory of fair play. Nozick states that you have benefited from the practice, and that you accept that it has been beneficial. But what happens if you do not, in fact, *like* it? If this is your position, the others have still put themselves out, and they have still done so with the intention of providing a benefit. How does that affect your obligation?

This issue arises with tacit consent as well. Remember, one example of tacit consent was walking down the public road. This might oblige you, at the very least, to contribute to maintaining the road, its street lighting and so on. But, although most people agree that public roads are a benefit, some people might disagree. You might wish that, instead of a tarmacked road, there was a dirt track, so that you could enjoy your four-wheel-drive or your horse riding better. You might be a stargazer, and wish that the roads were not lit up, because street lighting interferes with your ability to see the stars. So, things which are generally agreed to be beneficial by most people might actually harm others. It is very difficult, in such cases, to see where obligation comes from.

Natural duties

The final approach to securing political obligation is the natural duties approach supported by, among others, Jeremy Waldron (Waldron 1993) and John Rawls (Rawls 1971).

The idea of natural duties is similar to the idea of natural rights, discussed in the previous chapter. Just as some people believe that we have certain rights on account of the fact that we are human beings, so some legal and political philosophers have argued that, as human beings, we have certain duties which we are morally required to fulfil. In particular, Waldron and Rawls argue that we have a natural duty to justice. Rawls argues that 'first, we are to comply with and to do our share in just institutions when they exist and apply to us; and second, we are to assist in the establishment of just arrangements when they do not exist, at least when this can be done with little cost to ourselves' (Rawls 1971: p. 334).

We will put aside for now the important question of how to define justice (this is the subject of Part Two). Assume for now that we all know and agree which institutions are just. In such circumstances, would a theory of natural duty explain political obligation?

Remember, theories of political obligation attempt to preserve individual freedom and equality. Theories of natural duties succeed very well at this task – at least if they are liberal theories, based on a liberal theory of justice, as Rawls's is. Rawls's theory of justice is based precisely on freedom and equality. A just outcome or institution is one which conforms to freedom and equality. So, a natural duty to obey and establish just institutions is, at the same time, a natural duty to preserve freedom and equality.

Natural duty theory also does well at explaining why everyone is obligated to obey even laws they dislike. As long as those laws, or the institutions that enact them, are just then obligation ensues.

One important problem with the natural duties approach, described by Waldron, is that it is not clear why we should obey the state as opposed to any other just institution.

Two examples illustrate the point. The first example is the IRA in Northern Ireland. As well as fighting for a united Ireland, the IRA also engaged in vigilantism in Northern Ireland, and particularly in Belfast. That is to say, the IRA would identify and punish those who had committed crimes such as drug dealing and stealing. Imagine, for the sake of argument, that the IRA is very good at this – perhaps even better than the police. Members of the IRA are more embedded in the community than the police are, and so they know better what is going on and who is committing crimes. Suppose, then, that the IRA performs its vigilantism justly. It accurately identifies the perpetrators, and applies appropriate punishment. Does that mean that the people of Northern Ireland are obliged to obey the commands of the IRA?

The second example is given by John Simmons and quoted by Waldron. A Philosophy Society is set up to provide services for the community of philosophers. It publishes newsletters, assists needy philosophers, and keeps everyone informed of news in the philosophy world – jobs, publications and so on. What's more, it is entirely just – the leadership is justly elected, subscriptions are at a just rate, and its funds for needy philosophers implement a just distribution of wealth. One day, Simmons imagines, a letter from the society arrives through his letterbox, demanding that he pay a subscription in the name of his natural duty to support just institutions. Simmons has never asked to be a member of this society. Is he obliged to pay?

Waldron answers these examples by clarifying the duties we have to support just institutions. We are obliged to support those institutions which, firstly, do in fact act justly. This justice must be considered to apply to the institution taken as a whole. So, we might be able to eliminate the IRA by pointing out that, although its vigilantism is just, it is not just as a whole. It is a terrorist organization, its members are not elected, there are no mechanisms for accountability, and so on.

Secondly, we are only obliged to obey those institutions which are *most* able to act justly. This claim has three parts:

1 We are only obligated to obey institutions which are required by justice. That is to say, it must be necessary to justice that the institution exist. If there were no such institution, society as a whole would be unjust. This is why we are obliged to obey the law against murder, but are not obliged to pay the subscription to the philosophy society. A society with no law against murder would be an unjust society. On the other hand, although the philosophy society is internally just, it is not required by justice. A larger society which contained no philosophy society would not be unjust.

2 The second part of the requirement that the institution be the one most able to act justly is that there should be only one institution regulating any one aspect of life, so as to avoid conflicts. So, it would be unjust if the citizens of Northern Ireland had to obey both the IRA and the police, because those two institutions might make conflicting demands.

3 Finally, if there are several institutions competing for jurisdiction over one area, we are obliged to obey the one which is best at the function in question, and thus which is most likely to succeed. Usually, Waldron says, this will be the state – simply because the state has more resources than most other groups to maintain its rule and to discharge its functions effectively.

Still, it will not always be the case that it is the state that is best at performing a function, and Waldron's theory does entail that, if another institution is better, we are obliged to obey that institution rather than the state. Natural duties will often support a political obligation to obey the state, but not always.

Conclusion

The question of how we might justify political obligation is a crucial one, and there is more to be said about it than we can discuss here. For example, there is intense debate among legal positivists and natural law theorists about whether or not the authority of law is derived independently of morality, or whether unjust laws have as much authority as just ones. In general, theories of political obligation are a challenge to political philosophers: none seem to offer an entirely persuasive account of why we should obey the state and its laws, yet the vast majority of political philosophers (excluding anarchists) believe that we should. This chapter has discussed the strengths and weaknesses of three of the most important approaches to resolving this question. The issues raised in this chapter relate directly to more contemporary debates about justice and morality. It is to these debates that we will turn in Part Two.

Case study: Anarchism

Not everyone agrees that we need a state. Philosophical anarchism – found differently in the work of thinkers such as Peter Kropotkin, Pierre-Joseph Proudhon, William Godwin, Max Stirner, Mikhail Bakunin and Robert Paul Wolff – represents a fundamental challenge to the sorts of theories that we have discussed in this chapter. Anarchism is a diverse approach and has been defended in one way or another by libertarians, individualists, collectivists and communists. For all their differences, however, anarchists from different points on the political spectrum are nevertheless united in the general claim that all existing theories of political obligation of the kind that we have discussed thus far fail in their attempt to justify the authority of the state.

The reason for this is that such justification is impossible if we are to genuinely respect freedom and equality. States are *coercive*: they exist to force us to do things that we would otherwise choose not to do and, hence, they are straightforwardly antithetical to individual freedom. And they are hierarchical: they establish a class of rulers and a class of the ruled and, hence, violate equality. Theories of political obligation do little more than obfuscate and confuse the issue, they believe. Despite what the vast majority of political philosophers think, anarchists maintain, a thoroughgoing commitment to individual freedom and equality will ultimately require the rejection of the state as unfair, unjust and contrary to humane moral and political values.

Anarchism is a rich and diverse philosophical tradition which has, it must be said, become rather misrepresented in contemporary political discourse. Anarchism has for many people become synonymous with chaos, violent protest and riots. It is an open question as to the extent to which those involved in the riots that swept the UK in 2011 or in the violence associated with the anti-globalization movement and so on are drawing on a coherent set of ideas characteristic of philosophical anarchism. Nevertheless, anarchist critiques of the state (and, hence, all existing arguments which seek to explain political obligation) represent a profound challenge to many mainstream assumptions about the nature of authority, the legitimacy of state institutions, and the implications of a commitment to freedom and equality, which have not been wholly refuted by defenders of states.

Key ideas

Political obligation: The question of why, and on what normative grounds, we might be said to be required to obey the state and the laws that it passes.

Consent: The idea that the moral authority of political institutions and laws is rooted in the consent, either hypothetical or tacit, of the people who are to be subject to it.

Fair play: The idea that political obligation is justified by the idea of reciprocity. If you benefit from the fact that others have relinquished a degree of their own freedom in order to provide you with the benefits of living under a state, then it is only fair that you subject yourself to similar constraints.

Natural duties: The idea that human beings have certain moral duties that they are required to fulfil regardless of their particular preferences, or whether they have consented to the particular system of institutions under which they live. Natural duties tends to be linked to the idea of justice.

The state: The locus of political authority under which individuals live, and the source of laws. States need the authority to coerce their members to do things that they would not otherwise choose to do.

Dig deeper

Ronald Dworkin, 'The Original Position', in Norman Daniels (ed.), *Reading Rawls* (Oxford: Blackwell, 1975).

Ronald Dworkin, *Law's Empire* (Cambridge, MA: Harvard University Press, 1986).

H.L.A. Hart, 'Are There Any Natural Rights?', *Philosophical Review* 64 (1955), pp. 175–91.

John Horton, *Political Obligation* (London: Macmillan, 1992).

Ruth Kinna, *Anarchism: A Beginner's Guide* (Oxford: Oneworld, 2005).

George Klosko, *Political Obligations* (Oxford: Oxford University Press, 2005).

John Locke, *Two Treatises on Government* [1690] (Cambridge: Cambridge University Press, 1988).

Robert Nozick, *Anarchy, State, and Utopia* (Oxford: Basic Books, 1974).

Carole Pateman, *The Problem of Political Obligation* (Berkeley: University of California Press, 1979).

John A. Simmons, *Moral Principles and Political Obligations* (Princeton, NJ: Princeton University Press, 1979).

Jeremy Waldron, 'Special Ties and Natural Duties', *Philosophy and Public Affairs* 22 (1993), pp. 3–30.

Fact-check

1 Who argued that life in the state of nature was 'solitary, poor, nasty, brutish and short'?
   A   Jeremy Waldron
   B   David Hume
   C   Thomas Hobbes
   D   John Locke

2 What is the difference between Locke's and Hobbes's account of political obligation?
   A   Locke argues that actual consent is needed for obligation
   B   Locke argues that the state of nature is not necessarily the worst situation
   C   Locke has a more optimistic view of human nature
   D   All of the above

3 What sort of consent is Hobbes's theory based on?
   A   Hypothetical rational consent
   B   Tacit consent
   C   Actual consent
   D   Historical consent

4 Which of the following is an example of tacit consent?
   A   Accepting a government-provided student loan
   B   Asking police officer for help
   C   Voting
   D   All of the above

5 What is a natural duty?
   A   A duty to protect nature
   B   A duty that does not depend on consent
   C   A duty that people naturally want to fulfil
   D   All of the above

6 'You should obey the law because other people are obeying the law.' Which theory of political obligation is expressed in this quote?
   A   Fair play theory
   B   Natural duty theory
   C   Social contract theory
   D   Anarchism

7 Which of the following criticisms best applies to natural duty theory?
   A It does not succeed in obligating everyone
   B It does not succeed in showing why our obligations apply specifically to the state
   C It does not succeed in protecting freedom
   D It does not succeed in protecting equality

8 Which of the following criticisms best applies to social contract theory?
   A It is historically inaccurate
   B It is unrealistic
   C It cannot rely on meaningful consent
   D It does not succeed in showing why our obligations apply specifically to the state

9 Which of the following criticisms best applies to fair play theory?
   A It does not succeed in obligating everyone
   B It is historically inaccurate
   C It does not succeed in protecting equality
   D It does not succeed in protecting freedom

10 Which of the following best describes anarchism?
   A It is the belief that violence is good
   B It is the belief that all states are unjust
   C It is the belief that no one would consent to a state
   D It is the belief that existing theories of political obligation fail

Part Two

Contemporary
theories and
debates

9

Utilitarianism

It is now time to explore how political and moral philosophers used concepts in normative theories about justice, the roles and responsibilities of the state, and the obligations that individuals have toward one another. We begin with utilitarianism, which, until the publication of Rawls's *A Theory of Justice* in 1971, was the dominant normative theory of politics.

Utilitarianism is the idea that the right thing to do, or the just thing to do, is whatever brings about the greatest utility. Utility has been defined in different ways by different utilitarians, but in general it refers to something like welfare or happiness. So, utilitarianism can be thought of as the idea that the right thing to do is whatever maximizes total happiness in society. Different versions of utilitarianism have been defended by thinkers such as Jeremy Bentham, John Stuart Mill, Henry Sidgwick, Bertrand Russell and Peter Singer.

Consequentialism and deontology

Utilitarianism is a *consequentialist* theory. What this means is that, for utilitarians, the rightness or wrongness of an action is determined by its consequences. Something is wrong if and only if it brings about bad consequences, and right if and only if it brings about good, or perhaps even the best possible, consequences. If we want to know what we should do in a particular situation, we should consider what the consequences of various alternative acts are likely to be, and choose whichever action brings about the best consequences.

Consequentialism contrasts with *deontological* theories of justice or morality. Deontological theories hold that actions can be right in and of themselves, regardless of their consequences. Consequentialists argue that their approach provides a more attractive account of what constitutes moral behaviour than the deontological approach. For example, Kant makes the commonly held deontological claim that we are morally required to tell the truth. But imagine that you are disturbed one evening by someone desperately knocking on your door and asking to be given shelter because he is being chased by a violent would-be murderer. You let him in and, moments later, there is another knock on your door from the axe-wielding madman, who asks you if you have seen the first man. Telling the truth will result in murder. It seems clear that the morally right thing to do would be to lie and say that you have not seen the first man, so that the would-be murderer moves on and the man's life is saved.

According to consequentialists, this example shows that morality should be concerned with consequences rather than enforcing rules in and of themselves. Rules are only morally correct if they bring about desirable consequences. Since every rule will have exceptions, it makes more sense to abandon the idea that morality is based on rules in favour of the idea that morality is based on consequences. The right thing to do in any circumstance depends not on abstract, universal moral rules, but on the particular consequences of the alternative acts.

The central rule of morality is: 'Do whatever brings about the best consequences.'

Utilitarianism is a variety of consequentialism which defines the best consequences as those which maximize utility. Individuals and states are thus morally required to act in ways which maximize utility.

Utility

Utilitarians disagree about how best to define utility.

UTILITY AS PLEASURE

The most basic way of defining utility is simply by identifying it with pleasure, as Jeremy Bentham does. On this definition, you maximize someone's utility by maximizing their pleasure. It makes no difference what it is that gives them pleasure – whether the pleasure is long-lasting or temporary, whether it is brought about by scholarship and effort or by video games and drugs. Utility is the same as pleasure, and the morally right thing to do is whatever brings about the most pleasure.

> 'By the principle of utility is meant that principle which approves or disapproves of every action whatsoever, according to the tendency which it appears to have to augment or diminish the happiness of the party whose interest is in question... I say of every action whatsoever; and therefore not only of every action of a private individual, but of every measure of government... By utility is meant that property in any object whereby it tends to produce benefit, advantage, pleasure, good, or happiness... or to prevent the happening of mischief, pain, evil, or happiness to the party whose interest is considered: if that party be the community in general, then the happiness of the community: if a particular individual, then the happiness of that individual.'
>
> Jeremy Bentham, *An Introduction to The Principles of Morals and Legislation* [1879] (Elibron Classics Series, 2005), p. 2.

Spotlight: Bentham's body

Jeremy Bentham requested in his will that upon his death his body be preserved, placed in a wooden cabinet, and displayed as an 'auto-icon'. His request was granted. For several years Bentham's preserved corpse was kept by one of his disciples before being acquired by University College London in 1850. Bentham's body remains on public display there to this day.

This kind of approach has several problems. One problem is that, if pleasure is the ultimate value, we might miss out on things which are not pleasurable but which nevertheless seem valuable. For example, developing or understanding a scientific theory might be very difficult yet important. And many great artists like Van Gogh and Picasso famously found producing works of art stressful and difficult, but we still think that their endeavours had value.

Conversely, there is the concern that a life dedicated to the relentless pursuit of pleasure is actually rather empty and vacuous, and not very moral at all. Life is complex, we might say, and often characterized by moral dilemmas which are difficult to resolve. Should a woman made pregnant by a rapist have an abortion? Should we agree to the withdrawal of medical treatment for an incurably ill loved one in order to let them die with dignity? The idea that in hard cases like these, individuals should simply do whatever makes them happiest seems to miss the point, and reduces profound, complex, life-changing decisions like this to a selfish and barren calculation of costs and benefits.

Critics of utilitarianism like Robert Nozick, for example, have argued that there is more to life (and to morality) than the pursuit of pleasure and that, if we were to subordinate all of our various emotions and motivations to what gives us most pleasure, we would end up living not a moral life but a life of shallow hedonism, blown one way and another by casual whims and passing fads; a life that most people would reject if given the choice.

Case study: Nozick's 'experience machine'

Robert Nozick, in his book *Anarchy, State, and Utopia* published in 1974, argues strongly against utilitarianism, and in particular the idea that morality is all about maximizing pleasure. In doing so, he describes a thought experiment which has become very influential in debates about morality and ethics. Nozick asks us to imagine that scientists have created an 'experience machine'. The experience machine is a machine that you can be connected to which, through drugs and electrical stimulation of the nervous system, gives you any experience you want. When you are hooked up to the experience machine, you experience only what the machine tells you to experience. You do not realize that you are attached to the machine and that the experience is not real. As far as you are concerned, you really are a pop star, or a racing car driver, or irresistible to others, or whatever it is that you have programmed in.

Nozick asks us to imagine that we are given the opportunity to be hooked up to the experience machine for the rest of our lives, with the experience machine programmed to maximize our pleasure. If pleasure is the ultimate goal, then we all should jump at the chance. However, Nozick predicts that most people will not want such a life. He argues that most of us find the idea of such a life abhorrent, unpleasant and empty. If this is the case, then pleasure cannot be the ultimate value, and the premise of pleasure-based utilitarianism is undermined.

The main point of the example, for Nozick, is that it suggests that pleasure in and of itself is not the most important thing in life. Rather, we want to feel in control of our lives. We do not want to spend our days comatose on pleasure-giving drugs, we want to experience the world in all its complexity. We want to be free to make our own choices and mistakes, even if in doing so we end up experiencing less pleasure than we would if someone just gave us a pill, or hooked us up to a machine. Utilitarianism, he argues, ignores the desire of human beings to autonomously create their own lives rather than have lives or experiences given to them by someone else. It ignores the moral value of autonomy.

UTILITY AS PREFERENCE-SATISFACTION

Utility as pleasure is utility understood as some sort of mental state. If utility is the same thing as pleasure, then utility is maximized when the mental experience of pleasure is maximized. An alternative understanding of utility identifies it instead with preference-satisfaction. According to this alternative account, your utility is maximized when as many of your preferences as possible are satisfied, regardless of whether or not they bring you pleasure. If you want to be an artist, we maximize your utility by enabling you to be an artist, even if life as an artist turns out to be painful and unpleasant.

Utilitarianism, then, becomes the view that the morally correct thing to do is the thing which satisfies as many preferences as possible. Although this definition is removed from our base pleasures, it still leaves utility as a highly subjective concept. The correct thing to do will be that which maximizes preference-satisfaction, regardless of what those preferences are. You might have preferences which harm others, such as the preference to create computer viruses or sell illegal drugs, or you might have preferences which are bad for you. Some of your preferences might be based on false beliefs, such as the preference to smoke before its harmful effects on health were known, or the preference to stay in a relationship when you don't know that your partner is having an affair. Finally, some preferences may be socially constructed or influenced.

If utility is to be based on preference-satisfaction, then, we will have to decide what to do about these sorts of preferences. It seems clear that a person's utility is not maximized if we satisfy those preferences that are based on false information. At the very least, people need full information if their preferences are to reflect their utility. But what about those preferences to do harm to oneself which are based on sound knowledge, or preferences to harm others?

MILL AND THE HIGHER PLEASURES

John Stuart Mill uses both objective and subjective notions of utility. Mill wants to undermine the Benthamite idea that there can be no distinction between different types of pleasures. Mill rejects the idea that utility depends merely on some sort of mental state, or experience of pleasure, and argues instead that there can be higher forms of utility that do not depend on the immediate experience of pleasure. Mill terms this immediate experience of pleasure 'contentment', and he contrasts it with what he calls higher pleasure. Another way of putting the distinction is between higher and lower pleasures.

> 'Human beings have faculties more elevated than the animal appetites, and when once made conscious of them, do not regard anything as happiness which does not include their gratification... It is quite compatible with the principle of utility to recognize the fact, that some kinds of pleasure are more desirable and more valuable than others. It would be absurd that while, in estimating all other things, quality is considered as well as quantity, the estimation of pleasures should be supposed to depend on quantity alone.'
> John Stuart Mill, 'Utilitarianism' [1863], in John Gray (ed.), *On Liberty and Other Essays* (Oxford: Oxford University Press, 1991), p.138.

Mill is therefore interested in maximizing higher pleasure rather than lower pleasure. However, he does not define higher pleasures on entirely subjective grounds. If everyone in society liked football, for example, it would not follow that football is a higher pleasure, superior to more intellectual pursuits. Instead, Mill attempts to give a definite answer to the contingent and subjective question of what it is that most people prefer. 'It is an unquestionable fact', Mill writes, 'that those who are equally acquainted with, and equally capable of appreciating and enjoying, both, do give a most marked preference to the manner of existence which employs their higher faculties' (Mill [1863] 1991: p. 139). The famous example that Mill gives of this point is that: 'It is better to be a human being dissatisfied than a pig satisfied; better to be Socrates dissatisfied than a fool satisfied. And if the fool, or the pig, are of a different opinion, it is because they only know their own side of the question. The other party to the comparison knows both sides' (Mill [1863] 1991: p. 140). The idea, then, is that intellectual pursuits could actually be better than football because they use higher faculties, and that, if many people think otherwise, that is only because they have not properly experienced those pursuits.

There are numerous problems with Mill's view. For example, it seems very elitist to assume people like football more than intellectual activities only because they have made a mistake. But the main point is that Mill offers an alternative to utility understood as merely a subjective concept, and yet at the same time attempts to connect utility to people's actual preferences – albeit people who exist only hypothetically.

Spotlight: John Stuart Mill

James Mill, John Stuart Mill's father, was a passionate defender of utilitarianism. When John was born, his father educated him rigorously from an early age with the direct assistance of Jeremy Bentham, with the aim of creating a genius child who would champion the cause of utilitarianism after Bentham and his father were dead. He was kept away from other children, taught Greek at the age of three, and by five had read many classic texts including the works of Herodotus and Plato. By the age of ten, John had read Plato and Demosthenes in Greek and Latin, and at twelve, he had begun to tackle Aristotle's logic in the ancient Greek. John wrote poetry in his spare time and, at around ten years old, decided to write a continuation of Homer's *Iliad*. Given all this, it is perhaps no coincidence that Mill ended up not only a champion of utilitarianism, but also of what he called the 'higher pleasures'.

Act-utilitarianism

The most basic form of utilitarianism is known as act-utilitarianism. Act-utilitarianism is the idea that the morally correct thing to do in any situation is the precise act which will bring about the best consequences in that particular situation. In other words, we should base our actions on precise judgements about the likely consequences of acting in various ways in each individual case. So, when the would-be murderer knocks on your door and asks if you have seen his intended victim, you calculate that greater utility will be brought about if you say 'no', even if that is a lie. It follows that the morally right thing to do in that circumstance, according to act-utilitarianism, would be to tell the lie. There is no special moral reason to tell the truth. You are obliged to do so only if doing so maximizes utility.

What could be wrong with such a view?

UTILITARIAN CALCULATIONS ARE IMPOSSIBLE TO MAKE

The first problem with act-utilitarianism is a practical one. Many philosophers have pointed out that there is in fact no way of measuring utility. Even if we have decided on a particular definition of utility, still we will face the problem of comparing the utility of different people, and we have no way of doing so. Imagine, for example, that you are a government transport minister considering whether to build a new road through a village. The local residents of the village are strongly against the road, fearing that it will bring in traffic, noise and pollution. It will harm the residents' utility. Motorists who do not live in the village are, in general, in favour of the road, because it will provide a quicker route through the area. There are more motorists who live outside the village than there are residents of the village. However, each villager feels much more strongly against the road than each motorist feels in favour of the road, because it will affect each villager every day and whenever they are at home, whereas it will only affect motorists on those occasions when they use the road. If you are to make your decision on act-utilitarian grounds, what should you choose? How can you possibly measure the extreme disutility of the residents against the moderate utility of the motorists? How will you know which outweighs the other?

> 'The creed which accepts as the foundation of morals, Utility, or the Greatest Happiness Principle, holds that actions are right in proportion as they tend to promote happiness, wrong as they tend to produce the reverse of happiness. By happiness is intended pleasure, and the absence of pain; by unhappiness, pain, and the privation of pleasure.'
> John Stuart Mill, 'Utilitarianism', [1863] in John Gray (ed.), *On Liberty and Other Essays* (Oxford: Oxford University Press, 1991), p. 137.

UTILITARIANISM ALLOWS EVIL

We said earlier that one of the supposed attractions of utilitarianism is that it is an ethical theory based on what people actually do want, not on abstract ideas about what is supposedly good for people. As well as one of its strengths, this is also one of its weaknesses. We mentioned the possibility that some people could have preferences which harm other people, and act-utilitarianism is particularly prone to this objection. If the majority within a society will gain great utility from torturing a small minority, act-utilitarianism has nothing to say against the torture. If morality is based on utility, there can be no utility that is immoral. Torture would not be immoral if it maximized utility. Evil preferences, then, are given just as much weight as any others. Our moral intuitions, on the other hand, often give the opposite result – that an evil act is made *more* evil if someone gets pleasure from it. One of the objections to fox hunting in Britain is that it involves killing animals for sport, getting pleasure out of hunting. Opponents of hunting do not see the pleasure involved as lessening the evil, but as increasing it.

UTILITARIANISM DISREGARDS SPECIAL COMMITMENTS AND RELATIONSHIPS

Act-utilitarianism requires that we count the utility of each person equally, and that we do the thing that maximizes overall utility, regardless of precisely who is affected. What this means is that act-utilitarianism does not allow people to give preferential treatment to those people with whom they have a special relationship. People do not act morally if they base their actions on special commitments.

A famous example along these lines asks you to imagine that a building is on fire, and that there are two people caught in upstairs rooms. You have a ladder (and are the only person at the scene), but there will only be time to rescue one of the people before the building collapses. One person is someone who is of great use and utility to a great many people – perhaps a scientist on the verge of discovering a cure for cancer. The other person is your mother, who is very dear to you but who is of no special importance to society as a whole. If you are acting on act-utilitarian grounds, you will have to rescue the scientist and leave your mother to die. Indeed, you will be acting immorally if you rescue your mother, for you will not be bringing about the greatest utility.

Many opponents of utilitarianism have argued that this conclusion is absurd. Many argue that it cannot possibly be immoral to rescue your mother, given your relationship to her. Others argue still further that it would be immoral not to rescue your mother, given your relationship. Thomas Nagel argues in a version of this example that, if you even have to think about which person to rescue, you have already acted immorally as regards your mother. Special relationships, on this argument, should override utility-maximization. And if that is the case, act-utilitarianism cannot provide an adequate account of ethical individual or political action.

Act-utilitarianism does not only override special relationships based on love and family. It also undermines special relationships based on contract or agreement. If you agree to pay someone to paint your house, for example, but then (once they have finished the job) calculate that you would bring about greater general utility by giving the money to charity, then act-utilitarianism would require you to do so, and to deny it to the painter. The fact that you promised the money to him does factor in to the equation, in that you have to take into account the disutility caused by breaking the promise. But the promise is in no way an overriding reason to give him the money. But this surely violates our intuitions about the importance of promises, and also that it suggests that a world in which everyone is an act-utilitarian will be a very unstable, insecure, unpleasant one to live in. People could not count on being paid for jobs, or on having promises carried out, or on being told the truth, or on being rescued from burning buildings by their children. Again, we might find that an act-utilitarian world actually reduced utility, paradoxically. This fact has led to utilitarians proposing alternative forms of the theory.

Rule-utilitarianism

Most utilitarians, in response to the kinds of criticisms we have considered so far, have abandoned the idea of act-utilitarianism. In other words, they have abandoned the idea that individual people should make utilitarian calculations about individual acts.

Instead, they have argued that utilitarian calculations should not apply to specific *acts* but to the *rules* which regulate society. These rule-utilitarians hold that individuals should act in such a way as to follow those rules which will best maximize utility in society, taken as a whole and over the long term.

The idea behind rule-utilitarianism is not to consider each act individually, and not to judge a rule by its counter-examples or one-off incidences. Instead, we look at the bigger picture. If we do, rule-utilitarians argue, we will find that it maximizes utility if we obey moral rules such as 'always keep your promises' and 'always tell the truth'. We will live in a better society if these sorts of rules are followed. It follows, then, that we can retain our commitment to these sorts of moral rules and still be utilitarians. All that we need to do is to shift our perspective from the immediate and short-term to the longer-term, overall picture.

Rule-utilitarianism does seem to overcome many of the problems with act-utilitarianism. It can take account of the criticism that act-utilitarianism does not allow us to give special weight to personal relationships or commitments because it could be argued that utility is maximized if we follow a rule that tells us to give special weight to those relationships and obligations. However, it does so by dropping the appealing elements of act-utilitarianism or consequentialism that we started with – namely, responsiveness to particular contexts and circumstances. If we are supposed to follow the rules in all situations, we will have to tell the truth to the would-be murderer and let him carry out the attack. Rather than stick to the rule in this case, it seems more sensible to take account of the disutility that will result from this particular act – that is, to return to act-utilitarianism. But if we return to act-utilitarianism in this instance, why not in every other instance where the rule gives us an answer that reduces utility?

Conclusion

Utilitarianism has received a great deal of scholarly attention, and was the dominant normative approach within political philosophy until the publication of John Rawls's *A Theory of Justice* in 1971. Many variants of utilitarianism have been proposed, each giving a different answer to the questions we have raised in this chapter and posing many others. In the next chapter, we will discuss Rawls's influential critique of utilitarianism and his defence of a liberal alternative.

Key ideas

Utility: That value or property which utilitarian thinkers believe should be maximized, most commonly happiness, pleasure or the satisfaction of preferences.

Consequentialism: An approach to moral and political philosophy which understands actions to be morally right or wrong on the grounds of whether these actions have good or bad consequences. Consequentialist theories tend to be rooted in a particular conception of the good (such as utility or pleasure or happiness) and evaluate actions according to the extent to which they bring about, or impede, the realization of the good.

Deontology: Deontological theories stand in contrast to consequentialist theories. They hold that actions can and should be judged right or wrong in themselves, irrespective of the particular consequences that these actions may produce. Deontological theories thus ground morality not in the measurable consequences of particular actions but in rules derived independently of any particular conception of the good.

Act-utilitarianism: The form of utilitarianism which holds that utilitarian calculations should be applied to individual acts and decisions. Act-utilitarians believe that individuals should, when deciding upon what course of action to take in any given circumstance, consider which course of action would most increase utility.

Rule-utilitarianism: The form of utilitarianism which holds that utilitarian calculations should be used to derive the rules which govern a particular society, rather than each and every individual choice.

Higher and lower pleasures: John Stuart Mill's attempt to distinguish between different orders to pleasure in order to improve upon Jeremy Bentham's utilitarianism. Bentham understood pleasure as based entirely on the subjective desires of individual people. Mill thought that this led to counter-intuitive outcomes, and so tried to argue that certain pleasures had objective value.

Dig deeper

Derek Parfit, *Reasons and Persons* (Oxford: Oxford University Press, 1984).

John Rawls, *A Theory of Justice* (Cambridge, MA: Harvard University Press, 1971).

Samuel Scheffler (ed.), *Consequentialism and its Critics* (Oxford: Oxford University Press, 1988).

Amartya Sen and Bernard Williams (eds), *Utilitarianism and Beyond* (Cambridge: Cambridge University Press, 1982).

Peter Singer, *Practical Ethics: 2nd Edition* (Cambridge: Cambridge University Press, 1993).

John Skorupski (ed.),*The Cambridge Companion to Mill* (Cambridge: Cambridge University Press, 1988).

J.J.C. Smart and Bernard Williams, *Utilitarianism: For and Against* (Cambridge: Cambridge University Press, 1973).

Fact-check

1 What is consequentialism?
   A The view that every action has consequences
   B The view that consequences are the only important thing
   C The view that morality should be based on consequences
   D All of the above

2 Which of the following advantages best applies to utilitarianism?
   A It makes it easy to work out what the right thing to do is
   B It enables moral judgements to respond to specific circumstances
   C It corresponds to our intuitions about the right thing to do
   D Its followers agree about what it entails

3 Different utilitarians have given different definitions of utility. What is utility according to Jeremy Bentham?
   A Pleasure
   B Preference-satisfaction
   C Usefulness
   D Welfare

4 Who distinguished between higher and lower pleasures?
   A Jeremy Bentham
   B James Mill
   C John Stuart Mill
   D Robert Nozick

5 What is the best definition of rule-utilitarianism?
   A The view that utility is maximized if rules are followed
   B The view that we should act in accordance with the set of rules that best maximize utility
   C The view that we should act in accordance with the rule 'maximize utility'
   D All of the above

6 Why might utilitarians disagree about what to do?

    A   Because some might be act-utilitarians and some might be rule-utilitarians

    B   Because they might have different definitions of utility

    C   Because they might make different calculations about utility-maximization

    D   All of the above

7 Which of the following might be benefits of rule-utilitarianism over act-utilitarianism?

    A   It makes it easier to know what the right thing to do is

    B   It enables us to maintain many of our existing moral principles

    C   It is better for stability and trust

    D   All of the above

8 In what sense is utilitarianism egalitarian?

    A   Everyone's utility counts equally

    B   Equality is what maximizes utility

    C   Utilitarianism results in equal utility

    D   Utilitarianism rules out hierarchy

9 Why might utilitarianism be bad for minorities?

    A   Because minorities don't usually believe in utilitarianism

    B   Because utilitarians ignore the interests of minorities

    C   Because protecting minority interests might not maximize utility

    D   All of the above

10 Why might utilitarianism be bad for relationships?

    A   Because relationships are not accorded special weight

    B   Because relationships do not maximize utility

    C   Because relationships are unjust

    D   All of the above

10

Rawls's justice as fairness

John Rawls's work is crucial to contemporary political philosophy. His book *A Theory of Justice* (Rawls 1971) broke with the utilitarianism which dominated political and ethical theory at the time, and broke also with the trend in analytic philosophy to preach the redundancy of normative theorizing. Other thinkers had prepared the way: H.L.A. Hart (in jurisprudence) and Brian Barry (in political science) had begun to criticize the normative implications of utilitarianism (Hart 1961; Barry 1965). But Rawls provided not only a systematic, rigorous critique of utilitarianism, but also a persuasive, far-reaching and elegant defence of a liberal alternative. Rawls's justice as fairness is a canonical statement of liberal political philosophy. It is the theory against which virtually all subsequent work in Anglo-American analytic political philosophy is compared and tested.

In this chapter, we outline Rawls's principal ideas: his critique of utilitarianism, his theory of justice, and the philosophical machinery he employs.

Spotlight: Rawls and *The West Wing*

John Rawls is perhaps one of the few political philosophers who has influenced an American President, albeit a fictional one. An aide to Josiah Bartlett, the President in the TV series *The West Wing*, turned to John Rawls's theory of justice when attempting to construct a federal tax plan which would redistribute wealth from top earners to poorer families in order to subsidize education for low earners.

'To answer your question why the MD [Managing Director] should accept a greater tax burden in spite of the fact that his success is well earned is called a veil of ignorance. Imagine before you're born you don't know anything about who you'll be, your abilities or your position. Now design a tax system. That's John Rawls.'

Rawls's critique of utilitarianism

Rawls's conception of liberal justice is grounded in two criticisms of utilitarianism.

UTILITARIANISM IGNORES THE 'SEPARATENESS OF PERSONS'

The first problem with utilitarianism, Rawls argues, is that it takes the idea of an individual who is self-interested and rational and applies it to society as a whole. According to utilitarians, an individual has a variety of preferences and chooses the course of action which satisfies as many of those preferences as possible. Similarly, a utilitarian society should choose the course of action that satisfies as many of the various preferences of its many members as possible.

But Rawls argues that there is a crucial difference between an individual and a society. For any one individual it makes sense to say that the satisfaction of some preferences can compensate for the dissatisfaction of others: the fact that I am eating ice cream for pudding makes up for the fact that I could not also have cake. But this is not true for society as a whole. Utilitarianism at the social level imagines an impartial spectator, a perfectly rational individual who can observe the preferences of the members of society and then decide which should be sacrificed and which satisfied. In doing this, the impartial spectator treats the members of society not as separate individuals, but as parts of a whole. But members of society are separate persons. If I want public money to be spent on education but it is spent on defence, it is no consolation for me that those who supported defence are now happy. From the standpoint of the impartial spectator, their happiness outweighs my unhappiness, but from the individual's point of view there is no corresponding benefit. What this means, Rawls argues, is that utilitarianism ignores the separateness of persons. It treats people as if they were simply members of a group, and ignores their own individual moral worth and interests.

Moreover, Rawls argues that sacrificing the happiness of some people in order to increase the happiness of others is unjust. What matters to the utilitarian is the general level of happiness in society, rather than the level of happiness experienced by any one individual. So a utilitarian seems to have no moral objection to persecuting minority groups if in doing so we make the majority happier, for example. Indeed, utilitarianism seems to require such persecution! Similarly, if overall social utility could be increased by allowing public executions, the suppression of minority religions, or the imprisonment of climate change sceptics, utilitarianism seems to require the state to do these things. But, Rawls argues, such conclusions are counter-intuitive and wrong. Instead of leaving minorities open to mistreatment by majorities, a theory of justice should protect minorities by enshrining basic rights for all individuals which cannot be violated – irrespective of whether doing so would increase overall happiness. As Rawls put it '[e]ach person possesses an inviolability founded on justice that even the welfare of society as a whole cannot override' (Rawls 1971: p. 3).

UTILITARIANISM MISUNDERSTANDS THE RELATIONSHIP BETWEEN THE RIGHT AND THE GOOD

Rawls's second problem with utilitarianism is that it is a *teleological* theory, not a *deontological* one. Teleological theories start by stipulating the *telos*, or good, to which society as a whole should be aimed. They then derive principles of morality and justice from that good. For utilitarians, the good is utility, and so the *right* (the morally right thing to do) is whatever maximizes this good of utility. But, Rawls argues, modern societies are populated by citizens who have different views about what is good. Teleological theories ignore the fact that individuals have their own 'conception of the good' which may or may not be the same as anyone else's.

Furthermore, utilitarianism requires that everyone subordinate their own interests and desires to the one overall good of utility. It requires us to engage in utilitarian calculations in our daily lives, and in matters of personal morality. Hence, Rawls argues, it does not take seriously each individual's own personal motivations, moral convictions, or their attendant forms of moral reasoning: it views individuals not as ends in themselves but as means by which the wider end of society as a whole might be achieved. Should I go out to the shops or stay in and watch TV? Should I read a book or offer to mend my neighbour's fence? The answer to these questions for the utilitarian is always the same: I should do whatever would bring about the greater good for all. But, Rawls argues, it is not fair to require that everyone always put the general happiness of society above their own reasonably held interests. People may have moral convictions to act in ways which do not bring about the greatest happiness for the greatest number, or they might just want to engage in private pursuits which bring them, and not other people, happiness. Why should a gay or lesbian person be morally required to hide their sexuality in order to please lots of homophobic people? Why should a woman be morally required to submit to sexist norms in order to please a sexist majority?

The challenge for Rawls was to come up with an alternative to utilitarianism which was capable of respecting the separateness of persons, taking seriously the ideals and aspirations of individual citizens, and establishing a stable, cohesive society. He did so by rejecting the teleological approach of utilitarians like Bentham and Sidgwick, and turning instead toward the *deontological* approach favoured by Kant. Whereas a teleological approach such as utilitarianism derives the *right* from the *good*, a deontological approach such as Rawls's defines the right independently of, and prior to, the good. So, Rawls does not understand the right to be whatever maximizes some pre-determined good. Instead, the right is a *constraint* on action. It acts as a constraint on what conception of the good a person can reasonably pursue. So if a person's conception of the good requires treating others unjustly, then that conception of the good is ruled out. Rawls's argument thus requires us first to work out what justice is, and then to use this conception of justice (a) as a guide to the actions of social and political institutions, and (b) as a constraint upon the kinds of lives that people can legitimately pursue.

The original position and the veil of ignorance

So, how do we work out what justice is? Rawls asks us to imagine ourselves in a hypothetical situation called the *original position*. We can think of the original position as a position before there is a society. People in the original position get together to decide what the principles of justice should be in a society. In some ways, they are like contractors in the state of nature, deciding on social rules. However, they are not trying to decide whether it would be rational to form a society. They know that they will live in a society, so they are trying instead to decide how that society should be organized – what principles of justice it should adhere to.

To make the principles of justice *fair*, Rawls stipulates that the people in the original position must be deprived of certain sorts of knowledge about themselves and others. This deprivation of knowledge is called the 'veil of ignorance'. Rawls specifies three sorts of things that are concealed behind the veil of ignorance:

1 **Social status:** In the original position you do not know if, when you are in the society you are thinking about, you will be rich or poor, aristocratic or working class, a leader or a servant. You also do not know if you will have a job that is regarded as impressive or lowly, whether you will be thought of as being at the top of the heap or the bottom.

2 **Talent:** You do not know if, once you are placed in the society that you are planning, you will be clever or stupid, strong or weak, or what kind of work you will be good at.

3 **Conceptions of the good:** Your conception of the good is your set of ideas or beliefs about how you should live. In the original position, you are deprived of knowledge about your particular conception of the good. You do not know what you will believe once the veil of ignorance is lifted.

Why should fairness require the veil of ignorance? The idea is that people are more likely to choose principles of justice which are fair if they do so under conditions of ignorance.

Imagine there are two people and one cake. Each person is to have a portion of cake, and each person wants as much as possible for themselves. Only one person can cut the cake. In this situation, the fairest way of dividing the cake is if one person cuts it and the other person chooses which of the two slices to have. This way, the person cutting the cake knows that the other person will choose the biggest slice. It is therefore in the cutter's interest to cut the cake in half as fairly as possible, to make the two slices as similar as possible. If the person who cuts the cake does not know which slice she will get, she will cut the cake fairly. If, on the other hand, she knows which slice she will have, she will cut the cake unfairly – she will make her slice bigger.

A similar idea is behind Rawls's veil of ignorance. Because they do not know what sort of person they will be, the people in the original position will choose principles of justice that adjudicate fairly between different sorts of people. If you knew that you were going to be an upper-class atheist, you might choose a system of justice whereby upper-class atheists got more rights and resources than anyone else. However, if you knew there was a chance you might turn out to be a working-class Muslim instead, you might well think that things like rights and wealth should not depend on class or religion, and this would be a fairer outcome.

So, the idea of the veil of ignorance is to deny people knowledge of their particular circumstances: knowledge that they might use to bias the principles of justice in their favour. If they did that, the principles would not be fair. So, in order to develop fair principles of justice, it is necessary that people are ignorant of their particular circumstances.

However, some more requirements are needed if the original position is really to produce fair principles of justice. Think back to the cake example. Imagine if you were cutting the cake, and that you knew that your companion were very self-effacing. Although she likes cake very much, and would like as much cake as possible if she were on her own, her natural kindness and modesty leads her to put herself after others. So, if you cut the cake unevenly, she will take the smaller slice. Of course, if you know this, and if you are not troubled by matters of conscience, you will not cut the cake fairly. Instead, you will cut the cake into one small slice and one much larger slice, knowing she will take the smaller one. If she is asked to cut first, she will also cut unfairly, feeling that others are entitled to more than her.

If fairness is to be maintained in this sort of situation, everyone must be self-interested. That is to say, everyone must think only of their own position, and not of the position of others. So, Rawls makes this a further condition of the original position: in it, people are self-interested, and they are also rational. So, people in the original position calculate and prefer what is best for them. This way, the chosen principles will be fair.

It is very important to note that this does not mean that the principles chosen in the original position are based on selfishness and individualism, and that is the role of the veil of ignorance. Imagine we were all in a political philosophy lecture and we were asked, there and then, to agree on principles of justice to govern the lectures. If we were asked to do so using our self-interested rationality, each of us would argue selfishly for the principles that would most benefit us as individuals. Women would argue for principles favouring women, tall people would argue for principles favouring tall people, and so on. But if we used our self-interested rationality from behind the veil of ignorance, we would be forced not to be selfish but actually to think through what it would be like to be each and every person in the lecture. Because we do not know whether we will be male or female, tall or short, and so on, we have to imagine what it would be like to be each of those things. We might imagine that it would be difficult for a short person to be stuck at the back. We might imagine that if there were a rule that only women or tall people were allowed hand-outs, we would not like it if we turned out to be male or short. Far from encouraging selfishness, the original position encourages us to think what it would be like to be each and every different person. It therefore encourages us to be empathetic and kind – and, above all, fair.

So, we need to be deprived of certain information in order to ensure fair outcomes. But why should the veil of ignorance conceal talents, status, and conceptions of the good in particular? The reason why these three things are behind the veil of ignorance is simple and crucial: they are concealed so as to enshrine the key liberal values of *freedom* and *equality*, and so as to model the individual as free and equal.

The veil of ignorance protects *equality* by concealing talents and status. Talent and status are, according to Rawls, the two main forms of inequality. Talent, in this respect, can refer to anything that society values, be it intelligence, strength or the ability to sing or dance or manipulate the stock market. One reason why some people have more resources or opportunities than other people is that they are better at doing the sorts of things that are valued in society.

Status is another key factor in causing inequality. One's position in the class system can affect one's opportunity as regards education, jobs, housing and so on. One's position in the gender or race systems can affect one's success in the job market, how one is treated or perceived in popular culture, and how one is supposed to behave.

So, Rawls argues that a system of justice can only be one that respects equality if people's status and talent are not allowed to determine their life chances. Because status and talent are the two factors that have the greatest effect on equality, they must be abstracted from when choosing the principles of justice.

But why should the people in the original position not know their conception of the good? This time, the purpose is to protect *freedom*. Imagine if the principles of justice were to be chosen by people who *did* know their conception of the good. Imagine that 80 per cent of those people were fundamentalist Christians and the other 20 per cent were atheists or belonged to other religions. When these people come to decide on the principles of justice, the majority of Christians could impose Christianity as the official, compulsory religion of the society. If they know that they are fundamentalist Christians, they will argue that the state should require all citizens to be Christians, that it should provide only Christian teaching, and that it should punish any non-Christians. In such a society, there will be no religious freedom. People will not be able to choose or change their conception of the good. In such a society, even those who are Christians will not be free, since they will not be able to leave the faith.

Rawls argues that a crucial aspect of freedom is being able to choose and to change one's conception of the good. If this is the case, then the principles of justice will not protect freedom unless they are chosen independently of any conception of the good. So, conceptions of the good must be behind the veil of ignorance.

The original position, then, is set up specifically to safeguard and enshrine the liberal values of freedom and equality. It is not an open-ended way of deducing first principles. It starts from the substantive first principles of freedom and equality, and moves from them to principles of justice.

The two principles of justice

Rawls argues that parties in the original position would choose two principles of justice. He describes the two principles as follows:

▷ **First principle of justice:** 'each person is to have an equal right to the most extensive basic liberty compatible with a similar liberty for others' (Rawls 1971: p. 60);

▷ **Second principle of justice:** 'Social and economic inequalities are to be arranged so that they are both (a) to the greatest benefit of the least advantaged and (b) attached to offices and positions open to all under conditions of fair equality of opportunity' (Rawls 1971: p. 83).

These principles tend to be referred to using shorthand terms. The first principle is called the **equal basic liberty principle**. Principle 2(a) is called the **difference principle**, and principle 2(b) is called the **equal opportunity principle**.

Rawls also tells us how to resolve any conflicts between these principles. The equal basic liberty principle is the most important. Nothing can be done that violates it, even if it adheres to the other two principles. Next comes the equality of opportunity principle, and finally the difference principle.

> 'Justice is the first virtue of social institutions, as truth is of systems of thought. A theory however elegant and economical must be rejected or revised if it is untrue; likewise laws and institutions, no matter how efficient and well-arranged must be reformed or abolished if they are unjust. Each person possesses an inviolability founded on justice that even the welfare of society as a whole cannot override. For this reason justice denies that the loss of freedom for some is made right by a greater good shared by others. It does not allow that the sacrifices imposed on a few are outweighed by the larger sum of advantages enjoyed by the many.'
>
> John Rawls, *A Theory of Justice* (Oxford University Press, 1971), pp. 3–4.

The equal basic liberty principle

We have already said that conceptions of the good are concealed behind the veil of ignorance so as to enshrine the value of liberty. This does not go all the way to explaining, however, why those in the original position would choose the equal basic liberty principle. It might be equally fair to put all possible conceptions of the good into a hat and choose one at random for state enforcement. Why would those in the original position not do that?

The answer is that Rawls specifies that the people in the original position have a very strong interest in choosing their own conception of the good (that is, living a life that they themselves have chosen, as opposed to one that has been forced upon them). Their interest in that is so strong that it overrides all their other interests. Remember, the equal basic liberty principle takes priority over all the others. So, the people in the original position must think that it is more important to be able to choose their conception of the good than it is to have equality of opportunity or a high level of welfare. If it were possible to have more resources by limiting liberty – for example, by forcing all people to do whatever work is most productive at any one time – those in the original position would reject it. Their preference for liberty is one of the required features of the original position. Or, to put it in Rawlsian terms, people have an overriding interest in being able to 'frame, revise and rationally to pursue' their conception of the good. It is this interest that explains why the equal basic liberty principle is the most important.

In contrast to teleological theories like utilitarianism, then, Rawls's theory rules out principles of justice based on any particular conception of the good. It also rules out any argument that says that a particular value is more important than liberty. It is not open to anyone to say that their particular conception of the good is so important, or so correct, that it can be imposed. Even if Christianity, for example, were the one true religion, Rawls suggests that it is more important to allow people to choose a mistaken way of life based on an untrue religion than it is to follow the truth. People must be able to follow their chosen conception of the good, even if it is mistaken.

There are, of course, some exceptions to this rule. People will not be able to choose a conception of the good that involves limiting other people's liberty, because that would violate the first principle of justice. So, individuals may not impose their views on others by implementing Nazism or fundamentalist religion. Choice does not go that far. But, for individuals, the ability to choose is of paramount importance.

'The intuitive idea of justice as fairness is to think of the first principles of justice as themselves the object of an original agreement in a suitably defined initial situation. These principles are those which rational persons concerned to advance their interests would accept in this position of equality to settle the basic terms of their association.'
John Rawls, *A Theory of Justice* (Oxford University Press, 1971), pp. 118–19.

The equality of opportunity principle

In order of priority, the equality of opportunity principle comes next. We discussed the concept of equality of opportunity in depth in an earlier chapter, so we will not go into detail here. All we need to say at this point is that the equality of opportunity principle is derived from people's ignorance of their talents and status. Because in the original position people do not know what sort of characteristics they will have after the veil of ignorance is lifted, it is rational for them to require that positions be allocated only according to relevant criteria. If you don't know whether you will be black or white, middle or working class, it is rational to say that jobs or education or duties may not be allocated on the grounds of skin colour, and that people from different class backgrounds should have the same opportunities to develop the talents and skills that are needed for positions of advantage.

The difference principle

The difference principle is perhaps the most unusual and complex principle of justice. Remember, the difference principle states that 'social and economic inequalities are to be arranged so that they are ... to the greatest benefit of the least advantaged.' This is a very demanding principle. It means that inequalities are only allowed if they benefit the worst-off in society. They are not allowed if they benefit others, even if they do not affect the position of the worst-off at all.

Remember, in the original position, we do not know our own talents or the talents of anyone else. So we would reject inequality based on talents, because we may end up without talents that are valued. Rawls argues that we would want to protect individuals from being harmed by a lack of talent. We would want principles of justice that benefit the worst-off because once the veil of ignorance is lifted *we* might be the worst-off! Indeed, Rawls stipulates that the people in the original position must be very worried about the possibility of being badly-off. As a result the principles of justice must help the worst-off as much as possible, because that is the best way of securing equality.

One objection to the difference principle is that it is unfair to the talented. You might think that people deserve to be rewarded for their talents. For example, talented sportspeople, pop singers and actors are paid more than people who lack those talents. Rawls rejects this idea. He argues that natural endowments such as talents, health and so on are *morally arbitrary*: a matter of luck. A person has not done anything to deserve the talents they are born with, and so does not deserve more resources. For Rawls, we should pay some people more than others only if doing so benefits the worst-off. For example, if it were necessary to pay doctors more money to ensure that there were enough of them then doing so might be permitted, since having enough doctors benefits the worst-off.

Case study: Fair inequality not equality

It is important to remember, in the context of our discussion in Chapter 3, that Rawls does not seek to establish *equality*, so much as *fair inequality*. Rawls's scheme allows for inequalities to exist between the richest and the poorest members of society. Why does he do this? Why does he not simply argue that resources should be distributed equally among all members of society? One answer is, as we have said, that he does not think that that is what rational, self-interested individuals in the original position would choose. But that is not good enough because, as we have seen, Rawls constructs the original position in such a way as to get the outcomes that he thinks are consistent with justice. So: why does Rawls argue for fair inequality, rather than equality?

The answer is a controversial one, and one which has proven quite unpopular among more egalitarian and left-wing critics: he wants to provide an incentive for people with particular skills which could be of benefit to society to develop these skills and, hence, he wants to allow for the 'trickle-down effect'.

The trickle-down effect is the idea that allowing higher wages as incentives can actually benefit the worst-off, by ensuring that valuable jobs are done. If no inequality is allowed whatsoever, there will be no material incentive for anyone to work harder and increase their productivity. Without the prospect of higher pay, it does not make economic sense for companies or individuals to try to innovate, and improve the products they offer. As a result, the overall amount of resources available in the society will be lower than it would have been if inequality of income had been allowed. People will be not be working so hard, will be producing less, and will not be innovating to the same level that they would if they had an economic incentive to do so. There will also be fewer jobs as a result, and all this is bad for the worst-off. In some circumstances, inequalities provide incentives for people to innovate and start up new businesses, and this kind of activity benefits those who are worst-off by providing more jobs and wealth in the economy. Hence, Rawls argues that inequalities in wealth and income can be compatible with justice *as long as* they are justifiable to – and help improve the condition of – the worst-off.

Conclusion

There is a lot more to say about Rawls's theory, and we fill out the picture in the chapters to come. The central thrust of Rawls's theory is that we must take the interests and aspirations of individuals seriously. We should not subordinate individuals to the general good of others. Instead, principles of justice must respect individual freedom and equality. Rawls's principal achievements were to show the weakness of utilitarianism, and to provide a liberal theory of social justice which was egalitarian rather than libertarian. While traditionally many liberals argued that liberalism required a commitment to free markets, Rawls showed liberalism should instead be committed to egalitarian redistribution and state intervention. Parties in the original position would not choose free markets; they would choose to reject free markets in favour of an economic system which alleviated unfair inequalities through redistribution. Rawls's principles of justice defend the redistribution of wealth, income and power from the richest members of society to the poorest in the name of freedom and equality.

> A Theory of Justice *is a powerful, deep, subtle, wide-ranging, systematic work of political and moral philosophy which has not seen its like since the writings of John Stuart Mill, if then. It is a fountain of illuminating ideas, integrated together into a lovely whole. Political philosophers now must either work in Rawls' theory or explain why not... [I]t is impossible to finish his book without a new and inspiring vision of what a moral theory may attempt to do and unite; of how beautiful a whole theory can be.'*
>
> Robert Nozick, *Anarchy, State, and Utopia*
> (Oxford: Blackwell, 1974), p. 183.

Key ideas

Original position: The hypothetical situation in which persons consider and choose principles of justice, incorporating those conditions that Rawls believes it is necessary to impose upon the deliberative process in order to ensure that the outcomes are fair, and consistent with respecting the freedom and equality of all individuals.

Veil of ignorance: In order to ensure that the principles of justice chosen in the original position are fair, Rawls argues that we should not bring certain considerations into the deliberative process. Rawls therefore suggests that we should imagine that our status, talents and conception of the good are concealed behind a 'veil of ignorance'.

Conception of the good: The particular preferences, ideals, aspirations and values which make up an individual person's chosen way of life.

Separateness of persons: The idea that each individual is a person in their own right, with their own unique conception of the good, rather than simply an anonymous member of a social whole. Liberal justice seeks to respect the integrity of individual human beings as persons. Utilitarianism, according to Rawls, ignores the integrity of individual human beings by subordinating their interests and conceptions of the good to the overarching good of society as a whole.

Two principles of justice: The two principles which Rawls believes would be chosen in the original position. The first principle is commonly known as the equal basic liberty principle. The second is split into two parts: (a) the equal opportunity principle, and (b) the difference principle.

Dig deeper

Brian Barry, *Political Argument* (London: Routledge & Kegan Paul, 1965).

Brian Barry, *The Liberal Theory of Justice: A Critical Examination of the Principal Doctrines of* A Theory of Justice *by John Rawls* (Oxford: Clarendon Press, 1973).

Samuel Freeman (ed.), *The Cambridge Companion to Rawls* (Cambridge: Cambridge University Press, 2003).

Samuel Freeman, *John Rawls* (London: Taylor & Francis, 2007).

H.L.A. Hart, *The Concept of Law* (Oxford: Clarendon Press, 1961).

Thomas Pogge, *John Rawls: His Life and Theory of Justice* (Oxford University Press, 2007).

John Rawls, *A Theory of* Justice (Cambridge, MA: Harvard University Press, 1971).

John Rawls, *Collected Papers* (ed.), Samuel Freeman (Cambridge, MA: Harvard University Press, 1999).

Fact-check

1 What, according to Rawls, is wrong with utilitarianism?
   A Not everyone wants to be happy
   B Utilitarianism doesn't tell us what to do
   C Utilitarianism leads to unjust outcomes
   D Utilitarianism is old-fashioned

2 What is a deontological theory?
   A A theory that prioritizes the right over the good
   B A theory that prioritizes the good over the right
   C A theory that identifies the right with the good
   D A theory about teeth

3 Which of the following are concealed behind the veil of ignorance?
   A Your attitude to risk
   B Whether you are self-interested
   C Whether you are rational
   D Your status, talents and conception of the good

4 What is being decided in the original position?
   A Whether to form a society
   B Whether the state is justified
   C Whether one has a duty to obey the law
   D What justice requires

5 According to Rawls, which is the most important principle of justice?
   A The equal basic liberty principle
   B The equal opportunity principle
   C The sameness principle
   D The difference principle

6 Why don't talented people deserve to be paid more, according to Rawls?
   A Because talented people are often lazy
   B Because talented people don't help society
   C Because talents are morally arbitrary
   D Because wealth is morally bad

7 Why does Rawls rule out some conceptions of the good?

    A Because some conceptions of the good are mistaken

    B Because some conceptions of the good are unjust

    C Because some conceptions of the good do not promote utility

    D Because some conceptions of the good are only held by minorities

8 What are the fundamental principles at the heart of Rawls's theory?

    A Freedom and equality

    B Equality and utility

    C Freedom and wealth

    D Desert and freedom

9 Why might it be acceptable to pay doctors more than gardeners, according to Rawls?

    A Because being a doctor is more difficult than being a gardener

    B Because being a doctor is more useful than being a gardener

    C Because ill people deserve good doctors

    D Because the worst-off are harmed if there are not enough doctors

10 Which of the following does Rawls say is most important?

    A Being able to frame, revise and pursue your conception of the good

    B Being able to maximize your own position

    C Being able to do whatever you want

    D Being able to have whatever you want

11

Libertarianism

Libertarianism is a fundamental critique of egalitarianism in general, and of Rawls's theory of justice in particular. It has been defended by a number of political philosophers including Robert Nozick (1974) and David Gauthier (1986), and arguably represents the ideological core of political movements such as, among others, the Republican Party and the Tea Party movement in the USA. Broadly speaking, libertarians defend free markets and minimal states against the redistributive tendencies of egalitarian liberal theory. Indeed, the pre-eminent libertarian philosopher Robert Nozick wrote his *Anarchy, State, and Utopia* as a direct rebuttal of the liberal egalitarian redistributive state defended by Rawls. The book was published in 1974, three years after Rawls's *A Theory of Justice*, and set in motion a fierce debate between libertarians and egalitarians about the nature of freedom and justice which dominated political philosophy in the 1970s and early 1980s, and continues to this day.

In the rest of this chapter, we discuss libertarianism through the prism of its most significant advocate: Robert Nozick.

The limits on state action

For Rawls, remember, justice requires extensive redistribution according to the difference principle. According to Nozick, the Rawlsian state or any state which intervenes in free markets in order to redistribute wealth from the rich to the poor is unjust. This is because redistribution violates individual rights by forcing people to do things, and to give up their property, in ways that they do not choose. Nozick and other libertarians thus emphasize the *limits* that individual rights place on state action. The general claim of libertarianism is these limits are extensive: there is very little that a state may legitimately do.

Nozick's entitlement theory of justice

According to Nozick, justice is a matter of *entitlement*. The way to judge whether a particular distribution of resources is just is to consider whether people are entitled to the holdings they have. The way to do this is to consider how people came to acquire those holdings. Justice thus becomes a matter of finding out the history of a certain distribution. Nozick expresses this idea by saying that his entitlement theory is *historical*, not *end-state*.

An *end-state theory* of distributive justice is one in which the justice of a distribution is determined by looking at what people have at any particular point in time. Theories like Rawls's that call for the redistribution of wealth tend to be end-state theories: they consider the existing distribution, notice that some have more than others, and conclude that this is unfair and should be rectified.

In contrast, a *historical theory* of distributive justice is one in which justice is determined by considering how people came by their holdings. Nozick argues that end-state theories are problematic for two main reasons. Firstly, they are incompatible with liberty. Secondly, they fail to take account of the fact that goods are not 'manna from heaven'. They are made by people, and come into the world with ownership already attached. We will expand these claims later in the chapter.

There are three central elements of Nozick's entitlement theory of justice:

1 the initial acquisition of resources (that is, how people originally came by their holdings)

2 the transfer of resources (that is, the ways in which holdings might appropriately pass from one person to another)

3 the rectification of injustice (that is, what needs to happen if either (1) or (2) are seen to have been unjust).

The fundamental principle of Nozick's theory is: if each individual's holdings are just, then the overall distribution of holdings is just.

INITIAL ACQUISITION OF RESOURCES

The first question for a historical theory of justice is how it is that we can come to own anything in the first place. How can an individual or a company come to own natural resources, such as land or raw materials? Nozick's theory of how natural resources can be justly owned is a version of the theory of acquisition put forward by John Locke. Nozick assumes that initially, natural resources are unowned. People may appropriate these natural resources on a first-come, first-served basis, with one proviso: other people must not be made worse off. Nozick has a particular meaning in mind when he says that the position of others must not be worsened: someone is made worse off if they are no longer able freely to *use* something that they previously could use. The mere fact that someone else now owns that thing is not enough to make others worse off, on Nozick's account. This implies that there must always be some amount of unowned resource left, or that owners of a resource must allow some free use.

Nozick argues that people can often be made better-off if someone else appropriates a natural resource. Imagine that there is an unowned lake that people would like to use for fishing and swimming. However, the lake is polluted, so swimming is unpleasant and the fish are unhealthy. Because no one owns it, no one does anything about the pollution. Then Jack appropriates the lake. He charges people £5 per day to visit the lake, and uses £4 out of every £5 to clear up the pollution. The lake is much more pleasant to use, and people are very willing to pay the £5 – in fact, they feel that they are better off than they were before the lake was appropriated. So they would rather pay £5 to visit Jack's lake than visit a nearby unowned (and thus still polluted) lake for free.

According to Nozick, people also justly own the products that they create from their justly acquired natural resources. So, if Jack justly acquires the dirty lake, and then devotes his time and further resources to producing a clean lake, he is entitled to the clean lake that he has produced. Once the raw materials have been justly acquired, a person can transform them into products which she subsequently owns.

TRANSFER OF RESOURCES

Once people have justly acquired resources, they do not have to keep them. Resources may be transferred between people and, Nozick argues, as long as the transfers are just, the resulting distribution is just. The key aspect to a just transfer, for Nozick, is that it must be *voluntary*. So just transfers include gifts, inheritance, buying and selling, and payment for services and labour. There are no external, objective limits or definitions for what constitutes a just transfer. As long as the parties agree to it, it is just. So, if I agree to sell you my brand-new Rolls-Royce for £100, that is just. There is no force in the argument, for Nozick, that £100 is an unfair price and so the transaction was unjust. Crucially, for Nozick market transactions are just transactions.

RECTIFICATION OF INJUSTICE

Nozick accepts that the current distribution of resources in actually existing societies is not just, because it is not the result of just acquisitions and just transfers. He therefore proposes a principle of rectification: where there have been unjust transfers, there can and should be compensating transfers to rectify the injustice.

Nozick accepts that rectification will be exceedingly complex. He therefore concedes that it might be better to start with some other distribution, perhaps an equal distribution of resources. However, once we have reached a fair starting-point, we can let the principle of just transfers work freely. After a time there could, and probably would, be vast inequalities between people. It is these inequalities that liberal theories of distributive justice such as Rawls's are designed to mitigate. Nozick's argument is that there is no need rectify inequalities, no matter how vast, as long as they have come about through just transfers of justly held resources.

Redistributive taxation

We have seen, then, that Nozick argues that justice is a historical concept, determined by the question of whether people are *entitled* to their holdings. Their entitlement is determined by whether they acquired their holdings by one of the three just methods of acquisition: initial appropriation, just transfers, or rectification of injustice.

Of course, once just transfers get underway, inequalities will develop. While liberals advocate redistributive taxation in order to rectify certain inequalities, Nozick is firmly against such taxation. Indeed, Nozick argues that redistributive taxation is, normatively, equivalent to *slavery*. Since slavery is wrong, redistributive taxation must be wrong.

Spotlight: Tax Freedom Day

'Tax Freedom Day' is a term that is similar to Nozick's claim that taxation is like slavery. It refers to the first day that the average citizen can work 'for herself' after working to pay off her year-long tax bill. In the USA the day is calculated by the Tax Foundation think tank, who said that it fell on 9 April in 2010. That same year, the Adam Smith Institute calculated the UK Tax Freedom Day as occurring on 30 May.

Why does Nozick think redistributive taxation is like slavery? Redistributive taxation involves *coercing* the person who is taxed: forcing them to pay a certain amount of money to the state. If they refuse to pay they can be imprisoned. Now, for the most part, people get money by working for others – they are employed. This exchange of labour for money is just, for Nozick, because workers agree to it, and they agree to work precisely because they are paid. But if a worker has to pay tax so as to support redistribution, the worker is being forced to work unpaid. The worker will have to work extra unpaid hours in order to pay the tax.

Imagine a tax rate of 10 per cent. If Emma is paid £100 for 10 hours work she will be charged tax of £10. What this means is that Emma is forced to work unpaid for the tenth hour, because she has to give that hour's wages to the tax collector. This unpaid hour is, Nozick argues, like slavery: it is forced, unpaid work. And just as slavery is wrong and unjust, so redistributive taxation is wrong and unjust.

> 'The man who chooses to work longer to gain an income more than sufficient for his basic needs prefers some extra goods or services to the leisure and activities he could perform during the possible nonworking hours; whereas the man who chooses not to work the extra time prefers the leisure activities to the extra goods or services he could acquire by working more. Given this, if it would be illegitimate for a tax system to seize some of a man's leisure (forced labour) for the purpose of serving the needy, how can it be legitimate for a tax system to seize some of a man's goods for that purpose?'
>
> Robert Nozick, *Anarchy, State, and Utopia* (New York: Basic Books, 1974), p. 170.

Nozick acknowledges that without *some* taxation, there would be no society or state. So a just state would require people to pay enough (but *only* enough) tax to maintain things like defence, law and order, and perhaps also public goods like street lighting and road maintenance. But why isn't this form of taxation like slavery, if redistributive taxation is?

Because of the idea, embodied in the social contract, that it would be irrational not to form and maintain a state. Given this, basic taxation aimed at maintaining the minimal state (and no more) is understood as willingly, or voluntarily, given. It would be irrational not to give up a proportion of your holdings to support those institutions which protect your individual rights. This is not true of redistribution.

The very nature of redistributive taxation is that it takes money from the rich and gives it to the poor. Nozick argues that this unfairly discriminates between people who value leisure and people who value wealth. He writes:

> if it would be illegitimate for a tax system to seize some of a man's leisure (forced labor) for the purpose of serving the needy, how can it be legitimate for a tax system to seize some of a man's goods for that purpose? Why should we treat the man whose happiness requires certain material goods or services differently from the man whose preferences and desires make such goods unnecessary for his happiness? (Nozick 1974: p 170)

Redistributive taxation discriminates unfairly, whereas taxation for the minimal state is (or should be) paid for by all, and so is fair.

Redistributive taxation violates the Kantian (and liberal) maxim that no individual may be used as the means to achieve the well-being of another, while taxation aimed at supporting the minimal state provides goods that the people being taxed will themselves use or benefit from. People are ends in themselves; they are rights-bearing moral and political subjects: they should not be used as tools which can be used to ensure happiness or wellbeing for others. Progressive taxation violates this idea by assuming that rich people (and their holdings) can be used to improve the lives of other people.

Nozick is therefore committed to the idea that there should be no redistributive taxation. It follows that the needy will not be helped by the state. Nozick accepts this. However, he argues that the needy should still be helped, but by acts of voluntary charity, rather than by state coercion. He is willing to accept that the normative, moral obligation to perform acts of charity would be high in his society. He is merely against state coercion.

The principle of self-ownership

There are various objections to Nozick's argument that progressive taxation is like slavery. For example, we might start by asking: Why is slavery wrong? What is it about slavery that makes it wrong, and is redistributive taxation like slavery in the relevant sense? Is it sufficiently like slavery to make it fundamentally wrong and unjust? Nozick's answer, and his theory as a whole, is tied closely to the concept of self-ownership.

Self-ownership is the idea that each person has *full property rights* over herself: her body, her talents, her labour. Full property rights entail the right to sell oneself. So, for Nozick, it is justifiable to sell one's labour, even one's most intimate labour. So Nozick has no justice-based objection to prostitution, or surrogacy, or organ sales, or selling oneself into slavery.

Self-ownership provides the basis for many elements of Nozick's argument, and his critique of liberalism. It undermines the idea, crucial to the difference principle, that people's talents are morally arbitrary, so that people don't deserve the fruits of their talents. On the contrary, for Nozick people *own* their talents. It follows that people own the fruits of their labour and talents. As we have seen, Nozick argues that a person owns anything that she makes out of raw materials that she has justly acquired. If a person owns the materials, and owns herself and thus her labour, she owns the product of her labour. It is thus illegitimate to take products from people.

There are numerous problems with this view, but let us for now focus on two, provided by G.A. Cohen and Susan Moller Okin.

Case study: The eye lottery

A strong argument in favour of self-ownership and against egalitarian redistribution is Nozick's thought-example of the eye lottery. Nozick points out that if, contrary to his own views, we don't own our *natural* endowments, and if redistribution is required, there appears to be nothing to stop us from being forced to redistribute our natural endowments to others. For example, egalitarianism might require an eye lottery, whereby people lucky enough to be born with two good eyes could be forced to donate one of them to people who have none.

Nozick proposes that most will find the idea of the eye lottery (and the underlying idea that we should be coercively forced to redistribute our body parts to people who have need of them) horrendous. However, he says, the only way to prevent such a scenario is to adopt his theory of self-ownership. According to his theory, after all, we *own* our natural endowments, and we cannot legitimately be forced to donate our endowments to others even so as to bring about equality. Nozick believes that egalitarians face a choice. They must either accept that we do not own our bodies and that therefore we can be required to redistribute parts of them in the same way that we are required to redistribute social resources. Or, they can accept the idea of self-ownership and, hence, abandon the idea of redistribution.

COHEN AND SELF-OWNERSHIP

G.A. Cohen accepts that the idea of self-ownership is very attractive. However, self-ownership leads to extremely undesirable consequences, most obviously to significant inequalities of resources that are not mitigated by state help since there will be no welfare safety-net. Libertarianism also rules out state education and healthcare as these are essentially redistributive goods. All but the minimal state is abandoned. Cohen is a strong egalitarian, and shares with egalitarian liberals deep disgust for these consequences.

As we saw in Chapter 1, Cohen argues that poverty is actually a restriction of liberty, since those without money are subject to coercion. Cohen concludes that the concept of self-ownership must be abandoned, since it does inevitably lead to the undesirable consequences of inequality – which, in turn, leads to unfreedom. Redistributive taxation might be like slavery in that it restricts freedom, but poverty restricts freedom, too. Cohen argues that freedom should not be understood in purely 'negative' terms: it is not just about possessing rights; it is about being autonomous – in control of one's life.

> 'It is easy to think carelessly about the [Wilt Chamberlain] example. How we feel about people like Chamberlain getting a lot of money as things are *is a poor index* of how people would feel in the imagined situation. Among us the ranks of the rich and the powerful exist, and it can be pleasing, given that they do, when a figure like Chamberlain joins them. Who better and more innocently deserves to be among them? But the case before us is a society of equality in danger of corruption. Reflective people would have to consider not only the joy of watching Chamberlain and its immediate money price but also the fact, which socialists say they would deplore, that their society would be set on the road to class division. In presenting the Chamberlain fable Nozick ignores the commitment people may have to living in a society of a particular kind, and the rhetorical power of the illustration depends on that omission.'
>
> G.A. Cohen, 'Robert Nozick and Wilt Chamberlain: How Patterns Preserve Liberty', *Erkenntnis* 11/1 (May, 1977), p. 11.

OKIN AND SELF-OWNERSHIP

Susan Moller Okin argues that the thesis of self-ownership can be refuted, since it is incoherent. She points out that, if the thesis held, then mothers would own their babies. Babies are made from raw materials – sperm and egg – and gestational labour. A woman owns her own eggs, according to Nozick, and can justly acquire sperm (it is usually given freely by men!). She then transforms the sperm and egg, with nine months of demanding physical labour and risk, into a baby. Still more labour is required to transform the child into an adult capable of independence.

It follows that, on Nozick's account, all mothers own their children, and that no one owns themselves. Therefore, the principle of self-ownership is incoherent. If everyone is a self-owner, then no one is.

Against patterned distributions: freedom vs. equality

There is a final argument that Nozick makes against redistributive taxation: since liberty upsets patterns, maintaining any patterned distribution must necessarily restrict liberty. In other words, liberty and equality are incompatible.

Nozick makes this argument with a famous thought-experiment: the Wilt Chamberlain example. Wilt Chamberlain was a very high-earning basketball player in 1974, when Nozick was writing. Nozick asks us to imagine that we start with whatever distribution we prefer. Perhaps everyone has equal holdings, or resources are distributed to the difference principle, or according to the Marxist slogan 'From each according to his abilities, to each according to his needs'. Whatever your favourite distribution of resources is, start with that.

Nozick then asks us to imagine that Wilt Chamberlain is playing basketball, and that there is a pot placed at the entrance to the sports field with his name on it. Anyone who wants to watch Wilt play should put 25 cents into this box. Over time, one million people watch Wilt play, and all are happy to put their money into this box. The result is that Wilt has $250,000 more than anyone else. Nozick's claim is that nothing can be wrong with this final outcome. After all, everyone started with a just amount of money, and everyone acted voluntarily.

Nozick's point is not that Wilt deserves to be rich. Nozick is not relying on any controversial claims about Wilt deserving to profit from his talents. It would not matter if Wilt were untalented but still popular. Instead, the key point of the example is that, in order to prevent the inequality from arising, we would need to restrict the *audience*'s freedom. We would have to impose a law against giving 25 cents to a basketball player. In fact, we would have to impose a great many laws against transfers of resources.

Spotlight: Nozick on his private life

In an interview with Julian Sanchez (JS) in 2001 Nozick (RN) reflected on the connection between his philosophical libertarianism and his personal life:

RN: One thing that I think reinforced the view that I had rejected libertarianism was a story about an apartment of [*Love Story* author] Erich Segal's that I had been renting. [...] In the rent he was charging me, Erich Segal was violating a Cambridge rent control statute. I knew at the time that when I let my intense irritation with representatives of Erich Segal lead me to invoke against him rent control laws that I opposed and disapproved of, that I would later come to regret it, but sometimes you have to do what you have to do.

JS: Do the other professors pick on you because you're the 'libertarian kid,' so to speak? Has that been an albatross around your neck?

RN: No, not in the [Harvard] philosophy department certainly. (And I have been treated very well by the university administration.) Behind my back at the university, who knows what goes on, but not to my face. There was a time some years ago in the aftermath of *Anarchy, State, and Utopia* when it was probably the case that my social life was somewhat curtailed. There may have been many parties I wasn't getting invited to because people despised the views in my book. But if so, I didn't notice it very much at the time.'

Source: http://www.trinity.edu/rjensen/NozickInterview.htm

The problem with patterned theories of redistribution, which seek to determine exactly who gets what and why in any given society, is that they will inevitably be undermined by the choices that people make about how to spend the money they are left with *after* they have been taxed. The only way to solve this problem, and to maintain the redistribution stipulated by whatever theory of redistributive justice that is being used, is for the state to constantly police, and intervene in, the daily activities of its citizens and, hence, to substantially violate the freedom and individual rights of those citizens. This is why, if we value freedom, we must give up the idea of patterned theories of redistribution (like Rawls's difference principle, for example) in favour of free markets based on the voluntary transfer of resources from individuals to other individuals.

Conclusion

Libertarianism is a profound challenge to the fundamental assumptions of egalitarianism, particularly liberal egalitarianism, for it suggests that it is not possible to be committed to both liberty and equality. A project such as Rawls's is therefore doomed, if Nozick is to be believed.

Nozick's arguments are more problematic to some egalitarians than others. It is possible to avoid most of his critique if one is willing to reject the idea of freedom as being rights-based, and to argue that individuals are not entitled to the fruits of their labour. Nonetheless, Nozick's account does demonstrate that at least some versions of liberty are in tension with establishing – and, more importantly, maintaining – distributive equality.

'[Anarchy, State, and Utopia's] conclusions are not in the least unusual. They articulate the prejudices of the average owner of a filling station in a small town in the Midwest who enjoys grousing about paying taxes and having to contribute to "welfare scroungers" and who regards as wicked any attempts to interfere with contracts, in the interests, for example, of equal opportunity or anti-discrimination. ...[It is] quite indecent [that Nozick], from the lofty heights of a professorial chair, is proposing to starve or humiliate ten percent or so of his fellow citizens (if he recognizes the word) by eliminating all transfer payments through the state, leaving the sick, the old, the disabled, the mothers with young children and no breadwinner, and so on, to the tender mercies of private charity, given at the whim and pleasure of the donors and on any terms that they choose to impose.'
Brian Barry, 'Review of *Anarchy, State, and Utopia*', *Political Theory* (August 1975), pp. 331–2.

Key ideas

Libertarianism: A theory that prioritizes liberty and rights, rather than equality. Libertarians advocate a minimal state, which raises taxes only to provide law and order and national security, with few public services and no welfare state.

End-state theory: A theory, such as Rawls's, according to which justice is determined by the result or end-state of a series of transactions. A society is just or not depending on its outcomes for its members: how rich or poor they are at any given time. End-state theories will often seek to maintain a patterned distribution.

Historical theory: A theory, such as Nozick's, according to which justice is determined by the justice of the various transactions that take place on a daily basis. A society is just or not depending on whether it is the result of a series of just transactions.

Patterned distribution: A distribution of resources that conforms to some principle or pattern. Examples include absolute equality (everyone has the same), feudalism (wealth is in the hands of the nobility) or the difference principle (inequalities are permitted only if they benefit the worst-off).

Self-ownership: The idea that people's relationship to themselves is one of full property ownership. A self-owner may legitimately sell any part of herself: her body, her organs, her sexual services, her ideas, her labour or even her whole self in a voluntary slavery contract. The person is treated as property like any other. The focus on property rights means that self-ownership is not the same as autonomy or bodily integrity.

Dig deeper

G.A. Cohen, *Self-Ownership, Freedom, and Equality* (Cambridge: Cambridge University Press, 1995).

Cecile Fabre, *Whose Body Is It Anyway? Justice and the Integrity of the Person* (Oxford: Oxford University Press, 2006).

David Gauthier, *Morals by Agreement* (Oxford: Oxford University Press, 1986).

Susan Moller Okin, *Justice, Gender, and the Family* (New York: Basic Books, 1989).

Thomas Nagel, 'Nozick: Libertarianism without Foundations', *Other Minds: Critical Essays, 1969–1994* (Oxford: Oxford University Press, 1995), pp. 137–49.

Jan Narveson, *The Libertarian Idea* (Philadelphia: Temple University Press, 1988).

Robert Nozick, *Anarchy, State, and Utopia* (New York: Basic Books, 1974).

Peter Vallentyne, *Contractarianism and Rational Choice: Essays on David Gauthier's Morals by Agreement* (Cambridge: Cambridge University Press, 1991).

Jonathan Wolff, *Robert Nozick: Property, Justice, and the Minimal State* (Stanford, CA: Stanford University Press, 1991).

Fact-check

1 What is the difference between libertarianism and liberalism?

   A Libertarians reject the value of distributive equality

   B Libertarians reject the value of freedom

   C Libertarians reject rights

   D All of the above

2 What sort of freedom does Nozick defend?

   A Positive freedom

   B Rights-based freedom

   C Freedom as self-mastery

   D Freedom as autonomy

3 Why is Nozick's theory an 'entitlement theory' of justice?

   A It states that people are always entitled to whatever they have

   B It states that talented people are entitled to be rich

   C It states that a distribution is just if and only if people are entitled to their holdings

   D It states that people are entitled to receive redistribution of wealth

4 What, according to Nozick, is wrong with 'patterned distributions'?

   A They conflict with equality

   B They conflict with liberty

   C They conflict with charity

   D They conflict with security

5 What point does Nozick want to make with the Wilt Chamberlain example?

   A That liberty upsets patterns

   B That justice is based on desert

   C That inequality is a good thing

   D All of the above

6 What is self-ownership?

   A The claim that we cannot be the property of others without our consent

   B The claim that we should be allowed to sell our bodies

C The claim that we have full property-rights over our bodies

D All of the above

7 What limits does Nozick place on the appropriation of natural resources?

A Others must still be able to use some of that resource

B Others must still be able to appropriate some of that resource

C The environment must not be harmed

D Liberty must not be affected

8 Why, according to Nozick, is redistribution unjust?

A Because it is like slavery

B Because it violates the entitlement theory

C Because it attempts to uphold a patterned distribution

D All of the above

9 What is Nozick's solution to poverty?

A The welfare state

B The workhouse

C Charity

D Slavery

10 Why is libertarianism problematic for egalitarian liberalism?

A It suggests that poverty does not matter

B It suggests that freedom and equality conflict

C It suggests that we have no reason to help other people

D It suggests that freedom is unimportant

12

Luck
egalitarianism

An important aim of contemporary theories of social justice is to determine what counts as *fair* grounds for inequality, and what does not. Rawls's answer was that inequalities are only fair if they benefit the worst-off. Nozick argued that inequalities are fair if they arise from the free exchange of legitimately acquired resources. In this chapter, we discuss a third approach: luck egalitarianism. Luck egalitarianism is the idea that disadvantage is unjust if and only if it results from bad luck rather than from choice. Luck egalitarians therefore share Rawls's view that our lives should not be determined for us by factors over which we have no control, and incorporate a stronger emphasis on individual responsibility than can be found in Rawls. In this chapter, we discuss some of the different forms of luck egalitarianism that have been proposed, and some problems with the approach as a whole.

In this chapter, we discuss some of the different forms of luck egalitarianism that have been proposed, and some problems with the approach as a whole.

Luck in Rawls

There are many aspects of our lives over which we have little or no control. For example, we had no control over the parents we were born to, how much money they had, or how seriously they took our education. Similarly, we had no control over what talents we were blessed with. Rawls argues that, as these things were simply the result of good or bad luck on our part rather than a result of particular choices that we made, it would be very unfair if they had a significant influence on our life chances. It would be very unfair, for example, if some people got all the best jobs simply because their parents were rich, or if some children received very poor education simply on the grounds that their parents were poor.

'The natural distribution is neither just nor unjust; nor is it unjust that men are born into society at some particular position. These are simply natural facts. What is just or unjust is the way institutions deal with these facts. Aristocratic and caste societies are unjust because they make these contingencies the ascriptive basis for belonging to more or less closed and privileged social classes. The basic structure of these societies incorporates the arbitrariness found in nature. But there is no need for men to resign themselves to these contingencies. In justice as fairness men agree to share one another's fate. In designing institutions they undertake to avail themselves of the accidents of nature and social circumstances only when doing so is for the common benefit. The two principles [of justice] are a fair way of meeting the arbitrariness of fortune.'

John Rawls, *A Theory of Justice* (Oxford: Oxford University Press, 1971), p.102.

One of Rawls's principal aims was to outline a conception of justice which mitigated the influence that such unchosen factors play in our lives – characteristics like race, sex and class, as well as natural endowments like intelligence, ambition and talents, are 'morally arbitrary' precisely because they are *unchosen*: they are neither deserved or undeserved, and so should not influence the distribution of benefits and burdens in a society. Rawls argues that we should exclude such factors

from our deliberations about the distribution of benefits and
burdens (by putting them behind a veil of ignorance). Doing
so leads us to agree on a set of principles which emphasize
choice and responsibility over luck, and a principle of equality
of opportunity (according to which jobs are allocated on the
basis of relevant skills rather than ascriptive characteristics that
people do not choose).

There are two important problems with Rawls's argument:

IT DOES NOT SUFFICIENTLY TAKE INTO ACCOUNT INEQUALITIES CAUSED BY NATURAL ENDOWMENTS

For Rawls, the worst-off in society are not simply those who
have the smallest amount of money. The worst-off are those
who have the smallest amount of what Rawls calls 'primary
goods'. Primary goods are those goods that a person needs if
she is to follow her chosen conception of the good, whatever
that conception of the good happens to be. Money is a primary
good, because some amount of money is necessary to follow any
conception of the good. But there are other things that people
need to live good lives, things like rights, liberties, opportunities
and powers. These are primary goods that are distributed by
social institutions, and the worst-off are measured according
to their allocation of all of these social goods. So, in working
out who the worst-off people are, we need to know not just
how much money they have, but also how much power and
opportunity, and what rights they have.

However, these *social* primary goods are not the only things that
people need in order to be able to pursue their conception of
the good life. There are also *natural* primary goods, things like
health, intelligence, stamina, determination and so on. These are
the characteristics that Rawls argues are morally arbitrary, and
so do not entitle people to higher salaries. Nevertheless, he does
not allow natural primary goods to count when calculating who
the worst-off people are. This is for two main reasons:

▷ The first is the idea that justice is the first virtue of *social*
  institutions. In other words, principles of justice are supposed
  to tell us how social institutions should operate, how they
  should distribute benefits and burdens. Because natural

endowments are not distributed by social institutions, their distribution cannot be a matter of justice. It is not *unjust* that someone is born less intelligent than average. It is merely unfortunate. Justice concerns only the operation of social institutions.

▶ The second reason why natural primary goods do not count when working out who the worst-off people are is that it would be extremely difficult and costly to arrange society so that all inequalities benefit the worst-off, if the worst-off included people with debilitating handicaps, or who are paralysed or in a coma, for example. Including these people as the worst-off would mean that the state would have to distribute vastly disproportionate resources to them, thus undermining the difference principle.

While Rawls's claims may be true, it is still the case that his theory of justice would effectively ignore the potentially vast inequalities which arise out of the initial distribution of natural primary goods which are, as Rawls himself accepts, unchosen and therefore morally arbitrary.

IT IS INATTENTIVE TO THE NOTION OF INDIVIDUAL RESPONSIBILITY

A second concern, raised also by libertarians like Nozick, is that the difference principle rewards people who have less money as the result of their own choices. An example that is often given is that of surfers. Remember, the difference principle ensures that society is arranged so that inequalities benefit those who are worst-off. It makes no attempt to discriminate between people according to how they became worst-off. So, if a particular society contains hard-working, rich accountants, and beach-bum surfers who work just enough to be able to survive so that they can spend the rest of the time surfing, Rawls's account would say that the surfers are the worst-off. The accountants would not be allowed to earn more than the surfers just because the surfers have chosen their relative poverty. Instead, the difference principle makes the accountants subsidize the surfers, which does not seem very fair.

For these reasons, numerous thinkers have criticized Rawls's theory for failing to account for the moral difference between choice and luck. In what follows, we will concentrate on the most influential: Ronald Dworkin's luck egalitarian theory. Before doing so, let us first mention an alternative approach that he rejects.

Equality of welfare

Egalitarians are generally committed to ensuring equality. But equality of what? One option is welfare. Dworkin argues that equality of welfare is initially attractive because it seems to deal with the problem of the arbitrariness of natural endowments better than Rawls's theory of equality of resources. Consider the disabled, for example. Equality of resources is problematic once we take the disabled into account because disabled people require many more resources than able-bodied people just to reach the same levels of welfare. For example, someone who uses a wheelchair will require more resources than an able-bodied person if she is to be able to buy a car and enjoy the level of welfare that results from being able to travel independently. This is because the able-bodied person can purchase any car and drive it straight away, whereas the wheelchair user will have to spend a large amount of money having a car adapted, so that it can be operated without using foot pedals, for example. If we give both people the same amount of resources, there will be an inequality (of welfare).

If we care about this sort of inequality – if we think that it is just that disabled people ought to receive more resources than able-bodied people – then we might find the idea of equalizing welfare attractive. However, Dworkin argues that equality of welfare is undermined by the problem of *expensive tastes*.

This is the idea that different people will experience equivalent levels of welfare from different things, depending on their tastes. Some people will have tastes which are relatively cheap to satisfy, like tea and toast. Others will have very expensive tastes, like caviar and champagne. If our concern is to equalize welfare it seems that we should give the person with expensive tastes more resources than the person with cheaper tastes.

Most of us, Dworkin argues, will find the idea that a principle of *equality* requires us to give more money to someone so that she can buy champagne and caviar extremely counter-intuitive. He therefore argues that egalitarians should not be concerned to equalize welfare. What is needed, in contrast, is a different theory which captures the egalitarian intuition that some people (e.g. the disabled) need more resources than others but which does not fall prey to the problem of expensive tastes. Dworkin proposes an alternative theory of equality of resources to Rawls'.

Case study: G.A. Cohen on expensive tastes

Against Dworkin, G.A. Cohen argues that, in certain circumstances, the state ought indeed to provide people with expensive tastes with extra resources. The reason, again, concerns the relationship between luck and responsibility. Specifically, Cohen argues that the problem of expensive tastes can be solved by distinguishing between those expensive tastes which a person has voluntarily chosen to cultivate, and those that she finds herself with, through no fault or action of her own. According to Cohen, egalitarianism *does* in fact demand that we provide people with enough resources to satisfy those expensive tastes that they have no control over, but not those that they have deliberately cultivated.

Imagine that someone (Dworkin calls him Louis) deliberately cultivates a taste for champagne and caviar over tea and toast. Dworkin and Cohen agree that egalitarianism does not require that we fund this taste. However, imagine that Louis has a child, Louise, and that he brings Louise up on a diet of caviar and champagne. By the time Louise is fully grown, she cannot bear to eat anything but caviar and champagne. She has entrenched expensive tastes that she did not deliberately cultivate. If Louise falls on hard times, so that she cannot afford the caviar and champagne, Cohen's position is that, in some circumstances, the state ought to provide her with resources so that she can afford them, because her taste for them is not her fault. It is just her bad luck that she has those tastes.

Cohen therefore also rejects equality of welfare, arguing that egalitarianism should not be about the equalization of welfare, but instead the elimination of disadvantage.

Dworkin and equality of resources

Equality of resources does not mean, for Dworkin, simply that everyone should have the same amount or an identical set of resources. This is because people have different preferences, make different choices, about how to live their lives. Resources that are appropriate for one sort of life will not be helpful for another. For example, someone who wants to be a farmer will need a large amount of fertile land in the countryside, whereas someone who wants to open a shop will need a much smaller amount of built-upon land in the town. It follows, then, that if we are to take into account people's different choices about how to live their lives, we need to allocate them different sorts of resources so that they each have an equal chance at living out their choices.

HISTORICAL VS. END-STATE THEORIES OF JUSTICE REVISITED

The central claim shared by luck egalitarians is thus: inequalities are fair if they arise as a consequence of choices made by the individuals in question, and are unfair if they arise as a consequence of factors beyond their control. The aim of egalitarianism, luck egalitarians argue, is to compensate people for unchosen disadvantages (by ensuring that everyone has access to an equal bundle of initial resources) and *not* to compensate people for disadvantages suffered as a result of choices that they made. Luck egalitarianism therefore tries to do a better job of dealing with the tension between luck and choice that we find in Rawls by incorporating the idea of personal responsibility (for our choices) in a way that does not require libertarianism.

Dworkin explains his theory through a thought experiment (a bit like Rawls's original position) in which castaways on a desert island bid for an initial allocation of resources, depending on what kind of life they wish to lead. It is not possible to go into this in detail here. Suffice to say that Dworkin's conclusion justifies a luck egalitarian approach which is historical (in a Nozickean sense) rather than end-state (like Rawls's justice as fairness). People's choices count both in the allocation of the *initial* resources that everyone receives, and in determining the distribution of resources *over time*.

Imagine two people with equal resources, say, the same amount of land. The first person, Ben, decides to use his land just to farm enough food to survive. This leaves him with a fair amount of land, and a fair amount of time, to spend on leisure. So, he uses the rest of the land and the time to build a tennis court and play tennis on it. After five years, he has the same resources that he started with: he has made enough food to survive, but has not acquired any extra resources.

The other individual, Bonnie, has used her land solely for farming. As such, she has produced far more food than she can eat by herself, and she has traded her surplus with others. In order to do this she has had to work far longer hours than Ben, and has not been able to set aside much of her time or land for leisure. Still, after five years she has produced and traded enough food to acquire a great deal more resources than Ben. She has a separate piece of land on which she has built a luxurious house – or on which others have built her a house in return for food. Moreover, in the little leisure time she does have, she is able to play tennis on Ben's tennis court in return for giving him some of her surplus food.

In short, although they started out equal, they now seem to have *unequal* resources. Critically, Ben will now envy Bonnie's allocation of resources. They each began with the same amount. But now, Bonnie has much more than Ben. Does this mean, then, that the resulting distribution is inegalitarian?

Rawls argues that it does. Dworkin argues that it does not. If we are to be properly sensitive to people's choices, he argues, we must not consider Ben and Bonnie's comparative resources just as this one point in time, five years after the initial distribution. Instead, we must consider the resources that each has enjoyed over the whole five years. Bonnie has enjoyed the extra resources of her house and so on. But Ben has enjoyed the extra resource of a great amount of leisure time. He has had to work far less than Bonnie did, and this was the result of his choice. He decided that leisure was more important to him than acquiring extra resources. As such, he has to take responsibility for that choice. If he had wanted to acquire more resources, then he could and should have spent more of his time and land on farming. The fact that he chose to spend his time and land on tennis means that there is no injustice in his subsequent relative lack of resources. Whereas Rawls's difference principle would unfairly require Bonnie to redistribute some of her resources to Ben, Dworkin's approach requires Ben to take responsibility for his choices, and receive no extra help.

LUCK

So, one reason why people might end up with different amounts of resources is that they might choose to spend their resources and their time on different things. However, there could be another cause of inequality over time: luck.

Imagine two other people, Edward and Emily, who again begin with the same amount of land and who wish to use their land and time farming as much food as possible to trade with others. Imagine that Edward plants barley and Emily plants fruit. Both work equally hard. However, Emily's fruit crop is struck down by disease. Although she works very hard to save her crop, she is unable to do so. Simply as the result of bad luck, she is left with a far smaller, less valuable crop than Edward. What should a Dworkinian egalitarian do about this result?

In response, Dworkin distinguishes between two sorts of luck: *option luck* and *brute luck*. Option luck is the sort of luck that a person voluntarily, or optionally, takes on. For example, if you gamble £5 on a game of roulette, then the question of whether you win or not is a matter of option luck: you are subject to luck only as a result of the choice you took to play the game of roulette. Similarly, Dworkin gives the example of smoking: if you are aware of the health risks of smoking yet smoke for 20 years before developing lung cancer, then the fact that you developed cancer is the result of option luck. You voluntarily took the risk upon yourself.

In contrast, brute luck is unpredictable, and the risk of suffering from brute luck is involuntary. An example of bad brute luck might be being struck by lightning, or developing a form of cancer not thought to be linked to any particular behaviour and thus not thought to be avoidable by any particular behaviour.

Spotlight: The cost of bad choices

15 million people currently living in the UK are obese. According to the official report, 'Tackling Obesities: Future Choices' (2007), the *direct* cost attributable to overweight or obese individuals in the UK in 2007 was £4.2 billion, with the total annual costs of all obesity-related diseases (such as diabetes, stroke, heart disease and certain forms of cancer) reaching an estimated £17.4 billion. The same report estimated that, on current trends, the *direct* costs attributable to overweight and obese individuals would more than double (£9.7 billion), while total annual costs of all obesity-related diseases would reach nearly £30 billion, by 2030. This figure does not include the substantial *indirect* costs to the UK economy associated with obesity, arising from things like increased work absenteeism, increased likelihood of disability, early retirement, or death before retirement age. In the USA, the *direct* and *indirect* costs of obesity in 2009 were $147 billion, although recent research suggests that this figure will rise as high as $344 billion by 2018, accounting for 21 per cent of all healthcare spending.

This distinction between option luck and brute luck is central to the idea of luck egalitarianism. If people are to be held responsible for their choices, it seems appropriate that we should expect them to bear the costs of suffering from bad option luck, but not bad brute luck. So, for example, if you develop lung cancer as a result of your decision to smoke, then you have no grounds for asking society as a whole to bear the costs of your treatment. If, however, you develop lung cancer for reasons beyond your control (from passive smoking, for example), then you would have a prima facie claim to have your treatment paid for.

Of course, the problem with this approach is that it will often be very difficult to tell whether an outcome is the result of option luck or brute luck, and so it will be difficult to operate the appropriate transfers. Instead, Dworkin suggests that insurance can bridge the gap between the two concepts. If insurance is available, then people can choose whether to take it out. Insurance could cover all sorts of eventualities. It could cover unforeseen and unlikely occurrences of bad brute luck or, at a higher price, it could cover predictable and likely occurrences of bad option luck. However, if insurance is available, all forms of potential bad luck are transformed into cases of option luck. The option that people now take is whether or not to take out insurance. If Emily knows that her fruit might suffer from disease but decides to save the money and take out no insurance, she is effectively gambling on the trees not being diseased. If they are diseased, she will suffer from bad option luck – she chose not to take out insurance – regardless of how likely it was that they would be diseased. So, the availability of insurance rules out most forms of brute luck. It follows, then, that people can be held *responsible* for most bad luck that befalls them, for it was their *choice* whether or not to take out insurance.

> 'A person is exploited *when unfair advantage is taken of him, and he suffers from (bad)* brute luck *when his bad luck is not the result of a gamble or risk which he could have avoided. I believe that the primary egalitarian impulse is to extinguish the influence on distribution of both exploitation and brute luck.'*
> G.A. Cohen, 'On the Currency of Egalitarian Justice', in M. Otsuka (ed.), *On the Currency of Egalitarian Justice, and Other Essays in Political Philosophy* (Princeton, NJ: Princeton University Press, 2011), p. 5.

DISABILITY INSURANCE

Insurance, and the difference between option luck and brute luck, lie at the heart of Dworkin's approach to the question of inequalities in natural primary goods and, in particular, why disabled people should receive more resources than able-bodied people. Broadly speaking, Dworkin proposes that we place ourselves behind a kind of disability veil of ignorance. If we did so, it would be rational for each and every individual to put aside some of their initial starting resources into a common fund which would be used to provide us all with some level of welfare or compensation in the event that we were disabled, thus creating a social insurance scheme available to all who suffer from disabilities. We then take the amount that the average person would be willing to pay for such an insurance scheme, and levy that amount on each individual. The money raised is given to the disabled. Consequently, the disabled will not receive so many extra resources as to make them equal in welfare to the able-bodied, but they will receive a fair extra amount.

The practical upshot of Dworkin's luck egalitarian theory, then, is that we should distribute taxes and benefits in ways which are *endowment-insensitive* – i.e. which do not rely on people's natural endowments – and *ambition-sensitive* – i.e. that people receive an amount proportionate to the choices they have made about how to live their lives.

What is the point of equality?

In 1999 Elizabeth Anderson published an important critique of luck egalitarianism (Anderson 1999). She argues that luck egalitarianism suffers from three main flaws:

1 *It fails to treat people with equal concern and respect.* In particular, luck egalitarians must by definition refuse to help certain needy people, namely those needy people who are needy as a result of the choices that they made.

  People who need medical help because they chose to smoke and eat unhealthily all their lives are not entitled to help, for example, because it is their own fault that they are ill. Luck egalitarians therefore allow disadvantage and suffering and, hence, fail to show equal respect for those who are the victims of their own choices.

2 *The reasons it gives for helping the victims of bad brute luck are disrespectful.* Although those people who suffered from inferior natural endowments would be given help by a luck egalitarian state, they would be given help precisely because the state, and society in general, labels them as inferior. In other words, Anderson argues, the luck-egalitarian state expresses condescending and offensive pity toward those who have suffered from bad luck, because it has to identify and single them out as specially entitled to aid.

3 *It requires the state to make intrusive and demeaning investigations into, and judgements about, people's lives.* A luck-egalitarian state will have to collect information about people's choices and motivations, and will have to use that information to assess whether the person concerned made a reasonable or unreasonable decision. In refusing to assist people who are in need as a result of their own choices, the state effectively judges that such people made the wrong choices, that they used their freedom inappropriately. Although luck egalitarians attempt to ensure that people take responsibility for their actions, in effect they do so in a patronizing fashion, helping only those who choose wisely and smugly saying 'I told you so' to those who choose poorly.

> 'Recent egalitarian writing has come to be dominated by the view that the fundamental aim of equality is to compensate people for undeserved bad luck – being born with poor native endowments, bad parents, and disagreeable personalities, suffering from accidents and illness, and so forth... [I]n focusing on correcting a supposed cosmic injustice, recent egalitarian writing has lost sight of the distinctively political aims of egalitarianism. The proper negative aim of egalitarian justice is not to eliminate the impact of brute luck from human affairs, but to end oppression, which by definition is socially imposed. Its proper positive aim is not to ensure that everyone gets what they morally deserve, but to create a community in which people stand in relations of equality to others.'
> Elizabeth Anderson, 'What is the Point of Equality?', *Ethics* 109/2 (1999), pp. 287–337, at pp. 288–9.

Conclusion

Luck egalitarianism is a further refinement of the kind of liberal egalitarianism advocated by Rawls by political philosophers who share Rawls's general intuition about the importance of luck and choice, but who think that Rawls's own theory is incapable of dealing with this issue. Their contribution is to emphasize more strongly than Rawls the importance of individual responsibility when determining the distribution of benefits and burdens in a liberal society, and to further clarify what kinds of bad luck are worthy of compensation. In doing so, luck egalitarians believe that they improve upon Rawls's egalitarian theory of justice by providing a better solution to the question of how resources should be distributed among the worst-off, by clarifying who the 'worst-off' actually are, and who they are not.

Key ideas

Primary goods: Those things which, according to Rawls, all people will need in order to pursue their particular conception of the good regardless of what that conception of the good is. *Social* primary goods include rights and liberties, opportunities and powers, income and wealth, and a sense of self-worth. *Natural* primary goods include health and vigour, intelligence, imagination, ambition, appearance and other non-social factors.

Equality of welfare: The idea that the purpose of egalitarian justice is to ensure that all individuals experience the same level of welfare.

Expensive tastes: The problem, first outlined by Ronald Dworkin, that a theory of equality of welfare would require the state to subsidize the expensive lifestyle choices of some people in order to ensure that they experience the same level of welfare as others with cheaper tastes.

Equality of resources: Defended in different forms by John Rawls and Ronald Dworkin, among others, the idea that egalitarian justice should be concerned with ensuring that all people have access to those resources that they need in order to live a life that they believe to be worthwhile.

Brute luck and option luck: Brute luck covers those instances of good or bad luck over which the individual has no control. Option luck refers to those cases of good or bad luck which the individual has voluntarily brought upon themselves. In general, luck egalitarians believe that people should be compensated for disadvantages arising out of bad brute luck, but not bad option luck.

Dig deeper

Elizabeth Anderson, 'What Is the Point of Equality?' *Ethics* 109/2 (1999), pp. 287–337.

Richard Arneson, 'Equality and Equal Opportunity for Welfare', *Philosophical Studies* 56 (1989), pp. 77–93.

G.A. Cohen, *On the Currency of Egalitarian Justice and Other Essays in Political Philosophy*, ed. Michael Otsuka (Princeton, NJ: Princeton University Press, 2011).

Ronald Dworkin, *Sovereign Virtue: The Theory and Practice of Equality* (Cambridge, MA: Harvard University Press, 2002).

John Roemer, 'A Pragmatic Theory for the Egalitarian Planner', *Philosophy & Public Affairs* 22 (1993), pp. 146–66.

Samuel Scheffler, 'What is Egalitarianism?', *Philosophy & Public Affairs* 31 (2003), pp. 5–39.

Fact-check

1 What is the best definition of luck egalitarianism?
  A The view that luck should be equalized
  B The view that it is unjust to be unlucky
  C The view that inequality is unjust
  D The view that inequality resulting from luck is unjust

2 What is the role of luck in Rawls's theory?
  A Rawls argues that inequality resulting from luck is unjust
  B Rawls argues that inequality is always morally arbitrary because it results from luck
  C Rawls argues that natural endowments are always morally arbitrary because they result from luck
  D Rawls argues that social endowments are always morally arbitrary because they result from luck

3 How do luck egalitarians criticize Rawls's theory?
  A For failing to take account of the disabled
  B For failing to take account of those who choose not to work
  C For failing to place enough weight on personal responsibility
  D All of the above

4 What are expensive tastes?
  A Tastes for expensive things that are not necessary
  B Tastes that are expensive to satisfy
  C Tastes that are expensive to satisfy but which do not bring higher levels of welfare
  D Tastes that rich people have

5 What is the difference between brute luck and option luck?
  A People like option luck and dislike brute luck
  B Brute luck is more difficult to avoid than option luck
  C Option luck gives people more options
  D All of the above

6 Which of the following is an example of bad option luck?

   A   Being born disabled
   B   Losing the lottery
   C   Having poor parents
   D   All of the above

7 How does Dworkin distinguish between option luck and brute luck?

   A   Option luck should be compensated but brute luck should not
   B   Brute luck should be compensated but option luck should not
   C   Option luck should be allowed but brute luck should not
   D   Brute luck should be allowed but option luck should not

8 What is the role of insurance in Dworkin's argument?

   A   To transform brute luck into option luck
   B   To transform option luck into brute luck
   C   To provide a fair share of natural resources
   D   To eliminate all luck

9 What is wrong with luck egalitarianism, according to Anderson?

   A   It is disrespectful
   B   It is uncaring
   C   It fails to deal with oppression
   D   All of the above

10 Which of the following policies best fits with luck egalitarianism?

   A   Removing state-provided healthcare
   B   Ensuring everyone has equal wealth
   C   Providing universal healthcare
   D   Providing unequal access to state-provided healthcare

13

Communitarianism

The 1980s saw the emergence of a fundamental critique of liberal political philosophy: communitarianism. This critique concerns the individualist nature of liberalism. British and American politics in the 1980s was characterized by the rise of neoliberalism: individualism had replaced collectivism, free markets had replaced state planning, freedom had superseded equality, and the minimal state had replaced bureaucratic centralism. But many were concerned about this apparent triumph of liberalism. Traditional communities appeared to be breaking down, along with the collective bonds that held society together. In the rush to emphasize the *separateness* of persons, it seemed that liberals had lost sight of those *common* traits which *united* people together, and which gave a sense of identity and belonging. Communitarianism thus emerged as a critique of liberalism and libertarianism. It is the view that, by emphasizing individual freedom, liberalism and libertarianism undermine the shared sense of identity which people need in order to function as a society.

In this chapter, we discuss the communitarian critique of liberalism through the work of two thinkers.

Michael Sandel and the unencumbered self

The first, and perhaps most influential, communitarian thinker was Michael Sandel. Sandel's book *Liberalism and the Limits of Justice* (1982) criticized Rawls's theory of justice for its individualist and rationalist foundations. Sandel's critique is therefore of the metaphysical foundations of liberalism, in particular the conception of the self on which it is founded.

For Sandel, the liberal self is an 'unencumbered self'. Liberalism is grounded, he says, in a bizarre conception of persons as radically abstract individuals, isolated from all those desires, ideals, beliefs, aims and characteristics which in fact make people who they are. The individual behind the veil of ignorance in the original position is the paradigmatic unencumbered self: unencumbered by her status, her talents and, most importantly for Sandel, her conception of the good. As she does not know what her conception of the good is, she is not bound by its demands. She does not have to consider the moral requirements of her conception of the good when deliberating about justice. She is unencumbered – free from such considerations.

As we saw in Chapter 10, the cause and effect of placing one's conception of the good behind the veil of ignorance is to enshrine individual freedom – understood for Rawls as the freedom to choose one's own conception of the good. For Rawls, freedom to choose one's conception of the good is the most important principle of justice. As a result, Sandel argues, the idea of the unencumbered self assumes a moral status in Rawls's theory. For Rawls, the freedom to choose our own ends is more important than the ends in themselves. The right is prior to the good, in that no particular conception of the good may define or take priority over the principles of justice. For Rawls, then, the self should be conceived of as a chooser of ends. The individual can stand back from her conception of the good, and exist as a moral entity regardless of that conception of the good. An individual's identity is not defined by any particular conception of the good. It is, instead, unencumbered.

Sandel argues that the unencumbered self as it appears in Rawls is a *metaphysical* conception of the person. That is, Sandel reads the 'unencumbered self' thesis as being a thesis about the nature of personhood: the idea that people are not determined by their ends, but that they exist prior to their ends and that they choose those ends. It is this idea of the self that, Sandel argues, supposedly justifies Rawls's prioritization of the right over the good. The right must be prior to the good because individuals, and their ability to choose, are prior to their ends.

'The theme common to much classical liberal doctrine that emerges from the deontological account of the unity of the self is the notion of the human subject as a sovereign agent of choice, a creature whose ends are chosen rather than given, who comes by his aims and purposes by acts of will, as opposed to, say, acts of cognition... The antecedent unity of the self means that the subject, however heavily conditioned by his surroundings, is always, irreducibly, prior to his values and ends, and never fully conditioned by them.'
Michael J. Sandel, *Liberalism and the Limits of Justice* (Cambridge: Cambridge University Press, 1982).

Sandel thus interprets the Rawlsian conception of the self as a metaphysical theory about the inherently autonomous nature of personhood. There are, he says, three problems with such a view:

1 *It understands agency to be a voluntarist, rather than a cognitivist, process.* Firstly, the idea of the unencumbered self implies that a person voluntarily chooses her ends – that it is up to her which ends she will follow and which conception of the good she will adopt. In fact, Sandel argues, people often discover their conception of the good rather than choose it. They find that they believe in certain things, and that they hold certain values. For example, people do not usually choose which religion to follow by considering a variety of alternatives. Instead, they are usually born into a particular religion, which they learn about and operate in throughout their lives. Indeed, some religions and other conceptions of the good hold precisely that they are not chosen but inherited – children are automatically members. Human agency (the process of acting in the world) is therefore not simply a process of rationally choosing one's ends and then pursuing them, but rather one of pursuing the ends that are embodied in the various communities and groups to which we belong. The unencumbered self therefore misrepresents the relationship that people may have with their ends and, moreover, rules out certain conceptions of the good that are based not on choice but on inheritance.

2 *It suggests that persons cannot be constituted by their ends.* Secondly, Sandel argues that the idea of the unencumbered self means that a person must always be able to exist independently of her conception of the good. In other words, Rawls's theory cannot allow for the possibility that a person's identity could be constituted by her conception of the good. A particular value or end could never be integral to someone's identity. Sandel argues that this is an impoverished understanding of the self. Instead, he argues, it is often the case that we conceptualise ourselves through our ends and values, and that we experience conflict

between our values as a conflict in our identity. Christians, for example, are not people who happen to possess certain religious beliefs, rather, they *are* Christians: their beliefs (at least partly) constitute their identity. Rawls does not allow us to be constituted by our ends, and he therefore does not allow us to be constituted by ends that we have in common with others, by our membership of a community. Rather than being able to stand back from our ends, Sandel argues, we may not be able to understand ourselves without them. Moreover, many of the ends that constitute our identity will be communal.

3   *It rules out certain forms of political community.* Rawls envisages society as a system of co-operation for mutual advantage against a background of competing and contradictory conceptions of the good. In modelling the original position around this idea, Rawls effectively rules out the idea that a political society could be formed around a conception of the good, by people who share that conception. In other words, Rawls's insistence that the right must be prior to the good rules out any societies which are based on a particular good and organized so as to further it. So, although Rawls allows individuals to follow a particular religion, for example, he does not allow them to form communities which enshrine this religion in their political arrangements. Sandel argues that this is a highly substantive, non-neutral restriction, and one that rules out many conceptions of the good that involve the idea of political or communal embodiment.

Sandel's objections so far amount to the idea that, although Rawls's insistence on the primary importance of the individual's ability to choose her conception of the good is supposed to ensure *neutrality* between conceptions of the good, in fact the idea of the unencumbered self which is found in his theory means that many conceptions of the good are ruled out. To put it another way: Rawls's theory is neutral between all conceptions of the good which are consistent with a conception of the self as unencumbered in the way Sandel describes, but not neutral with regard to conceptions of the good (religious or secular) which invoke a different, less individualist understanding of personhood. Consequently, Sandel believes that Rawlsian liberalism fails on its own terms: it does not provide a principled means of managing the diversity that characterizes modern liberal societies in a way which avoids the state making judgements about the content of people's conceptions of the good.

INDIVIDUALISM AS INCONSISTENT WITH THE DIFFERENCE PRINCIPLE

There is a further problem with Rawls's theory, Sandel argues: the justification of the difference principle. The idea behind the difference principle, Sandel argues, is that the individual does not own her talents, in the sense of full property ownership. In other words, she is not entitled to the products of her talents. Remember, the difference principle is an extremely demanding principle of equality. It allows inequalities *only if* those inequalities benefit the worst-off. It is not legitimate, according to the difference principle, for an individual to be paid more than others because she is more talented, or because she somehow deserves higher pay because she has produced more than others.

This is because people's talents are morally arbitrary. You are not clever, for example, because you have virtuously tried hard to develop cleverness. Although education can have a significant effect, intelligence is something that people are born with and cannot control, beyond certain limits. It is just good luck if you are born clever, and bad luck if you are not. Talents are not deserved, they are morally arbitrary, the result of luck. As a result, Rawls argues, people do not deserve the *fruits* of their talents. They are not *entitled* to whatever they can produce through their efforts. Because the difference principle requires that the fruits of people's talents are shared among society, it must follow that people have no prior entitlement to the products of their talents, simply because they are *their* talents.

The problem with this argument, Sandel claims, is not that Rawls fails to show why people do not own their talents but that he gives us no reason to think that *society* has any greater claim over the products of people's talents. The difference principle amounts, in effect, to the claim that people's talents belong to society. Only then is it justifiable to distribute their products among society as a whole. However, the 'unencumbered self' thesis implies that individuals have no prior link to their community. Individuals are understood as existing prior to and separate from their communities. The whole basis of the unencumbered self is to distance individuals from communal attachments and obligations. Why then, Sandel asks, are our talents owned by society as a whole, when we as individuals are strictly separated from society? Sandel argues that liberalism makes us 'more entangled and less attached'. We are more entangled in that we must engage in extensive redistribution, donating the products of our talents to each other. We are less attached in that society is conceived of as a group of mutually disinterested, competing individuals, with no common goal and no prior communal obligations.

Sandel argues that the difference principle is a principle of *sharing*. It involves the idea that members of a society should share with each other, some giving the fruits of their labour to others in the name of their shared community membership. As a result, Sandel claims, the difference principle *must* presuppose some prior moral tie to the community. Why should we share with others in the community if we have no moral obligations to them and to the community? Who should we share with if there is nothing to bind us to other individuals in particular? If we really are to justify the extensive demands that the difference principle puts on us then, Sandel claims, we need to accept both moral obligations to the community and the existence of substantive ties to other members of the community, quite possibly based on a shared conception of the good.

Sandel's general point, then, is that Rawls gives insufficient weight to the importance of community. Community plays a role, for Sandel, in constituting our conception of the good, our identity, and our obligations of sharing. A state that is neutral between conceptions of the good, and a conception of the person as an autonomous chooser of her conception of the good, cannot capture the crucial role of community.

MacIntyre's critique of the Enlightenment

Another communitarian, Alasdair MacIntyre, extends the metaphysical critique of liberalism even further than does Sandel (MacIntyre 1981 and 1988). Indeed, he presents an elaborate and wide-ranging critique not just of liberalism, but of the entire set of philosophical and intellectual ideas upon which liberalism is founded. MacIntyre's critique of Rawls is therefore very radical. MacIntyre's problem with Rawlsian liberalism is not that it is internally inconsistent, or based on false premises, but that it is rooted in problematic Enlightenment ideas.

We mentioned the Enlightenment briefly in the Introduction. Broadly speaking, the Age of Enlightenment is a term that describes seventeenth- and eighteenth-century Europe, when philosophers, scientists, social scientists and others increasingly championed *reason* as the basis of all knowledge. Central to the Enlightenment was the idea that one could overturn established traditions and systems of knowledge through rational enquiry; that all authority, whether it be religious, political and so on, is only legitimate if it can withstand rational scrutiny. The Enlightenment challenged the idea that human beings should be divided by nations and cultures, since all people are united by a common rationality. Importantly for philosophy, it suggested that we could search for answers to moral and political problems by engaging in rational debate. We could give reasons for our moral judgements, and could construct rational arguments to support those judgements. When faced with a disagreement about an ethical principle, the Enlightenment method engages in rational argument to work out which ethical principle is supported by better reasons and reasoning. It is this, MacIntyre claims, that contemporary thinkers such as Rawls are trying to do: present rational arguments for ethical principles that can be justified universally and absolutely.

> '[W]e all approach our own circumstances as bearers of a particular social identity. I am someone's son or daughter, someone else's cousin or uncle; I am a citizen of this or that city, a member of this or that guild or profession; I belong to this clan, that tribe, this nation. Hence, what is good for me has to be the good for one who inhabits these roles. As such, I inherit from the past of my family, my city, my tribe, my nation, a variety of debts, inheritances, rightful expectations, and obligations. These constitute the given of my life, my moral starting point. This is in part what gives my life its own moral particularity.'
>
> Alasdair MacIntyre, *After Virtue: A Study in Moral Theory* (London: Duckworth, 1982), p. 220.

In fact, MacIntyre argues, contemporary moral debate, whether between academics or between citizens, can never be solved through rationality alone. MacIntyre concedes that it is possible to consider the extent to which an argument is internally consistent, and to engage in reasoning so as to make moral arguments more consistent. But once that is done ethical disagreements boil down to a disagreement about first principles, about substantive moral premises that cannot themselves be explained or justified.

Imagine, for example, that there is a country that is deeply divided into two opposing groups. These groups are on the brink of civil war. However, one particular charismatic leader is able to unite them. While she is in power, there is peace in the country. Unfortunately, the leader is also a criminal – she is involved in some sort of crime, perhaps money laundering or some other sort of corruption. In this case, *justice* requires that the leader be prosecuted, jailed and removed from office. On the other hand, *peace* requires that the crime is hushed up and that the leader remains in office, so that she can unite the otherwise warring factions.

In this sort of debate, MacIntyre would argue, the problem is not that those in favour of justice have an incoherent argument whereas those in favour of peace have a consistent one, or vice versa. The problem, instead, is that reason alone cannot resolve this dilemma. The debate boils down to substantive first principles that cannot be reconciled. There is no single way of deciding between, for example, the value of peace and the value of justice. They are *incommensurable*. Which one you choose will be based not on rational argument, but on personal preference. It will not be possible to explain, using rationality alone, whether peace or justice should be preferred.

MacIntyre therefore argues that the 'Enlightenment project', as he calls it, was a failure. It has eviscerated our moral lives, leaving us no way of making sense of the most profound moral questions in the world. Moreover, he argues, it has encouraged us to think that it is possible to construct moral arguments without any appeal to wider notions of the good life. Rawls's project – to come up with a theory of justice which can be justified independently of any substantive conception of the good – is bound to fail: in the absence of a theory of the good, or an overarching *telos* which describes the ends to which society and individuals should aim, society just becomes a collection of abstract individuals, each with their own particular conception of the good that they have plucked from the air, that no one can really explain to one another, and which cannot provide a resolution to complex moral dilemmas. As a consequence, substantive moral debate collapses into emotivism: the simple expression of what one thinks or feels at any one time.

To get over this problem, MacIntyre argues that we should reassert the importance of tradition. In the absence of universal agreement, we need to base first principles on the shared values and traditions of our community. Only community, MacIntyre argues, can provide the basis for resolving moral disagreements. Unless we are rooted in a particular community, we cannot give our moral judgements any rational basis. If we are to engage in meaningful philosophical debate, we need to know what our basic premises are, and we need to agree on those premises. Such agreement, MacIntyre argues, can only come from community and tradition. Tradition, as embodied in the communities of which we are a member, provides the *telos*, the conception of the good, toward which we should aim, and provides too a common ground over which moral disputes can be resolved by appeal to a shared moral vocabulary.

MacIntyre and Sandel are therefore united in rejecting Rawls's rejection of teleological moral theory: they argue that the rules which regulate social and political institutions should be rooted in a substantive conception of the good life. Both Sandel and MacIntyre have controversial (and different) ideas about what this conception of the good life should be. However, rather than go into this here, we focus instead on the wider point that MacIntyre and Sandel are making. Rawls believed that utilitarianism failed because it derived the right from the good: it had the wrong structure. MacIntyre and Sandel argue that Rawls was wrong. There may be particular problems with utilitarianism, but the problem is not that it is the wrong structure. The fact is, they argue, that we need to retain the idea of *telos*, for unless the rules which are to govern our lives are derived from an overarching conception of the good, they are derived from nothing at all.

Case study: Walzer and the spheres of justice

Another communitarian thinker, Michael Walzer, offers a critique of liberal theories of *distributive* justice (Walzer 1984). Walzer argues that liberal egalitarian arguments for the redistribution of wealth and resources wrongly assume that there can be one universal metric for working out how resources should be distributed. But there is not. There is no single criterion for distribution: goods may be distributed according to need, or desert, or wealth, or talent, or networks based on family, politics or club membership, or any combination of these and other factors. Consequently, Walzer argues, egalitarians' search for a single criterion of distribution is a mistake. Instead, goods should be understood as having their own spheres, within which they have their own criteria of distribution. In other words, different goods should be distributed for different reasons and in different ways. An appropriate distribution criterion for one good might be inappropriate for another, and that difference should be accepted. So, for example, we might distribute education according to educational merit, and healthcare according to medical need, and Ferraris according to wealth. We have different criteria for different goods. Different goods are distributed for different reasons.

Furthermore, Walzer argues, the way in which goods should be distributed is determined by the social meaning of these goods. Goods mean different things to different people in different contexts, and there is no objective truth about the meaning of any particular good. The meaning of a good may be understood very differently in different contexts. Bread, for example, could be understood as a form of food, or a sign of hospitality, or the body of Christ, depending on the context in which it is being used. So: how should we distribute bread? Or anything else? How can we determine whether someone has a 'need' for bread, or anything else?

Walzer argues that the criteria for the distribution of goods are provided by the particular social context in which these goods exist. Consequently, there is no universal, overarching set of criteria for working out who gets what other that provided by social context.

The reason this is so radical, of course, is it rules out the idea that there is any universal, persistent *need* for any particular good. There are no universal needs – only those needs which arise out of the social context in which people and goods exist. Therefore, there is no way in which a society could violate its members' rights by denying them a certain good – provided, of course, that the good was typically denied. Walzer's theory therefore appears to imply a radical relativism: justice and rights are determined by the society in question.

Conclusion

In this chapter, we have considered two communitarian thinkers, each of whom criticizes Rawls and liberalism. Sandel argues that Rawls's idea of the unencumbered self is a metaphysical idea of the nature of personhood, one which is both empirically incorrect and normatively flawed. In its place, Sandel offers an alternative conception of personhood which holds that persons are *constituted* by their conceptions of the good, which in turn come from their communities.

MacIntyre argues that rational argument about moral principles is simply impossible unless it takes place in the context of a community with a shared tradition and set of first principles. Both thinkers reject Rawls's approach of defining the right independently of, and prior to, the good, and seek instead to reclaim a teleological basis for our moral theorizing.

Both argue that the abstract individualism at the heart of liberalism is philosophically mistaken and leads to an impoverished and unattractive conception of politics and society.

In the next chapter, we will consider Rawls's response to these criticisms.

Key ideas

The unencumbered self: The idea – attributed to Rawls by Sandel – that the self exists independently of, and prior to, the various ends and values that it chooses for itself.

Voluntarist and cognitivist agency: Two differing views as to how persons act in the world, described by Sandel. The liberal (voluntarist) approach is premised on the idea of individual autonomy: the agent autonomously (and rationally) *chooses* a life for itself from the various options available and pursues that life until it decides to choose a different one. The communitarian (cognitivist) approach suggests that ends and values are not chosen voluntarily but, rather, are *discovered* through the process of learning about the various groups and communities of which we are members.

Moral incommensurability: The idea that a conflict between two moral claims or imperatives cannot be resolved by an appeal to norms of rational dialogue. For MacIntyre, the fact of moral incommensurability proved the failure of the Enlightenment project which, in undermining the authority of tradition, left humanity incapable of understanding their moral lives or resolving moral dilemmas.

Neutrality: The liberal idea that principles of justice, and the state, should not gain their authority from any particular conception of the good life and should, instead, aim to create social and political conditions in which different people can pursue their own conceptions of the good in their own way, within reasonable constraints.

Dig deeper

Daniel Bell, *Communitarianism and its Critics* (Oxford: Clarendon Press, 1993).

Amitai Etzioni, *The Spirit of Community: Rights, Responsibilities, and the Communitarian Agenda* (London: Fontana Press, 1995).

Alasdair MacIntyre, *Whose Justice? Which Rationality?* (London: Duckworth, 1986).

Alasdair MacIntyre, *After Virtue: A Study in Moral Theory* (London: Duckworth, 1994).

David Miller and Michael Walzer (eds), *Pluralism, Justice, and Equality* (Oxford: Oxford University Press, 1995).

Robert Putnam, *Bowling Alone: The Collapse and Revival of American Community* (New York: Simon & Schuster, 2000).

Michael J. Sandel, *Liberalism and the Limits of Justice* (Cambridge: Cambridge University Press, 1982).

Charles Taylor, *Philosophy and the Human Sciences: Philosophical Papers Vol. 2* (Cambridge: Cambridge University Press, 1985).

Charles Taylor, *Sources of the Self: The Making of the Modern Identity* (Cambridge, MA: Harvard University Press, 1989).

Michael Walzer, *Spheres of Justice: A Defence of Pluralism and Equality* (London: Basic Books, 1984).

Fact-check

1 What is the 'unencumbered self'?
  A A self that is unencumbered by possessions
  B A self that is unencumbered by a concern for justice
  C A self that is unencumbered by laws
  D A self that is unencumbered by a conception of the good

2 What, according to Sandel, is wrong with the unencumbered self?
  A It is not how people really are
  B It is not a valuable ideal to aspire to
  C It is incompatible with the value of community
  D All of the above

3 Why, according to Sandel, is the difference principle unworkable without a strong commitment to community?
  A Because, without community, there is no justification for sharing resources
  B Because, without community, there will be no way of enforcing the difference principle
  C Because, without community, there is too much ethnic diversity for redistribution
  D All of the above

4 What, according to MacIntyre, is wrong with liberalism?
  A It wrongly assumes that there can be any first principles
  B It wrongly assumes that first principles can be decided by rational argument
  C It wrongly assumes that the first principles can be freedom and equality
  D It wrongly assumes that there can be any rational arguments about justice

5 What is the right way to think about justice, according to MacIntyre?
  A By starting from the traditions of our particular community
  B By adopting our community's traditions without question
  C By doing whatever the majority want
  D There is no such thing as justice

6 What does MacIntyre mean by 'moral incommensurability'?

    A Moral values cannot be rationally evaluated against one another

    B Moral values cannot be easily communicated

    C There are no moral values

    D Moral values are less important than practical considerations

7 Who argues that there should be 'spheres of justice'?

    A Michael Sandel

    B Alasdair MacIntyre

    C Charles Taylor

    D Michael Walzer

8 What is the idea of spheres of justice?

    A That goods should be distributed in different ways

    B That goods should be distributed according to their social meanings

    C That there are no universal needs

    D All of the above

9 Why is the idea of spheres of justice communitarian?

    A Because communities endorse it

    B Because it connects distributions to community values

    C Because it rejects the unencumbered self

    D All of the above

10 Why is communitarianism problematic for liberalism?

    A It suggests that individuals are not the most important unit

    B It suggests that individuals have obligations to their communities

    C It suggests that individuals can legitimately be constrained by communal vales

    D All of the above

14

Political liberalism

In Chapters 10 and 13 we discussed Rawls's theory of justice and some criticisms made of it by communitarians. The communitarian critique essentially suggested that liberalism is a *comprehensive* doctrine: a doctrine based on a thick vision of the good life (as autonomous), certain controversial values (like freedom, equality, and individualism), and a metaphysical conception of the person, which together undermine its ability to remain neutral with regard to different conceptions of the good. Liberals have responded in different ways. Some have defended a comprehensive conception of liberalism (e.g. Raz 1986). We will discuss these liberals in the next chapter. Others, however, have suggested that liberalism should be understood as a *political* rather than a *comprehensive* doctrine (e.g. Larmore 1987 and 1995; Nussbaum 1999 and 2011).

These political liberals argue that liberal principles and institutions draw their authority from political agreements made by political actors rather than substantive conceptions of the good life or controversial principles. Political liberalism, they argue, satisfies the requirements of neutrality while also respecting the embeddedness of persons in communities. This approach was pioneered by Rawls in his later works – *Political Liberalism* (1993) and *Justice as Fairness: A Re-Statement* (2001) – and so our discussion of political liberalism in this chapter will focus on his contribution.

When Rawls and other political liberals say that liberalism is a *political* doctrine they mean three things: it is political not general, political not comprehensive, and political not metaphysical.

> '[T]he problem of political liberalism is: How is it possible that there may exist over time a stable and just society of free and equal citizens profoundly divided by reasonable though incompatible religious, philosophical, and moral doctrines? Put another way: How is it possible that deeply opposed though reasonable comprehensive doctrines may live together and all affirm the political conception of a constitutional regime? What is the structure and content of a political conception that can gain the support of such an overlapping consensus?'
> John Rawls, *Political Liberalism* (New York: Columbia University Press, 1993), p. xviii.

Liberalism is political not general

The first way in which liberalism can be political is in its scope. Political liberals argue that their theory applies only to the political sphere of society, or what Rawls terms the *basic structure*. As such, it is different from more general moral systems (like act-utilitarianism) in that it does not dictate the decisions that people should make in their daily lives. Instead it stipulates principles which regulate the institutions of society, the laws and other regulative bodies.

This is relevant to the communitarian critique in that it suggests that liberal principles should not be understood as applying to the internal workings of social institutions like churches, families, and so on. In the case of religion, for example, political liberalism requires that religions adhere to the principles of justice in the sense that they may not violate their members' freedom and equality *as citizens*. So, a particular religion may not make it illegal or impossible for its members to vote, or to compete for non-religious jobs under conditions of equal opportunity. The religion may not influence the law, so as to prevent its members from doing these things legally, and it may not forcibly prevent these actions by, for example, locking up its members. It must respect their freedom and equality as citizens.

However, within these limits the religion is not required to organize itself internally according to principles of justice. Religious positions, such as the priesthood, do not have to be allocated according to fair equality of opportunity so, for example, the Catholic Church may continue to insist that priests must be men. Similarly, the resources of the church do not have to be allocated according to the difference principle. In other words, people's freedom and equality is protected in the political sphere, in their role as citizens, but it is not protected *within* the church. Consequently, justice is political not general: it respects and protects people's ability to be members of groups which are not required to organize themselves according to liberal principles.

Liberalism is political not comprehensive

The second distinction is more controversial. Rawls argues that liberalism should not be grounded in any particular comprehensive conception of the good. So the authority of liberal principles is not provided by the truth of substantive (and controversial) first principles, but in reasonable agreements made between individual citizens.

This was Rawls's intention in *A Theory of Justice*, where he argues that the principles of justice should be chosen in the original position without knowledge of one's conception of the good. There he argues that autonomy, understood as people's ability to frame, revise and pursue their conception of the good, is the most important moral power that people have. In *Political Liberalism* Rawls revisited the question of how to justify liberalism given reasonable disagreement about conceptions of the good. Communitarians emphasize that some conceptions of the good do not prioritize individual autonomy. Political liberalism aims to show why even people who do not prioritize autonomy would agree upon a common regime of *liberal* institutions, as opposed to any other kind of institutions.

Rawls argues that liberalism can gain agreement between diverse people only if it is political rather than comprehensive. Political liberalism, with its focus on establishing a fair system of social institutions rather than on telling people how to live, gives different groups sufficient freedom to pursue their own ways of life. Liberal principles would be chosen, he argued, because they can be justified by an appeal to reasons that all people can accept, as opposed to reasons that only some people, with a particular conception of the good, can accept. They are *publicly justifiable* in a way that reasons arising out of comprehensive conceptions of the good life are not.

To see this Rawls asks us to imagine a hypothetical process of public deliberation conducted between people who wish to decide on the basic 'constitutional essentials' of a new society. This conversation is conceived to be between free and equal *citizens* rather than *persons* or *selves*: unlike the parties to the original position, parties to public deliberation are understood to be fully encumbered by their various conceptions of the good. Among parties to the agreement process, there will be an inevitable diversity of comprehensive doctrines, some of which will be mutually incompatible with others. Perhaps some people are evangelical Christians, others are Sikhs, others are atheists, others still will be utilitarians or Aristotelians. Now, the conversation will not get very far if each party to the agreement dogmatically seeks to draw up a constitution based on the truth of their own comprehensive conception of the good. Each will reject the other's vision of the future society.

In order for the conversation to continue parties need to modify the reasons they give, to make them more acceptable to others. They need to find reasons for or against proposals which do not rely on their own particular, controversial comprehensive values. They need to come up with what Rawls calls 'public reasons': reasons which could be acceptable to each member of the public, irrespective of their views about the good life. So, rather than arguing 'there should be a law against murder because the Bible tells us that murder is wrong', a citizen might argue 'there should be a law against murder because society will be extremely unpleasant and unfair if murder is permitted'.

The former is not a public reason because people who do not accept the authority of the Bible cannot accept it; the latter is, because it does not rely on controversial premises based on a particular conception of the good.

Rawls thinks that citizens who are motivated to find agreement on principles of political association would adopt these norms of public reason, and that such a process would produce a constitutional order underpinned by liberal principles. It would enshrine liberal constitutional protections of the kind defended by Rawls's basic liberty principle, such as free speech, free association, freedom of religion, and equal citizenship, while leaving people alone to live their lives as they see fit.

Liberal principles would therefore pass the test of public justifiability in a way that principles arising out of a particular conception of the good would not. A Muslim and a Christian, for example, may disagree profoundly over matters of religious truth, but they can both agree on the fact that it is important that they be able to practise their religion and so they can agree on the principle of freedom of religion. Climate change sceptics and environmentalists might disagree about the facts of climate change, but they can agree that they should not be persecuted for their particular views, and so can agree on a principle of free speech. Debate conducted between free and equal individuals about the fundamental character of the political order would, Rawls argues, produce a regime of institutions that are not grounded in any particular comprehensive doctrine and so can be acceptable to all.

The point of liberalism, then, is not to tell people how to live their lives, or how to understand their identity, or what values they must hold. It is to find principles of political association which are acceptable to all members of society *regardless* of their particular ideas about these things. The question for political liberals is not 'What form of society is required by the metaphysical conception of the autonomous self that we hold?' but rather 'What form of society, what regime of institutions, would be seen as legitimate by groups and individuals who fundamentally disagree about deeper questions about truth, the good life, and the nature of the universe?'.

This response did not satisfy the communitarians. After all, one of the key problems with liberalism for Sandel and MacIntyre was precisely that it elevated justice over and above all other moral considerations. Similarly, it is clear that the idea of public reasoning at the heart of political liberalism is not morally neutral, but is instead grounded in the principles of freedom and equality. As a consequence, Sandel's critique still stands. The political liberal process of public reasoning cannot be neutral with regard to *all* conceptions of the good: it can only be neutral between conceptions of the good that fit within a justificatory framework premised on individual freedom and equality. A Christian who is not interested in other people's freedom of religion might continue to insist that laws against murder (and other, more controversial laws such as laws about abortion or marriage) are justified and required only by the Bible. In this respect, Rawls's later formulation of liberalism seems to represent no improvement at all on his earlier one, as it seems just as inhospitable to religious, traditional and other 'non-liberal' conceptions of the good as his original theory of justice as fairness, described in *A Theory of Justice*.

'The norms of rational dialogue and equal respect do, of course, make a certain individualism overriding within the political realm. That is, the rights and duties of citizens must be specifiable in abstraction from any controversial ideals that they might share with others. But the two norms do not imply that a broader individualism concerning the very sources of value must pervade the whole of social life. Private associations cannot violate the rights of citizens. Yet they can continue to conduct their internal, extra-political affairs according to 'illiberal' principles – principles that deny their members equal rights and require them to defer to traditionally constituted authority... There seems no reason to think, therefore, that liberal neutrality, if understood in the way I have proposed, must harbor any special affinity for individualist views of the good life.'

Charles Larmore, 'Political Liberalism', in *The Morals of Modernity* (Cambridge: Cambridge University Press, 1995), pp. 140–41.

In response, Rawls accepts wholeheartedly that his theory rests on the values of freedom and equality. He also accepts that some comprehensive conceptions of the good are based on a rejection of those values. For example, Nazism is founded on inequality of the races, and totalitarianism is based on the rejection of individual freedom. Rawls accepts that his theory is based on values that rule out these comprehensive doctrines. Nevertheless, he argues that it is justifiable to rule out such doctrines, not for reasons based on alternative comprehensive conceptions of the good, but simply because they are not what he calls 'reasonable'. For Rawls, remember, society is a system of fair co-operation in which people with diverse conceptions of the good join together in a community of mutual advantage. Therefore, conceptions of the good which are contrary to the wider co-operative project fall beyond the scope of what can be tolerated in a liberal society.

So Rawls is open about the fact that justice as fairness rules out unreasonable conceptions of the good. However, importantly, he does not believe that groups must accept the good of autonomy, or understand the self as a 'chooser of ends' in order to be reasonable. Groups can reject the substantive *ethical* good of individual autonomy and still remain reasonable as long as they do not seek to constrain their members' *political* autonomy. That is, groups can organize themselves around principles other than autonomy (for example, they can be based on traditional hierarchies or can preach that obedience to a divine entity is more important than individual choice). The distinction between public and private in liberalism dictates, after all, that the state cannot force religious communities to organize themselves in ways which are contrary to their beliefs. However, what groups cannot do is seek to constrain their members' autonomy in the public sphere. Thus Rawls's liberalism is political and not comprehensive because its claims are about the *political* freedom and equality of *citizens*, not about the substantive value of freedom and equality in all spheres of life.

Case study: Can someone choose a non-autonomous life?

Political liberals like Rawls and Nussbaum believe that the state should not rule out non-autonomous lives. If someone chooses to live a life which is not autonomous, they argue, then they should be able to do so.

But is it possible for individuals to autonomously choose a non-autonomous life? This sounds paradoxical. But there are many examples of such a thing. For example, many women and men choose to join religious communities which radically curtail – or even deny entirely – their ability to choose how to live their lives on a daily basis. Nuns, for example, live their lives according to a strict routine, and their day-to-day lives are largely determined for them by their religious beliefs and by the rules of the convent. Similarly, men who join the priesthood, or who choose to join closed religious orders of one kind or another, do so in full knowledge that their lives will – from that moment on – require adherence to strict rules governing the way they conduct their lives, the choices they are able to make, and so on. And what about men or women who choose to join the armed forces? A principal point of the training process for the army, navy, or marines, for example, is precisely that it extinguishes any sense among new recruits that they are autonomous individuals. The army would not function as it needs to if everyone did whatever they wanted: army training specifically seeks to force people out of the habit of thinking for themselves and to obey orders instead. In all these cases, individuals make an *autonomous* choice, with full knowledge of the implications, to live a life in which they are required to give up some or all of their autonomy and submit instead to strict rules and rigid hierarchies of authority.

It is difficult to know what the liberal position on these or similar cases should be. In general, the political liberal approach is to allow people to choose a non-autonomous life but to make sure that they still enjoy the basic constitutional rights and freedoms associated with democratic citizenship. So, for example, they are considered autonomous from the point of view that no group of which they are a member can deny their basic liberal right to vote, etc. Comprehensive liberals, on the other hand, are much more sceptical of the idea that people should be allowed to live lives that are non-autonomous. For them, the *value* in a life arises out of the fact that it is autonomous. Hence, they would be more sympathetic to the idea that such lives should not be permitted. Neither approach is unproblematic, and neither seems to provide a clear answer to the question of what should be done about people who voluntarily give up the freedom that a liberal state is supposed to protect.

Liberalism is political not metaphysical

The final contrast is between the political and the metaphysical.

Sandel's critique of Rawlsian liberalism, remember, was that it was a metaphysical theory, grounded in a particular (and philosophically controversial) conception of the self as an autonomous chooser of ends. This, Sandel believed, meant that the theory could not satisfy its own requirement that the liberal state remain neutral with regard to the good. Rawls disagrees. The idea that the self is the autonomous chooser of ends is not supposed to be understood as a metaphysical claim about the nature of personhood, he says, but as a *political* claim. It is a claim about how we should regard people for political purposes. In other words, even if it is true in any particular case that an individual is constituted by her conception of the good, the state and other political institutions should not treat her in that way. They should not impose that conception of the good on her. They must still respect her as someone who may choose her conception of the good. The political institutions provide this respect by allowing her the equal basic liberties to continue pursuing her particular conception of the good or, should she wish, to change her conception of the good – even if such a change would mean a change in her identity.

Why should we treat people as choosing their conception of the good for political purposes, even if this is not how people really are? There are several possible answers to this question. The first answer would simply be to say that at least some people *are* autonomous choosers of their conception of the good, even if not everyone is like this. So, for example, someone who is brought up in a very religious household and who keeps that religion is not an autonomous chooser of her conception of the good – it is and has always been part of who she is. But another individual who is brought up in a very liberal household, given no clear direction about what she ought to do in life or what she ought to believe, might well settle on her conception of the good through choice. She might well try out a variety of lifestyles and values, and have a different conception of the good at different times. Such a person would be an autonomous chooser of ends, and so should be respected as such.

This answer goes some way to explaining Rawls's theory, but it does not go far enough. Firstly, it does seem to engage with Sandel's argument, which denies that people can be autonomous choosers of ends. In other words, it seems to involve us in an alternative metaphysical argument, rather than a distinctly political one. Secondly, it is not normative. It tells us what some people are like, but it does not tell us what our attitude to such people should be, and why the state should respect their choices rather than try to encourage or even coerce them to follow a particular way of life. We still need to know why the state *should* consider people as unencumbered selves for political purposes.

The answer to this question rests on the fundamental value of freedom, and the fact that, as a first premise, freedom is one of the most important principles in Rawls's theory (and in liberalism generally). The alternative to considering people as unencumbered for political purposes is, Rawls thinks, a coercive state, one which imposes a particular conception of the good on people and does not allow them to follow their conception of the good freely. In *Justice as Fairness: A Re-Statement*, he defines a community as 'a body of persons united in affirming the same comprehensive, or partially comprehensive, doctrine' (Rawls 2001: p. 3). The problem with a community, Rawls argues, is that it does not leave room for people to follow different conceptions of the good. It must coerce people into following the one particular conception of the good that the community is supposed to share. The reason that this would involve coercion is that societies inevitably, according to Rawls, contain what he calls 'reasonable pluralism'. In other words, people are always going to disagree about which conception of the good is best, and they will disagree for acceptable and understandable reasons. People have different values, and different ideas about how they should live their lives, and these differences cannot and should not be suppressed. As a result, we cannot unite around a particular conception of the good without limiting people's freedom, and coercing those who do not share it. Because freedom is a foundational liberal value, such coercion would not be acceptable. Our only alternative is to treat people, for political purposes, as people who do, may and should be allowed to choose their own ends.

So, justice is fairness is political in that its conception of the person applies only for political purposes. In this sense, it is contrasted with a metaphysical conception of the person. Rawls is not making any assertions about the metaphysical nature of personhood. His theory applies only to the way that people should be considered for political purposes. Specifically, people should be treated as free (and equal) in the political sphere or, as Rawls puts it, as *citizens*. This is why the process of public reasoning used to model the public justifiability of constitutional essentials is understood by Rawls and other political liberals to be conducted between *citizens*, rather than metaphysical persons. Principles of political association must be publicly justifiable to all those citizens who are to be bound by them, regardless of their wider conception of the good life. In return, all citizens, irrespective of their wider conceptions of the good, enjoy the same basic freedoms which are protected by institutions which draw their legitimacy from the shared notion of fairness rather than any particular comprehensive doctrine.

Conclusion

In this chapter, we have set out three ways in which theorists such as Rawls have argued that liberalism can and should be political. Firstly, liberalism is political not general: it is supposed to apply only to the basic structure of society and not to all spheres of life. We will critically examine this idea when we consider feminism. Secondly, it is political and not comprehensive: it is supposed to be independent from any conception of the good, and to be acceptable to people who hold a wide variety of conceptions of the good. Thirdly, it is political not metaphysical. Political liberals reject Sandel's assertion that liberalism relies on a metaphysical conception of the self.

We have therefore seen that the idea of neutrality is important and desirable to many liberals. However, not all liberals agree on its importance or its desirability. Indeed, many liberals reject political liberalism entirely, arguing that liberalism should not seek to be neutral with regard to non-autonomous ways of life but should, instead, encourage individuals to pursue certain kinds of lives over others. We will explore this issue in the next chapter.

'Montesquieu said that a bad book by a famous author causes a lot of trouble. In Rawls's case, the trouble arises because it is almost universally assumed that, if he now says that there were fundamental flaws in A Theory of Justice, he must... be right about that. Since there is also a widespread feeling that Political Liberalism does not succeed in fulfilling its stated task, the conclusion is naturally drawn that the whole Rawlsian project is fatally flawed. I have argued that Rawls's sweeping recantation is uncalled-for, and that the failure of Political Liberalism does not discredit A Theory of Justice. I believe that, as time goes on, A Theory of Justice will stand out with increasing clarity as by far the most significant contribution to political philosophy produced in this century. Only one thing threatens to obscure that achievement: the publication of Political Liberalism.'

Brian Barry, 'John Rawls and the Search for Stability', *Ethics* 105, pp. 874–915, p. 915.

Political liberalism: A conception of liberalism which holds that liberal principles should not be grounded in any particular conception of the good or 'comprehensive' doctrine. Rather, it should ground the authority of the liberal order in principles which are agreeable to all citizens regardless of their particular conceptions of the good life.

Comprehensive liberalism: An alternative conception of liberalism which holds that the authority of liberal principles is grounded in certain substantive principles (for example, personal autonomy), and that it is the role of a liberal state to encourage and protect these values.

Public reason: The hypothetical process of public deliberation envisaged by political liberals, and by Rawls in particular, in which citizens decide on the constitutional essentials of the political order. Used to model and clarify the notion of public justifiability and fairness.

Reasonableness: The requirement that citizens respect the norms of society as a system of fair co-operation, engage in the appropriate form of (public) reasoning about principles of political association, and accept the constraints laid down in the constitution. Those conceptions of the good which require their members to reject the requirements of reasonableness are, Rawls believed, beyond the scope of what a liberal democratic theory could tolerate.

Dig deeper

Brian Barry, 'John Rawls and the Search for Stability', *Ethics* 105 (1995), pp. 874–915.

William A. Galston, *Liberal Pluralism: The Implications of Value Pluralism for Political Theory and Practice* (Cambridge: Cambridge University Press, 2002).

Charles Larmore, *Patterns of Moral Complexity* (Cambridge: Cambridge University Press, 1987).

Charles Larmore, *The Morals of Modernity* (Cambridge: Cambridge University Press, 1995).

Martha Nussbaum, 'A Plea for Difficulty', in J. Cohen, M. Howard, and M. Nussbaum (eds), *Is Multiculturalism Bad for Women?* (Princeton, NJ: Princeton University Press, 1999).

Martha Nussbaum, 'Perfectionist Liberalism and Political Liberalism', *Philosophy & Public Affairs* 39/1 (2011), pp. 3–45.

John Rawls, *Political Liberalism* (New York: Columbia University Press, 1993).

John Rawls, *Justice as Fairness: A Re-Statement* (Cambridge, MA: Harvard University Press, 2001).

Fact-check

1 What is political about political liberalism?
    A   It is political not metaphysical
    B   It is political not comprehensive
    C   It is political not general
    D   All of the above

2 What is political liberalism usually contrasted with?
    A   Comprehensive liberalism
    B   Complete liberalism
    C   Controversial liberalism
    D   Communitarian liberalism

3 What would Rawls say justifies the political values of freedom and equality?
    A   They are true
    B   They are the values of liberal democratic societies
    C   They are the values that will bring about the greatest utility
    D   They are his favourite values

4 What is a public reason?
    A   A reason that does not rely on a comprehensive conception of the good
    B   A reason that everyone agrees with
    C   A reason that persuades everyone
    D   A reason that is objectively true

5 What makes a conception of the good unreasonable?
    A   It is based on false facts
    B   It is based on faulty reasoning
    C   It cannot coexist with different conceptions of the good
    D   It does not prioritize autonomy

6 What makes a person unreasonable?
    A   She is unwilling to co-operate fairly with others
    B   She is unwilling to change her mind
    C   She is not good at reasoning
    D   She is not a liberal

7 What would a political liberal say about cultural diversity?

    A   It undermines liberalism

    B   It is the basic premise of liberalism

    C   It has nothing to do with liberalism

    D   It is the same thing as liberalism

8 Why should the state treat people as autonomous, according to political liberals?

    A   Because autonomy is the highest value

    B   Because people are in fact autonomous

    C   Because people want to be autonomous

    D   Because coercion should be avoided where possible

9 What does Rawls mean by saying that his liberalism is political not general?

    A   It only applies to the basic structure

    B   It only applies to voting

    C   It only applies to politicians

    D   All of the above

10 Why, according to Rawls, is public reason a good thing?

    A   Because it contributes to social stability

    B   Because it contributes to public justifiability

    C   Because it enables deliberation between diverse people

    D   All of the above

15

Perfectionism and state neutrality

Should the state be neutral between conceptions of the good, leaving it totally up to citizens to decide what sorts of lives to lead and activities to pursue? Or is it the job of the state to encourage citizens to pursue better ways of life rather than worse ones, and to provide or subsidize valuable activities? We have already seen that political liberals argue that state neutrality is required, since that best promotes people's freedom to frame, revise and pursue their own conceptions of the good. We have also seen that communitarians criticize this aspect of liberalism, and argue that the state should promote the shared traditions of the community.

In this chapter, we consider objections to state neutrality from within liberalism. Liberals who reject neutrality are called comprehensive, or perfectionist, liberals.

> '[T]he ideal of impartiality in moral theory expresses a logic of identity that seeks to reduce differences to unity. The stances of detachment and dispassion that supposedly produce impartiality are attained only by abstracting from the particularities of situation, feeling, affiliation, and point of view. . . [It is] an impossible ideal, because the particularities of context cannot and should not be removed from moral reasoning. Finally, the ideal of impartiality serves ideological functions. It masks the ways in which the particular perspectives of dominant groups claim universality, and helps justify hierarchical decision-making structures.'
>
> Iris Marion Young, *Justice and the Politics of Difference* (Princeton, NJ: Princeton University Press, 1990), p. 97.

The policy implications of Rawlsian neutrality

Rawlsian state neutrality requires that the state does not make judgements about the relative value of competing ways of life. Policy and laws, according to political liberalism, cannot be justified by appealing to any comprehensive conception of the good. So the state may not fund particularly valuable ways of life, cultures, art forms, sports and so on, because they are valuable.

Let us now consider how Rawlsian neutrality would work in practice by comparing opera and pop music. Opera is both highly valued and under-supported. The cost of putting on opera is extremely high, and cannot usually be met by even expensive ticket prices. As such, opera is heavily reliant on state funding. It is quite possible that opera would not be performed if it were not for state funding, and very likely that, if it could be funded by ticket prices alone, prices would have to be too high for most people to afford. On the other hand, live popular music is an art form that can support itself through ticket prices alone. The potential audience is much greater than it is for opera, in that demand for tickets is much higher. As a result, then, the state does not usually fund the tours of pop and rock artists, and yet tours continue and make money regardless.

Most existing liberal states such as the UK, faced with these differences between pop music and opera, decide to provide public funding for opera and not for pop music. Such liberal states justify their decision by arguing that opera is an important and valuable art form, and that it must not be allowed to die out. Therefore, if opera cannot support itself through ticket sales, it must be publicly funded. Opera is an important good, such that it merits state funding. Pop music may or may not be an important good, but in any case it is able to fund itself. As such, there is no need for state funding of pop music.

This kind of reasoning is not, of course, peculiar to opera. Most existing liberal states fund many other valuable cultural activities: art galleries, museums, national sports teams, orchestras and so on. However, this sort of state funding is a violation of Rawlsian state neutrality. Funding opera requires the state to make value judgements about the worth of opera, and thus to promote a conception of the good that holds opera to be important. But not everyone agrees that opera is valuable, so by funding opera the state is not being neutral between those who value opera and those who do not. Whereas opera-lovers have their preferences subsidized by the state and thus by other members of society, pop-lovers have to bear the full costs of their preferences. By funding opera and not pop, the state is giving preferential treatment to opera-lovers. It is effectively giving their claims more weight than those of pop-lovers, and this violates the Rawlsian principle of state neutrality between comprehensive conceptions of the good.

But what, precisely, is state neutrality? There are two versions of the idea: *neutrality of effect* and *neutrality of justification*.

Neutrality of effect

Imagine that we live in a Rawlsian society which has no public funding for opera. Some people do value opera very much: it is central to their conception of the good. However, they are too few to provide the funding that opera needs to survive. As a result, with no state funding, opera gradually dies out and becomes a lost art form. On the other hand, pop music flourishes.

One might object to this state of affairs. The point of state neutrality is that everyone should be equally able to pursue their own conception of the good, regardless of whether others disagree with it. The state must recognize the fact of reasonable pluralism, and ensure that people are not unfairly prevented from following their conceptions of the good. But if opera dies out then opera-lovers are no longer able to follow their conception of the good. There is an inequality between the opera-lovers and the pop-lovers: the former cannot pursue their conception of the good, while the latter can. How neutral is this? Surely this is a society which favours pop at the expense of opera. If such a state wanted to be neutral, it ought to provide funding for the opera so that both groups could pursue their conceptions of the good.

This objection can be expressed as an argument in favour of neutrality of effect. A state without public funding for opera is not neutral *in effect* between those who value opera and those who value pop. Rawlsian so-called neutrality does not lead to outcomes that are neutral. On the contrary, active support of opera would best promote neutrality of outcome or effect.

However, there are four main problems with neutrality of effect.

1 *It is impractical.* If the state were to try to ensure that all its policies were neutral in effect, it would have to know in detail what the results of its policies would be in every possible circumstance. But the world is far too complicated for this sort of prediction to work. States cannot know exactly what motivates every individual, and so they cannot know precisely what the implications of any particular policy would be. It is simply impossible for a state to ensure neutrality of effect.

2 *It would require the support of conceptions of the good that few people share.* By its very nature, a policy of neutrality of effect would have to fund unpopular preferences, so as to

counterbalance the popularity of the alternatives. Indeed, the more popular the alternatives are, then the more the state will have to support the unpopular good.

3 *It unfairly subsidizes expensive tastes.* Remember, one argument for neutrality of effect was that some valuable ways of life, such as opera, cost more money than their supporters are willing to pay. Suppose, for the sake of argument, that opera could survive without state funding only if tickets cost £500 each. Opera-lovers are not willing to pay £500 to see an opera, and so the state steps in to fill the gap. However, if even opera-lovers do not think that opera is worth paying £500 each for, why should the state, and therefore taxpayers who don't like opera at all, think that it is worth this level of funding?

4 *It undermines the idea that people should be held responsible for their choices.* Given that we have finite resources, people have to accept that not all conceptions of the good will survive, and they must be willing to bear the consequences of their particular choices.

Neutrality of effect is not, then, the sort of state neutrality that liberals like Rawls advocate.

Spotlight: Subsidizing the arts

* In 2007–8 the entire budget for the UK Department of Culture, Media and Sport was £6.6 billion – just 1 per cent of total government spending. (Source: *the Guardian* and Institute of Fiscal Studies)
* The 19 free-to-enter museums and zoo of the Smithsonian Institution, Washington DC, USA receive 29 million visits per year. In 2012 the Smithsonian received $810 million from federal government. (Source: www.si.edu)

Neutrality of justification

The sort of neutrality that Rawls is in favour of can be called *neutrality of justification.* The important issue for Rawls is not the outcome of particular policies, but the way in which these policies are justified. The state may not fund opera because it is a valuable way of life, or because it is more valuable than pop music. It is not important that opera ends up on equal terms with pop music. It is just important that the state does not give greater weight to one form of music over another.

The reason for this is that Rawls argues that the principles of justice must be acceptable to people who hold a wide variety of conceptions of the good. The idea is that there can be an overlapping consensus on the principles of justice, which do not rely on any particular conception of the good. Any state that follows policies that are justified by reference to a particular conception of the good will not adequately accommodate alternatives. It will not respect the fact of reasonable pluralism.

As this was the subject of the last chapter, we move on to two criticisms of, and alternatives to, Rawlsian state neutrality: perfectionist liberalism and a politics of difference.

Case study: Catharine MacKinnon on state neutrality

In her landmark book *Toward a Feminist Theory of the State* (MacKinnon, 1989), Catharine MacKinnon writes:

> The state is male in the feminist sense: the law sees and treats women the way men see and treat women. The liberal state coercively and authoritatively constitutes the social order in the interests of men as a gender—through its legitimating norms, forms, relation to society, and substantive policies. The state's formal norms recapitulate the male point of view on the level of design. (MacKinnon 1989: pp. 162–3)

According to MacKinnon, the idea of neutrality is one way that the state promotes the interests of men. Neutrality in liberalism tends to be associated with negative freedom and non-interference: the state is neutral if it leaves things as they are. But, MacKinnon points out, if society is gendered then not interfering means leaving gender inequality in place.

Consider freedom of speech and pornography. In the USA, constitutional guarantees of freedom of speech have been taken to rule out any regulation of pornography. MacKinnon argues that pornography actually limits women's freedom of speech by representing women as passive beings who enjoy being raped and abused, meaning that women outside of pornography are often not believed when they say they have been raped. Freedom of speech might be better secured for women as well as for men, then, by regulating pornography. But state neutrality assumes that there is freedom of speech already, and that the state's job is not to interfere with it.

In general, state neutrality defends the status quo, with dire consequences for women:

> Rape law assumes that consent to sex is as real for women as it is for men. Privacy law assumes that women in private have the same privacy men do. Obscenity law assumes that women have the access to speech men have. Equality law assumes that women are already socially equal to men. Only to the extent women have already achieved social equality does the mainstream law of equality support their inequality claims. (MacKinnon 1989: p. 169)

As long as legislators and judges are primarily male, implementing constitutions and laws passed by men in situations of profound inequality, neutrality simply perpetuates that inequality.

Raz and liberal perfectionism

Comprehensive liberalism is an alternative to political liberal arguments for neutrality. It claims that liberalism should be grounded on valuable principles like autonomy. One influential variant of this approach is liberal perfectionism: the idea that 'it is the goal of all political action to enable individuals to pursue valid conceptions of the good and to discourage evil or empty ones' (Raz 1986: p. 133). Liberal perfectionism of this kind is most commonly associated with Joseph Raz. It also has much in common with the earlier comprehensive liberalism of John Stuart Mill.

> '[T]he autonomy principle is a perfectionist principle. Autonomous life is only valuable if it is spent in the pursuit of acceptable and valuable projects and relationships. The autonomy principle permits and even requires governments to create morally valuable opportunities, and to eliminate repugnant ones... A government which subsidizes certain activities, rewards their pursuit, and advertises their availability encourages those activities without using coercion.'
>
> Joseph Raz, *The Morality of Freedom* (Oxford: Clarendon Press, 1986), p. 417.

The liberal perfectionist claim that states should promote particular conceptions of the good is a straightforward rejection of state neutrality. What makes someone like Raz a *liberal* perfectionist (rather than, say, a communitarian) is that he does not argue that valid ways of life must be based on shared communal values. Instead, he argues that a valuable way of life is one that is based on *autonomy*. If a person is to lead a valuable life, it will be an autonomous one. In Rawlsian terminology, she will *actively* engage in framing, revising and pursuing her conception of the good. She will not passively follow her community and unthinkingly adopt a shared way of life. She will be the active author of her own life.

So, if the liberal perfectionist state is supposed to encourage valuable ways of life, then it follows for Raz that it will encourage autonomous ways of life. In this way, a perfectionist state retains its liberal character. It does not coerce people into following one way of life, but gives them the resources and encouragement to choose a way of life for themselves. Raz, then, is a comprehensive liberal in that he disagrees with the Rawlsian assertion that the state should be neutral between conceptions of the good that foster autonomy and those that deny it.

In practice, this means that Raz is willing to advocate paternalistic and interventionist state policies to a much greater extent than Rawls is, because he does not believe that the state should protect autonomy-denying ways of life. So, for example, certain sorts of cultural practices will not be allowed (see the chapter on multiculturalism for further discussion). He is more paternalistic because he is willing to involve the state in making value judgements about the value of different ways of life, and thus advocates that the state should fund and support some ways of life more than others.

The paternalistic nature of Raz's argument is more significant than it may initially appear. This is because he has a different, and more demanding, understanding of autonomy than many liberals, including Rawls. For Raz, autonomy is not just about choosing a way of life, it is about choosing a *valuable* way of life. If a person autonomously chooses a worthless life, her life is not valuable. The fact that she has chosen it is not enough. That is why governments should make value judgements about different ways of life – they need to ensure that there are many valuable options available, and possibly to rule out worthless or repugnant ways of life.

Choice is therefore a necessary, but not sufficient, condition for the living of a valuable life: people's choices could be misguided. The problem, of course, is: who gets to decide what is a valuable life if not individuals themselves? Raz argues that the state is best placed to make these decisions, based upon a reasoned evaluation of different conceptions of the good life, and the reasons people have for following them.

This is controversial but not unconvincing. It does seem that there are some ways of life that we know, pretty surely, are worthless. A life of addiction to heroin, for example, is not very worthwhile, and it is fairly uncontroversial that the state should at least discourage, if not actively forbid, such a life. Why should we allow people to make the mistake of becoming addicted to heroin, given all that we know about its extremely harmful effects? Surely it would be a dereliction of duty, not to mention a waste of human experience, not to act on the knowledge we have about the worthlessness of such a life? The problem, of course, is that once we depart from these extreme sorts of cases, the issues are much less clear-cut. We could probably agree that heroin addiction is worthless, but we are much less likely to agree about the relative merits of opera and pop, and the funding (if any) each should receive.

But Raz points out that perfectionist action does not have to be as extreme as prohibition. There may be some cases, such as heroin addiction, where the activity is sufficiently worthless to justify prohibition. However, there are other cases where state discouragement, perhaps in the form of taxation, seems more warranted. Actually existing liberal states do this sort of thing all the time. The policy of congestion charging is a good example. Driving into central London is not so worthless or morally repugnant as to justify a ban, but it is sufficiently undesirable to merit the use of a tax, to discourage people from doing it. Similarly, in the UK we have perfectionist taxes on tobacco, petrol and alcohol. We also employ perfectionist measures to discourage people in other ways. For example, we discourage gambling by setting a minimum age for participation. We discourage smoking by setting extensive limits on tobacco advertising. And, of course, similar measures apply to the encouragement of ways of life that we see as valuable. Public transport is subsidized, many art galleries and museums are free to enter, there are many free public libraries and subsidized leisure and fitness facilities.

Spotlight: Perfectionism vs. state neutrality

A discussion of perfectionism vs. state neutrality occurs between fictional Minister Jim Hacker (JH) and civil servant Sir Humphrey Appleby (HA) in the comedy series *Yes Minister*:

> **JH:** There's no difference between subsidizing football and subsidizing art – except that a lot more people are interested in football.
>
> **HA:** Our cultural heritage has to be preserved!
>
> **JH:** For whom? For people like you, you mean. For the educated middle classes. Why should the rest of the country subsidize the pleasures of the middle-class few? Theatre, opera, ballet. Subsidizing art in this country is nothing more than a middle-class rip-off!

(*Yes Minister* Series 3, Episode 7: 'The Middle-class Rip-off' (1982).

In other words, actual states do engage in all sorts of perfectionist policies. Most of them are not strongly opposed, and many of them are not even controversial. Few argue that tobacco should be untaxed and unregulated, or that public libraries should be run on free-market principles, with the consumer paying to use them. These facts seem to undermine the objection that perfectionist principles involve controversial and coercive imposition of state power over and above the will of the people. We often can agree about whether a way of life is more or less valuable and, when we can do so, Raz would insist that we ought to. For Raz, then, the role of the liberal state is clear: to provide for individuals, through direct or indirect means, a range of valuable options from which to use.

Young's critique of liberal neutrality

Iris Marion Young offers a critique of both neutrality and perfectionism (and hence, of political and comprehensive liberalism) from the point of view of a critique of domination and oppression. For Young, the ideal of neutrality that we find in the work of Rawls and other political liberals fails to take account of the differences between people, and forces people to reason in ways which ignore their felt emotions and experiences. In her phrase, it 'reduces difference to unity': neutrality refuses to recognize that people have deeply different lives, experiences and social roles. People have different races, genders, religions, cultures, sexualities, careers, classes, conceptions of the good. These differences, Young argues, should not be glossed over. They should not be placed behind a 'veil of ignorance' in order that they be excluded from our deliberations about justice, or excluded from the process of public reasoning about political principles and institutions. We should not try to pretend that there can be one, neutral standpoint that can reduce all these differences to unity, that can make all these people the same. There is no such moral standpoint. Instead, the correct way for us to approach questions of justice and public policy is through a process of deliberation between actually existing, situated people, people who are substantively different from one another and whose differences are recognized.

Because Young rejects the idea that there can be any truly neutral standpoint, it follows that the supposedly neutral state will actually end up representing one particular standpoint. This standpoint, Young argues, will be the standpoint of the majority group in society. In other words, the result of a policy of supposed neutrality is the perceptions of the dominant group are presented as universal and objective, and that subordinate groups are silenced and portrayed as inferior. Moreover, because the dominant standpoint is presented as a neutral standpoint, it cannot be challenged. Any attempted challenge can be refuted as a particularistic, selfish claim for special deviation from neutrality, rather than as a serious, principled alternative to the dominant viewpoint.

'A passively tolerant society says to its citizens: as long as you obey the law, we will leave you alone. It stands neutral between different values. A genuinely liberal society does much more. It believes in certain values and actively promotes them.'
David Cameron, 'Speech to the Munich Security Conference', 2011

Of course, if this argument holds, it applies even more strongly to Raz's perfectionism. Raz does not even claim to provide a neutral standpoint. Indeed, he argues that the whole purpose of government action is to discriminate between ways of life, and to promote some above others. Young would argue that this cannot be done without dominating and oppressing minority groups. She denies that there is any objective and universal standard of value. Instead, society is characterized by a number of diverse groups, each of which have their own, different, but *valid* perspective on life. Neither neutrality nor perfectionism can overrule these differences unless by suppressing diversity and undermining equality.

Conclusion

In this chapter, we have discussed how Rawlsian liberalism might be understood as neutral with regard to different conceptions of the good, and have outlined two important criticisms of liberal neutrality: a criticism made from within liberalism by comprehensive and perfectionist liberals who argue that liberalism should be grounded in a particular conception of the good life over others, and the criticism of comprehensive and political liberalism made by Iris Marion Young, who argues that liberalism entrenches dominant ways of life at the expense of minority values. We will pick this final point up in Chapter 17, in our discussion of multiculturalism.

Key ideas

Neutrality of effect: The idea that, in order to be neutral, the state would need to ensure that all the conceptions of the good that any individual might choose could be chosen.

Neutrality of justification: The idea that principles should be neutral in the sense that they are not justified by any particular comprehensive doctrine. This is the conception of neutrality defended by Rawls and other political liberals.

Perfectionist liberalism: A form of comprehensive liberalism premised on the idea that liberal states should promote ways of life which are valuable, and discourage ones which are not.

Dig deeper

Brian Barry, *Justice as Impartiality* (Oxford: Oxford University Press, 1990).

Catharine MacKinnon, *Toward a Feminist Theory of the State* (Cambridge, MA: Harvard University Press, 1989).

Thomas Nagel, *Equality and Partiality* (New York: Oxford University Press, 1995).

John Rawls, *Collected Papers*, ed. Samuel Freeman (Cambridge, MA: Harvard University Press, 1999).

Joseph Raz, *The Morality of Freedom* (Oxford: Clarendon Press, 1986).

Steven Wall, *Liberalism, Perfectionism, and Restraint* (Cambridge: Cambridge University Press, 1998).

Iris Marion Young, *Justice and the Politics of Difference* (Princeton, NJ: Princeton University Press, 1990).

Fact-check

1 What sort of state neutrality does Rawls advocate?
  A Neutrality of effect
  B Neutrality of justification
  C Neutrality of outcome
  D Neutrality of oppression

2 What, according to Rawls, should the state be neutral between?
  A Conceptions of the good
  B Conceptions of justice
  C Liberalism and anti-liberalism
  D All of the above

3 Which of the following could Rawls endorse?
  A Subsidizing opera because it is better than football
  B Subsidizing football because it is more popular than opera
  C Subsidizing opera because it would die out without subsidy
  D None of the above

4 Which of the following objections apply to neutrality of effect?
  A It is difficult to achieve
  B It is undemocratic
  C It is inefficient
  D All of the above

5 What is liberal perfectionism?
  A The claim that liberalism is perfect
  B The claim that liberals are perfect
  C The claim that liberals should defend state neutrality
  D The claim that liberals should reject state neutrality

6 What is liberal about Raz's liberal perfectionism?
  A It is based on autonomy
  B It is compatible with a variety of valuable ways of life
  C It does not try to coerce people into one particular conception of the good
  D All of the above

7 Which of the following would Raz endorse?
- **A** Subsidizing opera because it is a valuable art form
- **B** Subsidizing football because it is more popular than opera
- **C** Subsidizing opera because it is very expensive
- **D** All of the above

8 Why, according to Raz, is state subsidy sometimes justified?
- **A** Because state officials are cleverer than citizens
- **B** Because it is important to protect a range of valuable ways of life
- **C** Because liberty is unimportant
- **D** Because inequality of resources means that subsidy is required

9 Why does Iris Marion Young reject the idea of neutrality?
- **A** Because neutrality is impossible
- **B** Because neutrality conceals oppression
- **C** Because 'neutrality' tends to mean the views of the dominant
- **D** All of the above

10 Why is state neutrality bad for gender equality, according to MacKinnon?
- **A** Because women reject state neutrality
- **B** Because state neutrality leaves social inequality intact
- **C** Because political leaders are usually men
- **D** Because feminism conflicts with equality of justification

16

Multiculturalism

The question of whether, and how, liberal states should remain neutral with regard to different conceptions of the good is central to the debate about how states should respond to *cultural* diversity. Anglo-American political philosophy was dominated throughout the 1990s by debates about multiculturalism. Do cultural and religious minority groups have an equality-based claim for special treatment? Should certain groups be exempted from general laws if these laws can be shown to conflict with their cultural or religious beliefs? Is it appropriate for states to distribute public resources to religious and cultural groups in order to ensure their continued ability to practise their beliefs? Furthermore, does liberal toleration require tolerating illiberal cultures and practices? Should liberal states allow sexist religious groups to constrain the freedom of their female members through the enforcement of strict gender norms, or homophobic religious groups to punish or demean their members on account of their sexuality?

These questions summon fundamental *philosophical* debates about the nature and scope of liberal neutrality, the coherence of the liberal distinction between public and private, and the redistribution of resources in liberal states. They are also very important and controversial *political* questions. In this chapter, we outline the dominant philosophical defence of 'liberal multiculturalism' advanced by thinkers like Will Kymlicka and Joseph Raz, and then discuss some criticisms of it. It is important to distinguish multiculturalism as a fact from multiculturalism as a normative position. Viewed as a fact, multiculturalism refers to the existence of cultural diversity. As a normative position, multiculturalism refers to the idea that justice must take special account of culture, with special policies needed that go beyond standard, culture-blind liberalism. This chapter focuses on multiculturalism as a normative position. The criticisms discussed will be criticisms of this normative position, not criticisms of the fact of cultural diversity.

Spotlight: Canada

Canada is arguably the nation-state most committed to normative multiculturalism. Multiculturalism is affirmed in the Canadian constitution and at the federal level in the form of the 1988 Multiculturalism Act. The act affirms the social importance of immigration and of the diverse identities of Canada's immigrant population, as well as the rights of so-called 'first nations' groups such as the Inuit and Aboriginal communities. Multiculturalist policies in Canada have historically included the allocation of public funding for the maintenance of ethnic and cultural minority activities, the introduction of a 'multicultural' school curriculum, affirmative action for historically disadvantaged cultural minorities, and exemptions from dress codes, the most symbolic and obvious being the provision that Sikh members of the Royal Canadian Mounted Police could wear their turbans instead of the traditional head dress.

The argument for liberal multiculturalism

Defenders of liberal multiculturalism object to the 'traditional' liberal approach to cultural diversity on *practical* and *philosophical* grounds.

THE PRACTICAL OBJECTION

Until relatively recently, a broad consensus existed among liberals about the status of religious and cultural beliefs. Religion and culture were private in the sense that they were matters of conscience. As the liberal state does not enforce a particular conception of religious truth, so religious life was seen as appropriately belonging within the private sphere beyond the scope of the state. The liberal state should thus allow individuals to observe their religious beliefs, and to engage in the practices attendant to those beliefs, as freely as is commensurate with everyone else being able to do the same. Everyone may follow their religious beliefs, but no one may be forced to follow any particular religion. Most importantly, religious views would not figure in the justification of state authority, or in decisions made by state institutions about matters of public life (such as the redistribution of public resources). In Rawls's terms, such matters would be placed behind a 'veil of ignorance'.

This approach, while dominant, became controversial in the wake of the communitarian critique of liberalism because it appeared to favour some religions over others. In particular, it permitted the observance of religious beliefs which could easily fit within the private sphere, and ruled out the observance of beliefs which required public expression. But many religions require their members to do things which cannot be easily fit within what liberals call the private sphere. Religious believers may be required to observe certain practices *in public*. So the policy of universal equal concern via privacy imposes unfair burdens on some groups and not others, and fails to provide clear guidance on how the *public* disagreements arising out of religious diversity might be best resolved.

For example, Islam requires women to cover themselves in public, while Sikh men are required to wear turbans. Such requirements inevitably thrust religion into the public sphere and raise public policy dilemmas. Many liberals and feminists, for example, have suggested that the Islamic requirement that women be covered in public embodies sexist attitudes toward women and, hence, should be discouraged or even outlawed on the grounds of equality. The French government has recently passed a law outlawing the public wearing of the *burkha*. Similarly, the Sikh requirement that men wear turbans is a public requirement which gives rise to conflicts. Should Sikhs be allowed to wear their turbans in the workplace, for example? If wearing the turban is a core requirement of their religious beliefs, then allowing employers to ban Sikhs from wearing them in the workplace seems to represent a substantial constraint on their right to practise their religion and to pursue their own conception of the good free from interference. However, if employers are required to permit Sikhs to wear their turbans in the workplace, then what happens when doing so hinders their ability to do their job in some way? For example, should Sikh men be exempt from UK laws which require all builders working on building sites to wear protective helmets? Should Sikhs be exempt from rules which require police officers to wear helmets as part of their uniforms?

The traditional liberal claim that religion is private does not seem equipped to resolve these questions. Liberal states which take the protection of religious freedom seriously may have to ensure that members of religious groups receive special treatment to enable them to practise their religion on an equal basis. That is, to use terminology which we introduced in Chapter 1, liberal states must protect not just *formal* freedom of religion, but also the *effective* freedom to engage in religious practices.

Such a view has important implications for one area of policy in particular: the just distribution of resources. The traditional universalist liberal approach, most obviously exemplified in Rawls's justice as fairness, is clear: conceptions of the good should not affect resource distributions. Liberal multiculturalists argue that this approach entails the unjust 'benign neglect' of minority groups. Just as providing the disabled with the effective freedom to live a life that they have chosen on an equal basis with others might require the state giving them extra money or resources that are not available to non-disabled people, so providing members of minority groups with the effective freedom to engage in religious or cultural practices might require the state to give them money or other resources that are not available to others, like spaces in which to worship or time off to celebrate religious holidays.

The first objection to the traditional liberal approach to cultural and religious diversity is therefore that the liberal state must engage in deliberate and explicit reform of the public realm (through public policy and law) to secure for all individuals the effective, rather than merely the formal, freedom to practise their cultural and religious beliefs on an equal basis with others.

THE PHILOSOPHICAL OBJECTION

The second objection is more philosophical in nature: a person's culture at least partially defines their identity and, as such, is crucially bound up with their capacity to be free. This claim is made by liberal multiculturalists such as Will Kymlicka and Joseph Raz (e.g. Kymlicka 1991 and 1994). They argue that, insofar as liberalism is concerned to encourage individual autonomy (that is, one's ability to choose and pursue a way of life for oneself), then it must also be committed to protecting the integrity of those cultural values which provide the background against which these choices about how to lead one's life are taken.

Drawing on communitarian insights about the importance of community membership in shaping our ideas about the world and ourselves, multiculturalist liberals like Kymlicka argue that the state has a role in politicizing minority cultural groups *in the name of individual freedom*. Kymlicka argues that we live our lives within a particular cultural context of values and ideals which we inherit from our community. Our culture represents the background 'context of choice' which renders certain ways of life meaningful or meaningless, valid or invalid, desirable or undesirable, or moral or immoral.

Culture is thus crucial to individual autonomy because it provides the historical and normative framework within which we make choices about how to live our lives. Consequently, the liberal state must ensure that all individuals are able to access their culture, and to engage in those practices which ensure the survival of that culture, as a means to protecting individual autonomy.

> 'The decision about how to lead our lives must ultimately be ours alone, but this decision is always a matter of selecting what we believe to be most valuable from the various options available, selecting from a context of choice which provides us with different ways of life. This is important because the range of options is determined by our cultural heritage. Different ways of life are not just simply different patterns of physical movements. The physical movements only have meaning to us because they are identified as having significance by our culture, because they fit into some pattern of activities which is culturally recognized as a way of leading one's life...'
> Will Kymlicka, *Liberalism, Community, and Culture* (Oxford: Oxford University Press, 1989), pp. 164–5.

Kymlicka's argument has been incredibly influential in contemporary political theory, as it provides a specifically liberal justification for taking culture seriously. Kymlicka reconciles liberal individualism with communitarianism and defends a radical policy programme. He argues that the public recognition of cultural beliefs is necessary in order to satisfy the requirements of *equality*, *freedom* (understood as autonomy), and *neutrality*: if states simply treat all groups the same, and remove religious and cultural values from public deliberations about policies and justice, then there will be unfair burdens on some groups at the expense of others. For example, the timing of public holidays, the official language of the state, and default rules about uniforms will benefit some groups and not others. Typically, the groups which do worse will be small or weak minorities, many of which became small and weak as a result of suffering historical injustices in the past.

Liberal multiculturalism thus has radical *philosophical* implications. It also has quite radical *policy* implications. Three of the most important are:

1 It emphasizes the importance of rectifying historical injustice in general, and cultural and religious oppression in particular, to securing justice in liberal states. After all, if it can be shown that individuals need access to their culture in order to experience individual freedom, then the liberal state should be concerned for any individual who has, for whatever reason, been denied the opportunity of engaging in the life of their culture. Consequently, liberal multiculturalism suggests that members of first-nations or aboriginal populations in Canada, the USA, or Australia, who had their cultures all but wiped out by European settlers, might require group-specific rights enabling them to reclaim what they lost. Such rights might involve the ceding of territory, the right to establish certain social and political institutions, or the right to have their religious beliefs recognized in wider laws.

2 It suggests a shift from a policy of 'assimilation' (whereby all citizens are required to 'become liberals' in the sense that they accept the dominant liberal values of the state) to 'integration' (whereby the state 'recognizes' the divergent beliefs of its citizens and does not require people to relinquish their identities in order to create a homogeneous society).

3 It represents a critique of nationalism in general, and ethnic nationalism in particular, for excluding other, non-national forms of identity like culture and religion. In valorizing national symbols and national myths, states squash out minority identities and, hence, undermine the equality and freedom of minority groups.

Criticisms of liberal multiculturalism

The move toward liberal multiculturalism has been important and influential. It has also been controversial among politicians and academics alike. As mentioned above, the recent re-emphasis on common values and national unity in the face of terrorism and religious extremism has meant that the political agendas of many states have become less hospitable to multiculturalism. And many political philosophers have criticized liberal multiculturalism on a number of grounds. Three of the most important are discussed next.

MULTICULTURALISM MISUNDERSTANDS THE ROLE AND STATUS OF LAWS

Brian Barry criticizes what he calls the 'rule and exemption' approach employed by many defenders of multiculturalism (Barry 2001). This is the idea that the state may pass universal laws but must provide certain groups with exemptions from these laws if they impose disproportionate burdens on some people on account of their cultural or religious beliefs. For example, the UK has laws regulating the humane slaughter of animals which require that animals are stunned before they are killed. However, this requirement is incompatible with the Jewish (kosher) and Muslim (halal) methods of slaughter, which require that animals be killed by a single cut to the throat. Consequently, Jewish and Muslim groups are exempted from humane slaughter requirements on the grounds that those requirements place an unfair burden upon Jews and Muslims. Similarly, Sikh men who wear turbans are exempted from UK laws requiring workers on building sites to wear protective hardhats, and from laws requiring motorcyclists to wear protective helmets, on the grounds that these laws impose greater burdens upon Sikh men than non-Sikhs.

Barry argues that the rule-and-exemption approach is fundamentally misguided. He points out that *every* law imposes greater burdens on some people than on others. Laws against murder are more burdensome to people who would like to engage in murder than on people who would not. Laws against child abuse, littering, or fraud impose greater burdens on people who would like to engage in those practices than people who would not, and so on. The fact that a law is more burdensome on some people than others is not in itself a good argument for justifying an exemption.

> '"Culture is no excuse". If there are sound reasons against doing something, these cannot be trumped by saying – even if it is true – that doing it is a part of your culture. The fact that you (or your ancestors) have been doing something for a long time does nothing in itself to justify your continuing to do it... If slave-owners in the South had had access to the currently fashionable vocabulary, they would doubtless have explained that their culture was inextricably linked with the "peculiar institution" and would have complained that the abolitionists failed to accord them "recognition". But this simply illustrates that the appeal to "culture" establishes nothing. Some cultures are admirable, others are vile. Reasons for doing things that can be advanced within the former will tend to be good, and reasons that can be advanced within the latter will tend to be bad. But in neither case is something's being part of the culture itself a reason for doing anything.'
>
> Brian Barry, *Culture & Equality* (Cambridge: Polity, 2001), p. 258.

The point is not how or why certain groups should be exempted from universal laws, but whether there are *good reasons* for having a law in the first place. If there are good reasons for having a law protecting animals from inhumane treatment, for example, or requiring workers or motorcyclists to wear protective helmets, then these reasons stand even if they run contrary to the religious beliefs of certain members of society. If, on the other hand, the reasons for having the law are not found to be compelling enough to justify legislation then, Barry argues, the state should not legislate. But arguing that certain acts (like slaughtering animals inhumanely) are so wrong that they should be outlawed and then allowing some people (for whatever reason) to do them anyway, or that some acts are morally required and then arguing that some people should not have to do them at all, is muddled and incoherent.

The real question, therefore, is whether culture represents a good enough reason for having (or not having) a law. Barry does not think that it is. He believes that religious or cultural beliefs are 'expensive tastes' (of the kind discussed in Chapter 11). He does not believe they are unimportant: people can have religious beliefs, and they can believe them to be centrally important to their lives. However, if they are going to do so, he says, then they need to bear the *consequences* of doing so. Religious beliefs impose costs. If there are good reasons for having laws which protect animals from being slaughtered inhumanely, then groups whose beliefs run counter to these methods may have to bear the cost of not eating meat. Similarly, if there are good grounds for requiring people to wear motorcycle helmets or hardhats, then it may be that Sikhs have to bear the costs of not being able to ride motorcycles or becoming builders. Again, if there are not sufficiently weighty arguments in favour of having these laws, then we should not have them. But if there *are* sufficiently weighty arguments in their favour, then these arguments should stand, even if they impose costs on some people which not everyone has to bear.

Spotlight: *Laïcité* in France

In 1989 three French Muslim girls were suspended from (public) school for wearing their headscarves. This decision was initially reversed by the courts, as wearing headscarves was judged to be compatible with the French policy of *laïcité* (secularism). However, in 1990 three female students were suspended from school for wearing their headscarves. This time, the decision was supported by many teachers who called a strike in favour of the ban. In 1994 the government issued a memorandum proposing that it might be permissible to wear 'discreet' religious symbols (like crucifix necklaces) but not 'ostentatious' ones (like the hijab). This proposal angered many Muslims who saw it as unfairly allowing members of certain religions to express their faith in public and not others. Since 1994 more than a hundred female Muslim students have been either suspended or expelled for wearing their headscarves in class. These decisions have only been reversed on around 50 per cent of cases.

MULTICULTURALISM IS EITHER TRIVIAL OR MISTAKEN

A second criticism of multiculturalism is that it cannot respond coherently to illiberal practices. The basic insight of liberal multiculturalism is that many cultural and religious minority groups have values and practices which do not easily fit within a universalist conception of liberalism. Many cultures and religions have illiberal views regarding the status of women, for example, or homosexuality. Some allow their male members to marry many women, or to marry girls as young as 14. Still others engage in practices which involve physical harms such as ritual scarring or female genital mutilation. Critics of multiculturalism argue that liberalism should not be recast in order to make it easier for *illiberal* cultural and religious groups to violate liberal principles. Liberalism, after all, arose from the concern to protect individuals from the tyranny of history and tradition. Affording special status to cultural groups to engage in practices which violate liberal principles thus seems a backwards step which is incompatible with the core aims of liberalism. Kymlicka's argument in particular is vulnerable to this critique: individual autonomy will only be facilitated by cultures which value autonomy. Kymlicka responds by suggesting that the liberal state should not afford group specific rights to cultures which impose 'internal restrictions' on the freedom of their members (to express themselves freely, for example, or to receive an education).

The problem with this response is that it renders liberal multiculturalism either mistaken or trivial. If it provides justification for liberal states to allow cultural and religious minorities to treat some or all of their members in ways which violate basic liberal principles, then it is *mistaken*: liberalism cannot seek to afford such powers to cultural groups and remain committed to securing individual freedom and equality. If, on the other hand, it restricts the allocation of group-differentiated rights and other special treatment to groups which organize themselves around liberal principles, then it is *trivial*: liberal multiculturalism is not distinct from universalist liberalism.

CULTURE IS INDETERMINATE

Placing so much emphasis on culture is problematic, some critics have argued, because it is almost impossible to agree on what culture actually is. Culture is indeterminate in the sense that different thinkers disagree about not just its normative importance but its very *content*. Raz defines culture as the network of values and norms which provides the context in which we make autonomous choices. Kymlicka goes further, arguing that what people need in order to be autonomous are 'societal cultures' comprising 'not just shared memories or values, but common institutions and practices' (Kymlicka 1994: 76). But beyond this, there is very little engagement with the question of what a culture is, and no consensus about what distinguishes a cultural group from any other kind of group. Instead, liberals simply assert the fact of cultural diversity before moving on to debate the ways in which liberal states should resolve the political conflicts arising out of this diversity.

Liberal multiculturalists cannot avoid defining culture. We need to know what a cultural group *is* before we can afford it special rights. We need to know what it is about a *cultural* group, as opposed to any other kind of group, which renders us free, and what it is about cultural practices, as opposed to any other kind of practices, which are so important.

Case study: Jeremy Waldron's cosmopolitan critique of liberal multiculturalism

The debate within liberalism about multiculturalism is often presented as being between two warring sides. On the one hand, we have traditional, universalist liberal theories which ignore the importance of community and which, as a consequence, rob individuals of the resources they need to make meaningful, autonomous choices in the world, and fail to secure equality of opportunity for members of minority cultures. On the other hand, we have liberal multiculturalism which provides people with the resources they need to live freely, and accords members of minority groups special treatment through legal exemptions and so on, in the interests of equal opportunity. Having shown that radical abstract individualism is incompatible with freedom, liberal multiculturalists suggest, we are required to embrace multiculturalism and all the various policy implications associated with it.

Jeremy Waldron agrees that we need a context of choice, but disagrees that it is provided by a single, unified culture. Waldron offers an alternative conception of identity – a 'cosmopolitan' conception – in which an individual's identity, and hence her 'context of choice', is made up of fragments of many different cultures all at the same time. As members of liberal states, he says, we cannot help but experience different cultures all the time, and we necessarily construct our own identity in the context of this diversity. We will move around the world, reside in complex and diverse cities, listen to Italian opera on Japanese stereos while eating Chinese food; we might enjoy Belgian beer, American pancakes, French Impressionism, the novels of Haruki Murakami, Shakespeare, Islamic art, Irish folk music, and countless other things which come to us from different cultures and nations and historical traditions. In such a diverse cultural environment, it seems odd to suggest that we rely on a single culture for our identity and, hence, our freedom. On the contrary, Waldron suggests, in such a context of diversity 'each individual's identity is multicultural... [I]ndividuals can no longer in the modern world (if indeed they ever could) be understood as mere artifacts of the culture of the one community to which we think they ought to belong' (Waldron 1996: p. 114).

Waldron therefore agrees that liberals should be attentive to the importance of identity. But multiculturalists are wrong to say that this insight justifies a regime of multicultural minority rights. They are also wrong in assuming that liberals must choose between a *universalist* approach grounded in a *rejection* of the importance of community, and a *culturalist* approach which emphasizes the *importance* of community. It is possible, Waldron argues, to embrace a cosmopolitan universalist approach which rejects abstract individualism *and* multiculturalism.

Spotlight: The status of bullfighting

In 2011 the practice of bullfighting was accorded official cultural status in Spain by Prime Minister José Luis Rodriguez Zapatero, despite it being outlawed in Catalonia since 2010 on grounds of suffering. It is estimated that around 250,000 bulls are killed every year in bullfights, with Spain accounting for around 12,000 deaths. Furthermore, bullfighting in Spain is financed by public money: in 2008, the Spanish fighting bull breeding industry received grants amounting to 600 million euros.

Conclusion

Multiculturalism raises philosophical and political questions. It challenges the liberal assumption that culture and religion are merely 'private'. It raises important questions about the ability of liberal states to acknowledge difference at the same time as forging the kind of social unity that is necessary for the realization of other liberal commitments, like securing social justice and equal citizenship.

The key questions to bear in mind when thinking about liberal multiculturalism are: What is culture? What weight should an appeal to culture have in political decision making or deliberations about justice? What (if any) limits should be placed upon the ability of groups to engage in cultural practices? How does the freedom and equality of *groups* relate to the freedom and equality of *individuals* and, if the interests of individuals and groups conflict, how might these conflicts be resolved?

Key ideas

Context of choice: The idea, popular among liberal multiculturalists like Will Kymlicka and Joseph Raz, that culture is a prerequisite of individual autonomy in that it provides the context of values, norms, and ideals, and the linguistic framework, within which we make choices about how to live our lives.

Group-differentiated rights: The idea that the individual members of different cultural groups will have legitimate rights claims over different things, as a result of their cultural values.

Liberal multiculturalism: The idea that, in the interests of securing *individual* freedom and equality (and enshrining neutrality) liberal states are required to accord special treatment of one kind or another to cultural *groups* through such measures as legal exemptions or group-specific rights.

Liberal universalism: The 'traditional' liberal approach to religious and cultural diversity which considers culture and religion 'private' in the sense that they are matters of conscience. It embodies also the idea that all individuals should receive the same bundle of rights, that every individual is free to engage in whatever practices they wish as long as they do not violate liberal justice, and that no individual should be oppressed in the name of religious or cultural tradition.

Rule-and-exemption approach: The idea popular among liberal multiculturalists that it is a requirement of justice that individuals who suffer disproportionate costs from particular laws should, in certain circumstances, be given exemption from those laws.

Dig deeper

Clare Chambers, *Sex, Culture, and Justice: The Limits of Choice* (University Park, PA: Pennsylvania State University Press, 2008).

Chandran Kukathas, *The Liberal Archipelago* (Oxford: Oxford University Press, 2003).

Will Kymlicka, *Multicultural Citizenship: A Liberal Theory of Minority Rights* (Oxford: Oxford University Press, 1994).

Susan Moller Okin, 'Is Multiculturalism Bad for Women?', in J. Cohen, M. Howard and M.C. Nussbaum (eds), *Is Multiculturalism Bad For Women?* (Princeton, NJ: Princeton University Press, 1999).

Phil Parvin, 'What's Special about Culture? Identity, Autonomy, and Public Reason', *Critical Review of International, Social, and Political Philosophy* 11/3 (2008), pp. 315–33.

Anne Phillips, *Multiculturalism without Culture* (Princeton, NJ: Princeton University Press, 2009).

Joseph Raz, 'Multiculturalism: A Liberal Perspective', *Ratio Juris* 11/3 (1998), pp. 193–205.

Charles Taylor, 'The Politics of Recognition', in Amy Gutmann (ed.), *Multiculturalism and the Politics of Recognition* (Princeton, NJ: Princeton University Press, 1992).

Jeremy Waldron, 'Multiculturalism and Melange', in R. Fullinwinder (ed.), *Public Education in a Multicultural Society: Policy, Theory, Critique* (Cambridge: Cambridge University Press, 1996).

Iris Marion Young, *Justice and the Politics of Difference* (Princeton, NJ: Princeton University Press, 1990).

Fact-check

1 What is multiculturalism, as a normative position?
- **A** The theory that cultural diversity should be increased
- **B** The theory that cultural diversity requires modifying liberalism
- **C** The theory that cultural diversity requires rejecting liberalism
- **D** The theory that cultural diversity should be reduced

2 Which of the following might be cultural practices, according to multiculturalists?
- **A** Religious worship
- **B** Language
- **C** Gendered social roles
- **D** All of the above

3 What is wrong with the traditional conception of liberalism, according to multiculturalists?
- **A** It is not neutral between cultures
- **B** It rules out cultural diversity
- **C** It affirms the superiority of one culture
- **D** It is based on liberty, which is undesirable

4 Why do we need culture, according to Kymlicka?
- **A** Because diversity is good
- **B** Because liberal values are wrong
- **C** Because culture provides our context of choice
- **D** Because cultures are traditional

5 In Britain, turbaned Sikh men do not have to wear motorcycle helmets but everyone else does. What is this an example of?
- **A** The rule-and-exemption approach
- **B** A context of choice
- **C** An internal restriction
- **D** The rule of law

6 Why does Barry criticize the situation described in Question 5?
- **A** It undermines equality
- **B** It undermines liberty
- **C** It undermines multiculturalism
- **D** It promotes Sikhism

7 Why might a multiculturalist defend the situation described in Question 5?

    A   It shows that Sikhism is right

    B   It shows that liberalism is wrong

    C   It equalizes the burdens on motorcyclists

    D   It maximizes motorcycle riding

8 What sorts of cultures are particularly difficult for multiculturalist theory to accommodate?

    A   Homogeneous cultures

    B   Community-based cultures

    C   Illiberal cultures

    D   Minority cultures

9 What is cosmopolitanism as defended by Waldron?

    A   The view that cultures are irrelevant

    B   The view that cultures are essential

    C   The view that identity comes from many different cultures

    D   The view that identity comes from a specific, single culture

10 Which of the following is most compatible with multiculturalism?

    A   Valuing individuals and not groups

    B   Subsidizing groups to ensure their survival

    C   Ranking groups according to their merits

    D   Allowing the market to determine which groups survive

17

Feminism

The vast majority of societies contain profound inequality between men and women – even liberal democratic societies that supposedly enshrine equality. Millions of women currently live in societies which deny them freedom and accord them second-class status. In Saudi Arabia, for example, women are banned from driving cars, are required to cover all but their hands and eyes in public, and must have permission from their 'male guardian' to receive an education, open a bank account, travel, or get married or divorced. Orthodox Judaism forbids women from divorcing their husbands, but allows men to divorce their wives for any reason. In some states such as Afghanistan, rape victims can be required to marry their rapists in order to mitigate the shame that the victims have purportedly brought upon their families. Death by stoning is still a punishment for women found guilty of adultery in several states, including Iraq, Iran, Indonesia, Nigeria, Somalia and the Sudan. There are many more examples of the ways in which states violate the equality and freedom of women.

> 'I myself have never been able to find out precisely what feminism is: I only know that people call me a feminist whenever I express sentiments that differentiate me from a door mat or a prostitute.'
>
> Rebecca West, 'Mr Chesterton in Hysterics: A Study in Prejudice',
> *The Clarion* 14 November 1913.

Furthermore, it is wrong to assume that the subordination of women is peculiar to non-liberal states. Liberal states have also historically denied women equal rights. In Britain and the USA, for example, women could not vote, pursue careers on equal terms with men, or have an abortion until relatively recently. Progress has been made in many of these areas, and some of the most egregious forms of gender inequality in liberal societies have been addressed. However, it is a common mistake to assume that sexism is a thing of the past. Sexism remains a principal form of injustice in societies throughout the world, as shown in the statistics contained in boxes in this chapter. We still live in a world in which women are given lower status than men and are forced to endure indignities and inequalities not imposed on men. Equality between the sexes has not been achieved; feminists are those women and men who believe that it must be. There are many forms of feminism. However, for the sake of this chapter, it is possible to identify four principal themes which unite feminists. We discuss these in the next four sections.

Case study: Feminist diversity

While feminists are united in their general aim of alleviating the social, political, legal and economic inequalities which arise out of patriarchy, they have disagreed as to the ways in which this should be done, and what the priorities are for feminist academics and activists.

Feminism can be understood as having two distinct 'waves'. *First-wave feminism* occurred predominantly in the nineteenth century. One of its earliest advocates is Mary Wollstonecraft. Against the common wisdom of the time, Wollstonecraft argued that women possessed equal reason to men and that they should possess the same rights, in particular the right to vote (which was not granted

to all women over 21 in Britain until 1928, over a century later).
The work of first-wave feminists like Wollstonecraft significantly
influenced equality movements like the Suffragettes who used
direct political action as a means of securing greater equality for
women. First-wave feminism was thus primarily concerned to
secure equal political rights and formal equality.

Second-wave feminism emerged in the 1960s and 1970s and is
associated with the Women's Movement and the work of feminists
like Germaine Greer, Marilyn French, Betty Friedan, Simone de
Beauvoir, Catharine MacKinnon and Andrea Dworkin. Second-
wave feminism grew out of the realization that gender inequality
continued in liberal democratic states even though women in
those states had largely won equal legal rights. Second-wave
feminists thus focus less on establishing equal rights and equality
of opportunity, and more on revealing and reforming those
implicit social, political, legal and cultural forces which conspire
to discourage women from availing themselves of their rights or
taking up the opportunities available to them: the social forces
which discourage women from pursuing a career on an equal basis
with men even though they have the right to do so, for example.
Hence, second-wave feminism focuses not so much on the reform
of legal rules and policies, but on the wider social attitudes and
norms which guide our actions.

A further important division in contemporary feminism is between
liberal and radical feminists. *Liberal feminists*, such as Susan
Moller Okin and Martha Nussbaum, have argued that feminist aims
can and should be achieved through an application of mainstream
liberal ideas of justice, rights, and economic redistribution. The
principal aim for feminists, they argue, is to secure greater *justice*
for women, which means making sure that men and women do not
suffer unjust inequalities on account of their sex.

Radical feminists, like Andrea Dworkin, Catharine MacKinnon
and Sheila Jeffreys, urge that we reject the dominant liberal
discourse concerning justice for its failure to address many of the
most profound examples of gender inequality in the world, such
as rape, sexual harassment, trafficking, domestic abuse, and
female sexuality. They focus instead on reforming unequal power
relationships and ending violence against women.

The existence of patriarchy

Translated literally as 'rule by the father', patriarchy is the term feminists use to describe the system of values, norms and practices which encourage and perpetuate the subordination of women. Feminists do not see the patriarchal subordination of women as something done *by* all men *to* all women. Rather, they see it as something which shapes the lives of men *and* women.

Men and women learn who they are, what they believe, and what forms of behaviour are appropriate in the context of the society in which they live. From birth boys and girls are taught how to behave and what it means to be a success or a failure. We learn quickly what kind of behaviour is worthy of praise and reward, and what kind is worthy of punishment, and we learn too that we can be rewarded and punished by many different people in many different ways: our parents, our teachers, our peers, our friends, our work colleagues, the police, community leaders, religious leaders, and countless others. All, in their own ways, influence our actions and shape our choices. Consequently, feminists argue, if the overarching values of a society are sexist (as they have been throughout the majority of human history), then men and women will internalize sexist attitudes. If society shapes our identities, then the people produced by sexist societies will be sexist.

Patriarchy (and, hence, sexism) is not simply the fault of men, then. It is something which works to the benefit of men, but which is internalized and strengthened by men *and* women. Women and men are both encouraged, through explicit and implicit means, to adopt certain kinds of identity, to make certain kinds of choices, and to behave in particular ways. However, the roles that men are encouraged to adopt tend to have a much higher social status than those that women are encouraged to adopt. This is patriarchy. It is the idea that men and women are encouraged by society to adopt certain roles but that, overwhelmingly, male roles are accorded much higher status, respect, and economic worth than those of women.

Feminism aims to (a) *reveal* the nature and extent of patriarchy, and (b) *undermine* patriarchy. Feminism promotes gender-neutral social and political attitudes, values, and practices which do not systematically demean the views and activities of women.

Sex and gender

Throughout history *social* roles have often been justified by an appeal to *biological* differences between men and women. For example, Kant and Aristotle both argued that women were 'naturally' unsuited to certain kinds of life: both believed that women were incapable of engaging in the kind of reasoning required by politics and, hence, that women should not be consulted about political matters. Nietzsche believed that women were 'naturally' weak and, hence, were inferior to men. And Hegel, in *The Philosophy of Right*, argued that women 'are not made for activities which demand a universal faculty such as the advanced sciences, philosophy, and certain forms of artistic production' (Hegel [1820] 1973: p. 263).

Extreme claims of this kind are less common now, but the idea that women and men are 'naturally' suited to different occupations or lifestyles persists. For example, the relative lack of women in top jobs in many liberal democratic states has been attributed to the purported fact that women are naturally less competitive than men, and the fact that women still take on the vast majority of child care and domestic duties in the household (while their partners pursue their careers) has been attributed to the 'fact' that women are naturally more caring and men are more ambitious.

Feminists respond in two ways. *Firstly*, they argue that essentialism of this kind is bound up with historically antiquated, patronizing and offensive perceptions of what men and women *can* or *cannot* do and, hence, what they *should or should not* be allowed to do. They point out that we no longer justify unequal treatment of other social groups on the basis of essentialist arguments. Historically, racists have claimed that black people are naturally aggressive or lazy, or that Jews are naturally greedy. However, egalitarians rightly reject these claims and the unjust policies associated with them. Feminists argue that justifying unequal treatment of women by an appeal to natural difference should be rejected for the same reasons.

Secondly, feminists argue, even if there *are* entrenched differences between the sexes, society and politics should be reconfigured so as to value women. It is one thing (and very controversial) to say that, for example, women engage in politics in a different way to men. It is quite another, however, to say that in doing so they engage in politics in the *wrong* way and that, therefore, women should not be accommodated in political debates. Put bluntly, if women engage in politics differently to men, feminists insist that the appropriate response is to change the male-centric way that politics has been conducted, a bias based on centuries of male dominance and female oppression.

Spotlight: More evidence for patriarchy

* At least 47,000 women are raped in Britain every year (Fawcett Society). More than a quarter of the British public believe that women are either partially or totally responsible for being raped if they wear 'sexy or revealing clothing'. In Britain, two women every week are killed by their partners or ex-partners. At least 1,500 women are illegally trafficked into Britain every year, most of whom are forced to work in the sex industry. Globally, one in three women has been beaten, raped, or abused in her lifetime (Amnesty International).
* 1.9 million cosmetic surgery operations were conducted in one year (2009) in one country alone (the USA). Of these, 90 per cent were conducted on women.

Many feminists thus insist on a distinction between sex and gender. Sex refers to the biological differences between women and men: differences in body parts, chromosomes and reproductive biology. Gender refers to the differences between women and men that are social: differences in appearance norms, career choices and so on. Feminists argue that most observable differences between women and men are differences of gender rather than sex. Since gender differences are social they can be reduced, or at least made fairer, by social action.

For example, it is a difference of sex and not gender that only women can gestate and breastfeed. But it is a difference of gender and not sex that women's careers are disproportionately affected by parenthood. It is society and not nature that structures paid work in such a way as to be incompatible with caring for children, and that imposes stronger norms on mothers than on fathers to be available to their children. This gender inequality could be reduced by social policies such as changing ideals of paid work and promoting fathers' parenting, without affecting sex differences of gestating and breastfeeding.

Feminists therefore argue that we should not try and explain gender differences purely in terms of biology. Millions of women undergo painful and invasive cosmetic surgery operations not because of some biological urge, but to conform to *social* standards of beauty. Women are under-represented in top jobs because of enduring attitudes about the 'natural' role of women, and their natural strengths and weaknesses. It is not because of some biological predisposition toward raising children rather than engaging in paid work that women have historically devoted their lives to domesticity and motherhood while men have not. And it is not a genetic need to procreate which leads so many men to rape so many women every year, but widespread social attitudes about male and female sexuality.

The importance of power

Feminists emphasize the importance of power. In particular, they criticize the liberal view of power as something possessed primarily by the state. For feminists, power is exercised not only in a one-dimensional sense (to use Lukes's terminology) but also in a three-dimensional sense: social norms powerfully shape our lives by shaping our choices. Power is often invisible and exerted in ways which we might not easily see or understand: power is not just about making us do what we do not want to do, but about making us actually *want* to do certain things.

Consider again the example of cosmetic surgery. Hundreds of thousands of women a year willingly pay surgeons huge amounts of money to have them increase the size of their breasts, eradicate wrinkles, or remove fat from their abdomens. Cosmetic surgery is a multi-million dollar global industry, and the reason for this is that there is a genuine market demand for it. Women who undergo cosmetic surgery procedures do not do so, on the whole, against their will: they do so because they feel that it would make them happier or more confident. But why is confidence and happiness linked so strongly to body image for so many women? How does a situation arise in which, in order to feel confident and happy, so many women feel the need to pay someone to cut them open, insert foreign objects in their bodies, or inject chemicals into them? Norms about body image, beauty, and sexiness are powerful motivators to action: they encourage men and women to make choices and adopt certain kinds of lifestyles, and to reject others.

Social norms exert pressure on us in countless other ways. They shape our attitudes about what to wear, how to act, what to say and when to say it, what jobs to pursue, and so on. Every social context has a set of norms which shape our choices. And, again, if these norms are sexist, then women will be encouraged to act, and to understand the world, on sexist terms. Patriarchy has the power to make women complicit in their own subordination by encouraging them to want things and to develop views about themselves and the world which further entrench their own inequality.

Societies which reward women for being thin and youthful, for example, create in their female members a desire to be thin and youthful which is real, not imagined. Similarly, societies which reward women for giving up their independence in favour of marriage, or subordinating their careers to those of their husbands, create in women a genuine, not imaginary, desire to get married and to put their husbands' careers before their own. Thus, gender roles are internalized by men and women, and handed on to future generations through socialization, peer pressure and tradition not because men and women are consciously seeking to keep women 'in their place' (although some might do this), but because social norms have a power over us which we feel but do not always recognize.

Given this, many feminists have criticized liberalism's approach to equality. While liberal feminists like Susan Moller Okin and Martha Nussbaum try to address gender inequality within the liberal tradition, radical feminists like Andrea Dworkin and Catharine MacKinnon, and post-structuralist feminists like Iris Marion Young, argue that in holding 'justice' to be the principal subject of political inquiry liberals miss the point, and shift normative debates in a direction that makes them unable to deal with the most devastating aspects of gender inequality.

Radical feminists argue that inequality is important not simply because there are not enough female chief executives or Members of Parliament, but because women are subjected to violence. For feminists like MacKinnon and Dworkin, the point is that the *three*-dimensional power embodied in social norms translates very quickly into the use of *one*-dimensional power by men over women. Men are more likely to rape and abuse women if women are routinely portrayed in the media and elsewhere as submissive, sexually available, and subordinate.

'Liberal individualism seems to be a good view for feminists to embrace. For it is clear that women have too rarely been treated as ends in themselves, and too frequently treated as means to the ends of others. Women's individual well-being has far too rarely been taken into account in political and economic planning and measurement. Women have very often been treated as parts of a larger unit, especially the family, and valued primarily for

> *their contribution as reproducers and caregivers rather than as sources of agency and worth in their own right.'*
>
> Martha Nussbaum, *Sex and Social Justice* (Oxford: Oxford University Press, 2000), p. 63.

> *'[Liberalism has] yet to face either the facts or the implications of women's material inequality as a group, has not controlled male violence societywide, and has not equalized the statues of women relative to men. . . [I]f liberalism 'inherently' can meet feminism's challenges, having had the chance for some time, why hasn't it?'*
>
> Catharine MacKinnon, '"The Case" Responds', *American Political Science Review* 95/3 (2001), p. 709.

The personal is political

Finally, feminists are critical of the traditional liberal distinction between the public and the private. They argue that this distinction undermines *equality*. Historically women have primarily occupied the 'private' or domestic sphere: while men went out to work, women stayed at home as wives and mothers. Consequently, if the private sphere is beyond the scope of the state then women's lives are beyond the scope of the state. And yet, feminists point out, a great deal of power, including oppressive and abusive power, operates in the private sphere. The principal focus of liberal political thought has been to determine the appropriate limits of state power and confine it to the public sphere. But feminists argue that power cannot be contained within a circumscribed public sphere. It is everywhere, including those parts of our lives which are often considered to be private in the sense that they are beyond the scope of politics and the state: the family, for example, or religion.

Power pervades every area of our lives. Consequently, feminist politics is more *holistic* than traditional liberal politics: it asks us to examine our settled convictions, and to seek reform, across the full range of human experience, and to broaden our understanding of 'the political' into areas like the family which many think should be considered apolitical or non-political.

Conclusion

Feminism asks us to broaden our understanding of the political into all those areas in which power, in all its different forms, resides. It is therefore a critique of many approaches to political philosophy and political science. Most importantly, it urges us to re-examine the many ways in which society is characterized by deeply entrenched attitudes about men and women, handed down through generations.

It is sometimes said that feminism is redundant now that women have achieved equality. However, women have not achieved equality, even in the most enlightened and progressive of societies. Once the scale of gender inequality is grasped, once the negative stereotypes associated with feminists are dispensed, and once the subtlety and importance of feminist insights into society, politics, power and equality are more fully grasped by more people, perhaps more men and women will identify as 'feminist'.

Key ideas

Patriarchy: Literally translated as 'the rule of the father', more generally used by feminists to describe the overarching attitudes and norms which serve to encourage and perpetuate the inequality of women.

Gender: The socially constructed (as opposed to biologically determined) identities held by men and women, shaped by social norms, widespread attitudes, etc.

Social construction of preferences: The idea that our choices are at least partly shaped by overarching social norms and that, in sexist societies, women will be encouraged to make choices which are against their wider interests.

Public/private distinction: Central to liberalism, the idea that it is possible to distinguish a 'political' from a 'non-political' realm. Generally viewed with scepticism by feminists, who argue that our whole lives are 'political'.

Sex: The biological categories of male and female, determined by physical features such as chromosomes, genitals and reproductive organs.

Dig deeper

Clare Chambers, *Sex, Culture, and Justice: The Limits of Choice* (University Park: Pennsylvania State Press, 2008).

Andrea Dworkin, *Pornography: Men Possessing Women* (London: Women's Press, 1981).

Germaine Greer, *The Female Eunuch* [1970] (London: Harper, 2006).

G.W.F. Hegel, *The Philosophy of Right* [1820], trans. T.M. Knox (New York, Oxford University Press, 1973).

Catharine A. MacKinnon, *Towards a Feminist Theory of the State* (Cambridge, MA: Harvard University Press, 1989).

Martha Nussbaum, *Sex and Social Justice* (Oxford: Oxford University Press, 2000).

Susan Moller Okin, *Justice, Gender, and the Family* (New York: Basic Books, 1989).

Natasha Walter, *Living Dolls: The Return of Sexism* (London: Virago, 2010).

Fact-check

1 Which of the following is the best definition of patriarchy, as the term is used in contemporary feminism?
   A A society in which men are in charge
   B A society in which men hate women
   C A society in which men are feminists
   D A society in which men are advantaged

2 According to feminism, how does patriarchy manifest itself?
   A Through social norms
   B Through patterns of wealth
   C Through patterns of violence
   D All of the above

3 What is the difference between sex and gender?
   A Sex is biological, gender is cultural
   B Sex is cultural, gender is social
   C Sex is genetic, gender is political
   D Sex is personal, gender is political

4 What is implied by the sex / gender distinction?
   A That some differences between men and women can be changed
   B That some differences between men and women cannot be changed
   C That some differences between men and women should be changed
   D All of the above

5 Why does power matter to feminism?
   A Because feminists want to have power over men
   B Because feminists argue that there is power in gendered norms
   C Because feminists argue that power is not important
   D Because feminists think that power is the most important thing

6 Which of the following is *not* usually part of the feminist claim 'the personal is political'?

    A The private sphere is a sphere of power

    B The private sphere is traditionally identified with women

    C Politics should pay more attention to the private lives of politicians

    D Politics should pay more attention to the family

7 Which of the following claims best encapsulates liberal feminism?

    A Men and women should be free to do as they please

    B Men and women should be given equal freedoms

    C Men and women are exactly the same

    D Equality requires a profound shift in gender norms and behaviour

8 Which of the following claims best encapsulates radical feminism?

    A Men and women should be free to do as they please

    B Men and women should be given equal freedoms

    C Men and women are exactly the same

    D Equality requires a profound shift in gender norms and behaviour

9 Feminists might endorse any or all of the following, but which of the following reforms would best meet the demands of liberal feminists?

    A Having more female leaders than male leaders

    B Ending male violence against women

    C Equal rights for women and men in the workplace

    D Women working in the home, men working outside the home

10 And which would best meet the demands of radical feminists?

    A Having more female leaders than male leaders

    B Ending male violence against women

    C Equal rights for women and men in the workplace

    D Women working in the home, men working outside the home

18

Global justice

Consider the following facts:

▷ 25 per cent of the world's total financial assets are currently controlled by the wealthiest 0.2 per cent of the world's population.

▷ The gross domestic product (i.e. the total of everyone's income) in the poorest 48 nations is less than the combined wealth of the world's three richest people.

▷ 50 per cent of the world's population (3 billion people) live on less than £1.60 a day.

▷ Of the 2.2 billion children in the world, 600 million live in extreme poverty.

▷ One-third of all deaths (18 million people a year) are caused by poverty.

What should we think about facts such as these? Why should political philosophers care about the fact that the vast majority of the world's wealth is concentrated not merely in a few very rich nation-states, but in the hands of very few very wealthy *individuals* living in certain wealthy nation-states, while millions of people living in poorer nations suffer under conditions of devastating poverty? And what, if anything, should we think about the fact that around the world numerous states routinely imprison, torture, and murder their citizens for crimes such as peacefully protesting against the government, campaigning for democracy, or having the wrong religious beliefs?

Questions such as these have come to assume a central place in contemporary political philosophy. If Anglo-American political philosophy was dominated in the 1970s by debates about the distribution of wealth, in the 1980s by debates about communitarianism, and in the 1990s by debates about multiculturalism, then the 2000s might arguably be seen as the decade in which political philosophers chose to reflect upon the international implications of their normative theories. The increased interest in international issues among political philosophers has been partly driven by the growing sense among political theorists and political scientists that politics can only really be understood in an international or global context. With the rise of supranational institutions like the United Nations, the International Monetary Fund (IMF) and the World Bank, political structures like the European Union (EU), multinational corporations, and the increased global influence of non-governmental organizations, pressure groups, lobby organizations, and other bodies, as well as the globalization of liberal markets and the rise of other global issues such as the war in Iraq, the war on terror, 9/11, and climate change, normative debates about social justice have been increasingly framed in international terms.

The key question for political philosophers is whether principles of justice can be *universal*. Universal principles of justice would allow us to criticize and perhaps punish unjust regimes, using sanctions, trade embargoes, or even military force. But if justice is *relative* rather than universal then other regimes may be immune from outside criticism. If justice can be different in different societies then any attempt to interfere in the affairs of other states may simply be unjust.

Questions of global justice are fundamental, then. From where do we derive our ideas about good and bad, right and wrong? *Particularists* claim that we derive them from the shared values of our particular cultural or national community. On the other hand, *cosmopolitans* argue that principles of justice and morality apply to all people in all circumstances.

In the second half of this chapter we examine the distinction between particularism and cosmopolitanism in more detail. But first we introduce the concepts of statism and state sovereignty.

Statism

The assumption underlying the conduct of global politics in the modern era, originating in the Peace of Westphalia in 1648, is that states are sovereign. According to this view, known as *statism*, the world is divided into nation-states which are *sovereign* in the sense that they should be free to manage their own internal affairs without external interference from other bodies, including supranational institutions, corporations, and other states.

The idea of sovereignty occupies an important place in international law. It protects nation-states from interference by other states or institutions, and ensures that nation-states are self-determining or self-governing. Statism is therefore a basic assumption of real-world global politics. And yet as an ideal it is problematic. Consider four problems with the idea of sovereignty that underpins statism.

SOVEREIGNTY PERMITS INJUSTICE

Illiberal states can appeal to state sovereignty as a defence for doing things which violate liberal principles, such as oppressing their citizens, denying them basic rights, treating them unfairly, or even killing them in the name of some greater good. This is the wrong way around. We should not be protecting the right of groups (e.g. nations or states) to oppress their members. We should instead be protecting the rights of individuals not to be oppressed by their states, by recognizing basic standards of justice which apply to all people regardless of where they live.

SOVEREIGNTY PROTECTS UNDEMOCRATIC REGIMES

A democratic state, one that acts in accordance with the will of the people, has moral grounds for its domestic policies: it has been given a mandate by the people who will be affected by those policies. So the idea that a democratic state should be left alone has widespread appeal. But it is less appealing to suggest that *undemocratic* states should enjoy the same protection. It is not clear why the international community should extend the privileges associated with state sovereignty to regimes which maintain power through corrupt or undemocratic means. Liberal and other critics of the idea of state sovereignty argue that international law gives too much scope for undemocratic states to claim the same protections against external interference in their affairs as democratic ones.

SOVEREIGNTY ENTRENCHES INEQUALITY

According to current international law, if a nation-state discovers that it has desirable resources within its territory (such as diamonds or oil) then, following state sovereignty, it can claim *ownership* of those resources. But is it fair that a particular nation-state and its members should automatically be the *owner* of the natural resources within its territory? Is it fair, for example, that the 12 countries which make up OPEC (Organization of Petroleum Exporting Countries) control 79 per cent of the world's oil reserves, effectively allowing the heads of those states to set the price of oil for the whole world, simply because they happen to have been lucky enough to live on pieces of the Earth's surface which contain oil? Similarly, does the fact that the USA has discovered vast new oil reserves in Alaska give it the right to extract that oil even though doing so would devastate the environment, landscape, and wildlife in that area? They currently have the *legal* right to do so, as their rights in international law are grounded in the idea of sovereignty.

However, is it morally right that they have the legal ability to act in such a way, or is there an argument for *constraining* national sovereignty in this case in the interests of preserving the Alaskan ecosystem?

'In the case of natural resources, the parties to the international original position would know that resources are unevenly distributed with respect to population, that adequate access to resources is a prerequisite for successful operation of (domestic) cooperative schemes, and that resources are scarce. They would view the natural distribution of resources as arbitrary in the sense that no one has a natural prima facie claim to the resources that happen to be under one's feet. The appropriation of scarce resources by some requires a justification against the competing claims of others and the needs of future generations. Not knowing the resource endowments of their own societies, the parties would agree on a resource redistribution principle that would give each society a fair chance to develop just political institutions and an economy capable of satisfying its members' basic needs.'

Charles R. Beitz, *Political Theory and International Relations* (Princeton, NJ: Princeton University Press, 1979), p. 141.

SOVEREIGNTY CONFLICTS WITH GLOBALIZATION

The fourth objection to statism is that its premise, that global politics is conducted among self-interested, sovereign nation-states, can no longer be coherently defended. This is partly because the world now faces problems like climate change which cannot be solved unless states put aside their self-interest and work for the good of the collective good of the world's population as a whole. But it is also because (as a result of globalization) national governments are increasingly incapable of exercising sovereign control over important areas of public policy. The most obvious example is economic policy. Liberal markets transcend national boundaries; trade is genuinely global, with deals being made electronically among people all over the world. Consequently, as the recent global financial crisis has shown, whole national economies can be plunged into recession as a result of decisions made by people on the other side of the world, who are not elected, and who are not subject to political scrutiny. It is therefore a simple fact that in the world today states cannot be said to have sovereign control over their own economies.

Cosmopolitanism and particularism

These criticisms of statism raise the more fundamental question of the origin and status of moral principles. We can distinguish two approaches to this question: particularism and cosmopolitanism.

PARTICULARISM

Particularists believe that morality and justice originate in the shared values of a community, be it a religion, culture or nation. Particularists argue that people are situated in communities which shape their understanding of themselves and determine the context in which they act. Hence, these communities shape the way we think, the way in which we understand the world, and *the way we think we should and should not act*.

Furthermore, particularists argue, we have moral obligations to people in our community that we do not have to outsiders. Just as we have moral obligations to our own families that we do not have to other people's families, so we have moral obligations to members of our own nation that we do not have to members of other nations (Miller 1995). Particularists differ in their attitude toward the possibility of international standards of justice. Some, like David Miller, argue that national values provide the basis for our morality but that certain 'minimal' standards of morality exist between nations (Miller 1995). Others, like Michael Walzer, believe that no such international standards can exist (Walzer 1983). Nevertheless, particularists tend to be sympathetic to the idea of sovereignty, arguing that it is each nation's sovereign right to live according to its own moral values and manage its own affairs.

Particularists tend to see the search for universal principles of justice and morality as *politically* mistaken, as doing so represents little more than the desire of one group to impose its values on another, and *philosophically* mistaken, in the sense that community membership determines the way in which we think about and discuss morality. Not everyone reasons about morality and politics in the same way: when thinking about morality we reach for concepts and vocabularies which make sense to us, but which might not make sense to others. Liberals frame their claims in terms of things like rights and individuality and rationality, while others might appeal to things like humility or hierarchy. Or, many people might appeal to notions like 'freedom' and 'equality' but have entirely different understandings of these ideas.

So particularists are sympathetic to sovereignty as the result of fundamental claims about the nature of morality rather than simply for political expediency. They defend a global politics in which different nation-states are allowed to act in accordance with their own moral values.

COSMOPOLITANISM

Cosmopolitans, on the other hand, argue that universal standards of morality and justice are possible and necessary. They reject the particularist story about the origins of morality, and replace it with their own. For cosmopolitans morality does not originate in community values but in universal, claims about the ways in which individuals should be treated. Cosmopolitan liberals argue that the authority of normative statements comes not from an appeal to particular traditions or *shared* values, but from the fact that they can be accepted as reasonable by people who have *different* values and traditions. Hence, when thinking about global justice, we must put aside our national membership, and seek what is right for all people, rather than what is merely right for our nation.

Some liberal cosmopolitans, such as Charles Beitz (1979) and Thomas Pogge (2008), argue that Rawls's theory should be applied globally. They argue that our national identity should be put behind the Rawlsian veil of ignorance. Just as deliberators in the original position do not know what religious, ethnic or cultural group they belonged to, so they should not know their *national* group. So parties in the original position would agree upon a set of principles which have global scope. Rawls thus provides liberal cosmopolitans with a tool for criticizing the actions of unjust states, although Rawls himself does not develop his theory in this way (Rawls 1999).

Cosmopolitans uphold the universalist liberal idea embodied in documents like the Universal Declaration of Human Rights: it is the wellbeing of individual human beings, not nations, that matters. State violations of freedom and equality are therefore unjust and should not be permitted in the name of national values or state sovereignty. They are unjust because, in Rawlsian terms, they would not be the subject of agreement in the original position and, as such, they would be rejected as principles by which the global order might be arranged.

Case study: Two varieties of cosmopolitanism

Peter Singer's utilitarian cosmopolitanism

Peter Singer is a utilitarian, and so his approach to global poverty is grounded in consequentialist moral theory. He focuses on the moral duties of individuals rather than states. In his article 'Famine, Affluence, and Morality' (Singer 1972), Singer asks: What should we think about the fact that so many people in the world suffer the effects of devastating poverty? Singer's answer is radical, but grounded in two intuitively uncontroversial claims: that (a) 'suffering and death from lack of food, shelter, and medical care are bad', and that (b) 'if it is in our power to prevent something bad from happening, without thereby sacrificing anything of comparable moral importance, we ought, morally, to do it' (Singer 1972). Singer argues that if we accept these claims, which we should, then we must radically rethink our attitudes toward the plight of needy individuals. For, he says, it requires that we will need to give a far larger proportion of our money to charity than we currently do: in fact we will need to give all the money that we would otherwise spend on things which are less morally important than reducing global poverty.

This effectively means that we must donate our entire disposable income to the global poor. If, having provided for your basic needs, you have £10 to spare, you are morally required to give it to people elsewhere who are in poverty (through charitable donations, for example) rather than spend it on something that you would enjoy. Similarly, if you have £30, or £300, or £3000 left over, you ought morally to donate this money to people who are suffering the effects of poverty, rather than spend it on yourself. Singer argues that if we are in a position to prevent one or more people somewhere suffering the effects of poverty, then we are acting immorally whenever we choose not to do so in favour of buying something nice for ourselves like a meal out or an iPad or a new car. Singer's conclusion is that accepting the two claims with which he begins means that we are morally required to give away as much of our wealth as is compatible with us not suffering the effects of poverty ourselves.

Thomas Pogge's liberal cosmopolitanism

Thomas Pogge is a liberal who draws upon Rawls's work to inform a universal cosmopolitan conception of global justice (Pogge 2008).

Pogge argues that the unequal distribution of wealth and resources among states in the world today results from treaties, conventions and institutional structures created and strengthened by rich states. These rich states could reform these conventions and institutions so as to alleviate the inequalities which result in so many people living in poverty. The fact that they are not doing so is immoral. Rich states are not passive bystanders: they have used their power to secure their own national self-interests at the expense of other, less powerful states. Given this, rich states ought morally to take steps to rectify the disadvantage experienced by people living in poor states by working together to (a) reform global and international institutions and (b) contribute a proportion of their wealth to a common fund which would be used to eradicate poverty. In particular, Pogge challenges the common claim that the eradication of poverty would be too expensive. He does so by proposing that nations pay a tax on the resources they use or sell (what he calls the 'Global Resources Dividend'). Pogge estimates that a dividend of only 1 per cent would raise around $300 billion a year, equivalent to $250 per person in the world's poorest quintile.

> 'Three facts make the great ongoing catastrophe of human
> poverty deeply problematic, morally. First, it occurs in the
> context of unprecedented global affluence that is easily sufficient
> to eradicate all life-threatening poverty... Second... global
> inequalities... are increasing relentlessly... Third, conditions of
> life anywhere on earth are today deeply affected by international
> interactions of many kinds and thus by the elaborate regime
> of treaties and conventions that profoundly and increasingly
> shape such interactions. Those who participate in this regime,
> especially in its design or imposition, are morally implicated in
> any contribution to ever-increasing global economic inequality
> and to the consequent persistence of severe poverty.'
> Thomas Pogge, *Politics as Usual: What Lies Behind the Pro-Poor Rhetoric*
> (Cambridge: Polity, 2010), pp. 12–13.

Global poverty: humanitarianism vs. global coercive redistribution

How do particularists and cosmopolitans respond to the
radical inequalities in resources, wealth and opportunities
which exist between nation-states in the world today? Do rich
states have a moral obligation to redistribute wealth to poorer
states? More specifically, do rich *individuals* living in rich
states have an obligation to give a proportion of their wealth
to poor *individuals* living in poor states?

Currently, the global distribution of resources results from
exchanges among individuals and organizations (either through
global markets or private philanthropy) or states (through
humanitarian aid). The humanitarian model operates a bit like a
global form of libertarianism among states: states are considered
the owners of resources which they can use as they please. Any
attempt to tell states what to do with their own resources is a
violation of their sovereignty and a constraint on their freedom
and is, therefore, unjust. Hence, it is largely up to states whether
they choose to distribute any of their resources to poorer states.
Sovereign states, like Nozickean individuals, work out for
themselves whether they can afford to give charity and are free
to set the terms of their aid.

This humanitarian model is consistent with particularism and the idea of sovereignty, but has been widely criticized for the same reasons that Nozick's libertarianism has been criticized. It leaves the poor subject to the whims of the rich and fails to take seriously the needs of people living in poverty; it assumes that states are entitled to the resources that they currently hold (even the natural ones which they were lucky enough to find within their territory); and it means that states can, if they wish, give nothing at all without moral reproach.

Furthermore, the humanitarian model strengthens power imbalances between rich and poor states by allowing rich states to place conditions on their aid. For example, recipient states are often required to pay substantial interest on loans that they are offered, and aid money from organizations like the IMF and the World Bank is often conditional upon recipient states introducing free market reforms. Often, poor states are forced to choose between accepting these conditions or losing the much-needed aid entirely.

In applying Rawlsian liberalism at a global level, cosmopolitan liberals like Thomas Pogge, Charles Beitz and Brian Barry offer a much more radical approach. Placing national identity behind the veil of ignorance has profound implications for international justice and the relations between states: it means that Rawls's two principles of justice are applicable *at a global level*. States are not simply left to decide for themselves how many of their resources they will give to poorer states, rather they must redistribute their resources in accordance with the two principles of justice. Just as individuals in a Rawlsian scheme are not entitled to benefit from talents that they acquired by luck, so states are not entitled to benefit from the natural resources that they were lucky enough to discover on the land they happen to inhabit. Conversely, states that do not happen to possess valuable national resources should not suffer unfair hardships.

So cosmopolitanism rejects the voluntaristic basis for the humanitarian model, and rejects the claim that international obligations of justice cannot exist. Instead it argues for the establishment of a global system of redistribution whereby rich states redistribute resources according to something like a global difference principle. As such, cosmopolitanism rejects the idea that states should have sovereignty over matters of international justice and calls instead for states to be forced to comply with the principles of justice that would be agreed upon in a global original position. Principles of justice act as constraints upon the pursuit of self-interested ends by *states* at the *global* level just as they act as constraints upon the pursuit of self-interested ends by *individuals* at the *domestic* level. In the realm of economic redistribution, their relations with other states, and their treatment of their citizens, then, states in a cosmopolitan system would be required to constrain their actions in accordance with liberal principles, and to respect the freedom and equality of all individuals.

Conclusion

There is, of course, a lot more to be said on this issue. Not all liberals are cosmopolitans, for example. And not all cosmopolitans are liberals (some, like Peter Singer, are utilitarians). And not all cosmopolitan liberals commit to Rawls's difference principle. Indeed, although many cosmopolitans use Rawls's work to justify global principles of justice, Rawls himself rejected cosmopolitanism!

Nonetheless, we hope to have done enough here to reveal some of the complexities, and the importance, of the debate concerning the relations between states. These debates between universalist cosmopolitans and particularists are of profound importance. They matter philosophically, and the political implications of the debate affect each and every person on the planet.

Key ideas

Cosmopolitanism: The normative position, held by many universalist liberals and utilitarians, that individual human beings are the basic subjects of philosophical reflection on questions of global justice, and that the wellbeing of individuals cannot be trumped by the wellbeing of groups, communities or nations.

Globalization: The claim that people and countries of the world are becoming increasingly connected and interdependent.

Particularism: The idea, associated with a communitarian conception of identity and politics, that moral rules originate in the shared values of the community and that, therefore, no universal standards of morality are possible.

Sovereignty: The idea, embodied in current international law and politics, that nation-states should, as far as possible, be left alone to manage their own internal affairs free from external interference.

Universalism: The idea that moral statements hold true for all people, and not just for members of particular communities.

Dig deeper

Brian Barry, 'Statism and Nationalism: A Cosmopolitan Critique', in Ian Shapiro and Lea Brilmeyer (eds), *Global Justice* (New York: New York University Press, 1999).

Charles Beitz, *Political Theory and International Relations* (Princeton, NJ: Princeton University Press, 1979).

David Miller, *On Nationality* (Oxford: Oxford University Press, 1995).

Thomas Pogge, *World Poverty and Human Rights: Cosmopolitan Responsibilities and Reforms*, 2nd edn (Cambridge: Polity, 2008).

Thomas Pogge, *Politics as Usual: What Lies Behind the Pro-Poor Rhetoric* (Cambridge: Polity, 2010).

John Rawls, *The Law of Peoples* (Cambridge, MA: Harvard University Press, 1999).

Joseph Raz and Avishai Margalit, 'National Self-Determination', *Ethics in the Public Domain: Essays in the Morality of Law and Politics* (Oxford: Clarendon Press, 1994), pp. 125–145.

Peter Singer, 'Famine, Affluence, and Morality', *Philosophy and Public Affairs* 1 (1972), pp. 229–43.

Yael Tamir, *Liberal Nationalism* (Princeton, NJ: Princeton University Press, 1995).

Kok Chor-Tan, *Justice without Borders: Cosmopolitanism, Nationalism, and Patriotism* (Cambridge: Cambridge University Press, 2004).

Michael Walzer, *Spheres of Justice: A Defence of Pluralism and Equality* (New York: Basic Books, 1983).

Fact-check

1 What is statism?
- **A** The claim that global politics is static
- **B** The claim that states have a duty to bring about global justice
- **C** The claim that states should have sovereignty
- **D** The claim that states are increasingly interdependent

2 What is cosmopolitanism?
- **A** The claim that global politics is static
- **B** The claim that states have a duty to bring about global justice
- **C** The claim that states should have sovereignty
- **D** The claim that states are increasingly interdependent

3 What is globalization?
- **A** The claim that global politics is static
- **B** The claim that states have a duty to bring about global justice
- **C** The claim that states should have sovereignty
- **D** The claim that states are increasingly interdependent

4 What is particularism?
- **A** The claim that moral principles are particular in scope
- **B** The claim that moral principles are not particular in scope
- **C** The claim that moral principles are particularly important
- **D** The claim that moral principles are not particularly important

5 What is universalism?
- **A** The claim that statism is universal
- **B** The claim that all states should have equal rights
- **C** The claim that all people should have equal rights
- **D** The claim that globalization is universal

6 Which of the following best describes the existing international order?
- **A** Statist
- **B** Universalist
- **C** Cosmopolitan
- **D** All of the above

7 Which of the following are not compatible with cosmopolitanism?

   A Globalization

   B Universalism

   C Global redistribution

   D Statism

8 What is state sovereignty?

   A The idea that states should have monarchs

   B The idea that states should be left to themselves

   C The idea that states should be democratic

   D The idea that states should help the global poor

9 Which of the following defends the most extensive duties to help the global poor?

   A Peter Singer

   B David Miller

   C Thomas Pogge

   D Robert Nozick

10 Which of the following argues for a global difference principle?

   A John Rawls

   B Peter Singer

   C Charles Beitz

   D Robert Nozick

19

Intergenerational justice

As concerns about the environment continue to grow among scientists, activists and politicians, political philosophers have increasingly asked questions about the kind of obligations of justice which may or may not exist between generations. Do we have moral obligations to future generations? Do currently living people have obligations toward people who do not yet exist? If so, what kind of obligations could these possibly be?

It is very difficult to ground such obligations in any philosophically rigorous way, and it is especially difficult to generate obligations toward future generations within a traditional liberal egalitarian normative framework. How can liberalism, premised upon the fundamental assumption that everyone should be able to live a life that they believe to be worthwhile and which they have chosen for themselves, remain compatible with the idea that present generations should be forced to constrain the pursuit of their own ways of life in the interests of securing the same right for people who do not live, and who may not live for 100, 1000 or 1,000,000 years?

And what about previous generations? Do states and currently living individuals that have benefited from past oppression have a moral responsibility to rectify these historical injustices? Does the current US government have a moral obligation to compensate today's native Americans for the seizure of their ancestors' land? Do the Canadian or Australian people owe a debt of justice to the descendants of those aboriginal peoples who the first white settlers slaughtered or expelled from their land?

In order for claims of historical injustice to make sense, we have to understand people as members of distinct historical communities whose descendants bear the consequences (or enjoy the benefits) of acts committed by different people in the past. Actions have moral implications which are held to apply across generations and not just to the people who engage in them. This was precisely the area of tension at the heart of one form of intergenerational justice in particular, affirmative action, which we discussed in Chapter 4. Defenders of affirmative action argue that people living *now* have a moral obligation to rectify injustices suffered by people *in the past*. But claims about affirmative action are, as we saw, controversial and complex, partly because they seem to violate the wider liberal concern for *individuals* by understanding people as bearers of a particular historical identity which they share with people in the past.

Debates about intergenerational justice thus problematize many of our assumptions about equality, freedom, obligation, and the nature of duty. As we have covered some of the issues concerning historical injustice in our discussions about equality, we focus in this chapter on the issue of what obligations *current* generations have toward *future* generations.

'Distributive justice among contemporaries and within the boundaries of a state has been at the centre of the dramatic revival of political philosophy in the last quarter century. Extending the inquiry into the nature of distributive justice beyond these is a natural and inevitable development. But I think that there is also something to offer to those who are not interested in pursuing these questions for their own sake.

> *It is surely at least something to be able to assure those who*
> *spend their days trying to improve the prospects of future*
> *generations that such measures do not represent optional*
> *benevolence on our part but are demanded by elementary*
> *considerations of justice... [T]he application of ideas about*
> *justice that are quite familiar in other contexts have radical*
> *implications when applied to intergenerational justice, and...*
> *there is no reason why they should not be.'*
>
> Brian Barry, 'Sustainability and Intergenerational Justice', *Theoria* 45/89
> (1997), pp. 43–65, at pp. 64–5.

Spotlight: Baby-boomers

In his book about intergenerational justice, the UK government minister David Willetts argues that British 'baby-boomers', those born just after World War II, are disproportionately well-off. For example, people born between 1956 and 1961 will receive more from the welfare state than they have paid in (118 per cent) since they have benefitted from measures such as universal state pensions, free NHS prescriptions, and free university tuition and maintenance.

Utilitarianism and the 'repugnant conclusion'

In his book *Reasons and Persons* (1984) Derek Parfit suggests that neither liberalism nor utilitarianism, the two dominant approaches to understanding morality and ethics, are particularly well-suited to dealing with intergenerational justice. Take utilitarianism, for example. Parfit argues that utilitarianism cannot secure justice for future generations and actually results in what he calls the 'repugnant conclusion'. The general idea is this: the utilitarian maxim that we are morally required to create the 'greatest happiness for the greatest number' encourages us to create an enormous population of not very happy people.

Parfit points out that utilitarianism is concerned to create the greatest aggregate welfare *overall*, not to secure the greatest welfare for *each and every individual*. The implications of this are very significant. Imagine that we rank quality of life on a 1 to 10 scale, where 1 represents the worst quality of life imaginable and 10 represents the best. Now imagine two societies. One has a population of 10,000, with each individual member having a quality of life rated at 8, which is very high indeed. That society has an aggregate welfare score of 80,000. The other society has a population of 100,000,000, but each individual has a quality of life rated at 1, the lowest it can possibly be. This second society has an aggregate welfare score of 100,000,000, far in excess of the first. So on utilitarian grounds the second society is best. It does not matter to the utilitarian that members of the first society are healthy, have access to clean drinking water, good public services, literature, music, live in a democracy and so on, while members of the second society are malnourished, unhealthy, and live in a corrupt and tyrannical society which terrifies and oppresses them. The point is not how much welfare each individual has, but how much the society has *as a whole*. The 'repugnant conclusion' that utilitarians are led to when considering the question of intergenerational justice, therefore, is that we would do best from a moral point of view to deliberately increase the future population of the world as much as possible, even if in doing so we condemn the individual members of that world to terrible lives.

Liberalism and 'person-affecting' moralities

Parfit argues that liberalism also faces problems when dealing with future generations. We will discuss Parfit's argument first, in the context of wider debates about intergenerational justice, before discussing a broader set of concerns in the latter half of this section.

OBLIGATIONS TO WHOM?

Morality creates obligations. If it is morally wrong to deliberately harm another person, then I have a moral *obligation* not to harm another person. If it is morally wrong for a state to imprison its citizens without trial, then the state has a moral *obligation* not to imprison its citizens without trial.

Obligations are *relational*. They define what one individual, group or entity (like the state) can or should do with regard to another individual, group or entity: *I* have an obligation to *you*, the *state* has an obligation to its *citizens*, and so on. Furthermore, if I fail to fulfil my obligations to you (for example, by deliberately harming you) then I have acted immorally and, hence, am appropriately liable to be criticized and, in certain circumstances, punished.

But what if I do something which will not harm anyone who is currently living, but which is likely to harm people who will live in the future? Who am I harming by driving a gas-guzzling SUV which pumps out vast amounts of petrol fumes? Who am I harming if I refuse to recycle my rubbish, or refuse to reduce the number of long-haul flights I take? The harm caused to current generations by these acts is negligible. The real costs of these actions will be borne by future generations, that is, people who do not yet exist. But how can we be said to have obligations to people who do not exist?

Parfit argues that 'person-affecting' moralities based on ideas like harm or rights cannot deal easily with intergenerational moral claims precisely because in such claims no person is being affected. I cannot harm someone who does not exist, nor can I violate their rights. Remember, the question is not just what moral claims we have to the *next* generation, i.e. to existing children. The problem at hand is what obligations we have, if any, to people who do not currently exist and who may not exist for hundreds of years.

The question is not just a matter of abstract philosophy. It is also at the heart of contemporary debates about environmental policy. Take the question of whether Britain should increase its reliance on nuclear power, for example. Your position on this question will depend largely on how far into the future you think we should look when contemplating obligations to future people. Defenders of nuclear power argue that it is the least environmentally damaging way of generating the power that we need: it produces comparatively low levels of greenhouse gases and, hence, contributes far less to climate change than more traditional forms of energy production, while remaining far more productive and efficient than other forms of renewable energy like wind or solar power. Critics, however, point out that nuclear power produces toxic waste which cannot be destroyed and which remains lethal for up to 240,000 years (in the case of plutonium-239). All this waste needs to go somewhere, they argue, and at some point we will run out of places to put it, leaving future generations with the terrible problem of what to do with these deadly chemicals. So the question is: do we prioritize the needs of the not-too-distant future generations, adopt nuclear power, and not concern ourselves with the terrible problem we are causing for the people who come later? Or do we prioritize the needs of more-distant future people, reject nuclear power, and adopt instead forms of energy production which are less efficient and more harmful to the environment in the shorter term?

The philosophical issue is not so much *what* we should decide about issues like this, but *how* we should decide. First, we need to know how to weigh the needs of actually existing people with the needs of future people. This in itself is very philosophically complex, for the reasons alluded to in the introduction to this chapter. Liberal societies are premised on the idea that individuals should be able to pursue their own conception of the good without coercion. But this view seems incompatible with the idea that individuals should be radically constrained in the kinds of lives they can lead in order to protect the interests of people who will exist in the future. If I want to lead a life which includes driving a classic car even though it belches out petrol fumes, or if I want to replace my mobile phone for the newer version every year even though this is incredibly wasteful, or if I want to eat strawberries or bananas all year round even though this means having them flown to my local supermarket from across the world, then surely a liberal system should protect my ability to do so. Obviously, I should not do things which directly harm others but beyond that I should be free to make my own choices and to live the life that I wish. However, it is precisely this kind of individualist, consumerist approach which, according to environmentalists, has resulted in the degradation of the environment and placed future generations in such peril. Taking seriously the needs of future generations seems to require radical constraint of the lifestyles that many individuals throughout the world continue to choose. Coercion on such a scale needs to be justified and, in a liberal system, it needs to be justified in person-affecting terms (e.g. harm) which, as Parfit has pointed out, is very difficult.

THE FATE AND IDENTITY OF FUTURE PEOPLE

One possible response to the problem of obligations is this: although we do not know *exactly* who will exist in the future, we nevertheless know that *some people* will exist. And we know that these people (whoever they are) will need certain things like clean air, drinking water, and so on.

However, this argument leads to yet another set of problems. Decisions made by currently living people not only affect the *number* of people that exist in the future, their *health*, and the kind of *lives* they are able to live, but also (1) precisely who exists in the future, and (2) whether or not anyone exists at all. Let us discuss these claims in turn.

(1) Exactly who has a right to exist in the future?

Choices about who to have children with, and when to conceive, determine precisely which humans are created. In choosing to have a child with person A rather than person B, I bring about the child produced by myself and A, and deny forever the existence of the child that would have been produced by myself and B. Furthermore, in conceiving a child with A *today* I bring about the existence of a completely different child to the one that I would have brought about had A and I conceived it next week, next month, or next year – or even one minute later. The chance of any given sperm meeting any given egg, so as to create any specific human, are minute. None of us would exist if anything in the past had been different.

Parfit suggests that this fact has profound implications for intergenerational justice as it leads to what he calls the 'non-identity problem'. The non-identity problem is that we cannot meaningfully say that any of our actions *harm* future people because the future people in question owe their very existence to our actions. For example, imagine we choose to deplete rather than conserve the Earth's resources. The people who come several generations after us will have difficult lives in that depleted world. However, we can only say that we have *harmed* those people if it is possible to imagine a world in which *those same people* were not forced to live under the conditions that we have created. But there is no alternative world in which these same people exist but in better circumstances, because every different action today affects who is born in the future.

So, the effect of choosing differently (for example, to conserve rather than deplete the Earth's resources) would not have saved the 'harmed' future people from being harmed. Rather, it would have simply denied them existence and created different people instead. The normative upshot of the non-identity problem, Parfit argues, is that we cannot coherently apply notions like harm in an intergenerational context.

(2) Do future generations have a right to exist at all?

Earlier we assumed that some people will come after us, even if we cannot know exactly who they will be, so we can consider the idea that we might have obligations to those people. But future generations will only exist if current generations create them. It would be entirely possible for no future generations to be brought into existence. So, do we have a duty to ensure that future people live? Or, to put it the other way, do non-living people have a right to be brought into existence?

The idea that we do not have a moral responsibility to perpetuate the existence of the human race is perhaps counter-intuitive. But it is an important question to ask once we have realized that the existence of future generations is itself the consequence of a collective decision by the current generation. If environmentalists and others are right that future generations will suffer profound hardships as a result of the degradation of the environment, why not solve the problem by ensuring that there are no future generations? That way, members of the current generation could live as they please, even if this includes activities devastating to the environment, without having to worry that they are harming anyone or infringing anyone's rights. Indeed, if the environment has already been degraded to such an extent that even radical action would make little difference to the plight of future generations, perhaps we should limit the number of future people who have to live under such unpleasant conditions. Until recently, the Chinese 'one child policy' prevented many married couples from having more than one child so as to limit population growth. Is this a good policy? Should we in fact go further and ban people from having children completely on the grounds that bringing a child into a world which we know is already irreversibly damaged is an immoral act?

Spotlight: Better never to have been?

In his book *Better Never to Have Been*, David Benatar argues that it is wrong to bring people into existence. This is because people are *not* harmed by *not* being brought into existence – you cannot harm someone who does not exist – whereas people who are brought into existence suffer in all sorts of ways, ranging from serious harms such as pain and disease to everyday annoyances such as hunger or tiredness. On balance, then, it is better not to create someone since then there is no risk of harm.

There are many competing considerations, such as the wellbeing of existing people and their rights to reproduction, bodily integrity and privacy. But the important point is that the very question of whether or not there should *be* future people is something that we can reflect upon philosophically.

A liberal response: Rawls's 'just savings principle'

Can we find a liberal answer to problems of intergenerational justice? The problem for critics worried about intergenerational justice is that liberalism is deliberately *ahistorical*. This, after all, is the main reason why liberalism is rejected by conservative and communitarian thinkers: liberal morality is derived from hypothetical agreements made by rational individuals who are specifically stripped of any aspect of themselves which might identify them as a person located in a particular generation, or who lives in a particular historical community. There is, in the original position, no past or future. There are just the abstract individuals with whom we happen to be deliberating. We do not know where we or anyone else comes from, we do not know when we are living or when this conversation is taking place, and so on. In such a circumstance, we cannot reflect upon the requirements of justice for past or future generations because all the information that we would need in order to do so is placed behind the veil of ignorance. Thus, communitarians and conservative thinkers reject liberalism as a way of determining moral obligations and look instead to the morals arising out of one's membership of various *historical* communities (e.g. nation, culture, etc.).

'[G]enerations are not subordinate to one another any more than individuals are. The life of a people is conceived as a scheme of cooperation spread out in historical time. It is to be governed by the same conception of justice that regulates the cooperation of contemporaries. No generation has stronger claims than any other... [P]ersons in different generations have duties and obligations to one another just as contemporaries do. The present generation cannot do as it pleases but is bound by the principles that would be chosen in the original position to define justice between persons at different moments of time... The derivation of these duties and obligations may seem at first a somewhat farfetched application of the contract doctrine. Nevertheless, these requirements would be acknowledged in the original position, and so the conception of justice as fairness covers these matters without any change in its basic idea.'

John Rawls, *A Theory of Justice* (Cambridge, MA: Harvard University Press, 1971), pp. 291–3.

Liberals, on the other hand, have suggested that abstract reasoning is perfectly suited to dealing with intergenerational concerns. As we saw in our discussion of affirmative action, it is precisely the fact that deliberators in the original position are not understood as located in any particular historical group that allows them to reflect appropriately about, for example, the just response to claims of historical oppression. Deliberators in the original position are not banned from discussing the importance of identity, or whether justice requires rectifying past injustices suffered by certain groups. They are only banned from knowing whether *they* are members of that group. Thus, the agreements they strike will deal with historical injustice, but they will do so in ways which ensure against mere self-interest.

Rawls makes a similar claim about future generations. The original position can deal with intergenerational justice because in it no one knows which generation they are a part of (or, to put it in Rawlsian terms, what stage of development the economy has reached). This information is behind the veil of ignorance. So, Rawls argues, parties in the original position would not decide that one particular generation or group could consume all the world's resources, leaving none for those who come after them, because they might be members of that later generation. Thus people in the original position would agree that everyone should constrain their own consumption of the Earth's resources and put some aside for future generations. Rawls calls this the 'just savings principle': liberal justice requires that currently living individuals constrain the pursuit of their conception of the good in order that they leave sufficient resources for future generations to live worthwhile lives.

Rawls does not stipulate the 'just savings rate' (that is, how much of the Earth's resources should be kept back). Hence, he does not answer the difficult question of exactly *how much* individuals might be required to constrain their pursuit of their conception of the good. Nevertheless, he does offer a response to at least the first criticism made above: he argues that the liberal state is justified in imposing constraints upon individuals in the pursuit of their particular conception of the good because these constraints would be agreed by parties in the original position. The constraints are therefore *fair* and, hence, consistent with individual freedom.

Case study: The moral status of children

The principal focus of this chapter has been to discuss intergenerational justice in the context of what obligations, if any, currently living people have with regard to future people. But there are also important questions to be asked about the obligations of justice that exist between different generations that exist at the same time.

The most obvious example is the moral status of children and, specifically, what obligations adults have with regard to children. Liberalism has historically found the status of children rather problematic. Liberals hold a conception of the individual as free, equal and rational. They believe that no individuals should have a life forced upon them by others, and they also believe that power only has authority if has been, or could be, consented to by those subject to it. The fact that children, especially very young children, are neither free nor able to consent to the forms of authority under which they live is problematic, then.

For example, we might think that children have rights. But this is problematic if we believe that rights are grounded in some particular human quality like reason or autonomy – qualities which children do not straightforwardly possess. We do not generally think that children should be allowed to opt out of going to school even if they have a strong preference for doing so, and most liberal democratic states deny children certain basic civil rights (like voting).

The general view among liberals is that it is right to treat people below a certain threshold age differently to people above that age because children are not yet rational, autonomous choosers. They need to have the benefit of skills, abilities and experience before they are capable of making a genuinely reflective judgement about who they want to be and what kind of life they want to lead. Children need education, then, in the broadest sense, in order that they become the kind of rational autonomous individuals that the liberal system requires. Hence, we think that it is right that, for example, the state coerces children into getting an education, and that they and their parents are appropriately liable for punishment should they not attend school.

But this common view only leads to further problems. For example, it states that the ability to reason appropriately about the world, about who should govern us, and about what kind of life someone wants to lead are all dependent upon the possession of certain abilities, skills or knowledge which are thought to be sufficiently acquired by, say, the age of 16, or perhaps 18. But this is controversial, as it ignores the obvious fact that many under-18s will be in a position to make a more informed decision about many aspects of their lives than many over-18s. For example, in Britain adult citizens who suffer severe learning and other mental disabilities are entitled to vote but no under-18, regardless of their cognitive abilities or intelligence, is allowed to do so. It is not obvious that this policy should stand *if we accept that the right to vote is contingent upon the possession of certain cognitive faculties.*

More generally, however, the idea that we should deny children certain political rights in this way seems to violate a wider assumption in liberalism that access to civil or political rights of one kind or another should *not* depend upon particular capacities or knowledge, but should instead be *universal*. The idea that basic rights should be possessed only by people with the right skills or abilities is generally rejected by liberals in favour of universal rights and freedoms possessed by all. After all, the claim that some people and not others are able to exercise rights and freedoms has historically been used to exclude women, black people, aboriginal peoples and other 'minorities' from public life, and to deny them equal political or moral status. But if we cannot legitimately deny adults moral equality on the grounds that they lack relevant qualities or faculties why can we systematically deny such status to all children?

Conclusion

This chapter has introduced some of the challenges that arise when we subject widespread assumptions about our obligations to future generations to philosophical scrutiny. There are other, more recent, liberal interventions into this debate, and there is much more to be said about, for example, the non-identity problem, utilitarian approaches to intergenerational justice, and intergenerational harm. However, this chapter, just like this whole book, is aimed at encouraging you to reflect upon the assumptions implicit in public discourse about justice and politics, and to form your own opinions in the light of their complexity.

Key ideas

The repugnant conclusion: The conclusion necessarily drawn by utilitarians that the greatest *overall* utility in the future is created by radically increasing the general population, thus dramatically reducing the utility experienced by each and every *individual*. Argument made by Derek Parfit.

Non-identity problem: Identified by Derek Parfit, the problem posed for our moral theorizing about intergenerational justice and morality by the fact that the choices of current generations determine the identity of the people who are born in the future.

Person-affecting moralities: The idea that morality imposes obligations between individuals and that, therefore, person-affecting moral systems are incapable of dealing coherently with the moral claims of future generations because obligations cannot exist between people who exist and people who do not.

Just savings principle: The idea, suggested by Rawls, that parties in the original position would rationally agree to constrain their pursuit of their conception of the good in order to ensure that future generations have access to sufficient resources to live free and worthwhile lives.

Dig deeper

Brian Barry, *A Treatise on Social Justice, Part 1: Theories of Justice* (Hertfordshire: Harvester-Wheatsheaf, 1989).

David Benatar, *Better Never to Have Been: The Harm of Coming into Existence* (Oxford: Oxford University Press, 2008).

Andrew Dobson (ed.), *Fairness and Futurity: Essays on Environmental Sustainablility* (Oxford: Oxford University Press, 1999).

Stephen M. Gardiner, Simon Caney, Dale Jamieson and Henry Shue (eds), *Climate Ethics* (New York: Oxford University Press, 2010).

Peter Laslett and James S. Fishkin (eds), *Justice between Age Groups and Generations* (London: Yale University Press, 1992).

Derek Parfit, *Reasons and Persons* (Oxford: Clarendon Press, 1984).

David Willetts, *The Pinch: How the Baby-Boomers Took Their Children's Future – And Why They Should Give It Back* (London: Atlantic, 2010).

Fact-check

1 Who first wrote about the 'repugnant conclusion'?
- **A** John Rawls
- **B** John Locke
- **C** David Parfit
- **D** Derek Parfit

2 What is the repugnant conclusion?
- **A** Utilitarianism advocates making miserable people
- **B** Utilitarianism advocates making people miserable
- **C** Liberalism advocates making miserable people
- **D** Liberalism advocates making people miserable

3 Why, according to Parfit, does liberalism find intergenerational justice problematic?
- **A** Because liberalism is a person-affecting morality
- **B** Because there are no existing people currently being harmed
- **C** Because obligations are relational
- **D** All of the above

4 Why is it harder to account for our duties to future people than our duties to currently living people?
- **A** Because future people do not vote
- **B** Because future people may not care about the environment
- **C** Because future people may not exist
- **D** Because future people are not autonomous

5 'We should care about climate change because climate change harms future generations.' What is wrong with this argument, philosophically?
- **A** We cannot harm people who do not yet exist
- **B** Climate change may not happen
- **C** Future generations may be selfish too
- **D** All of the above

6 Why is it difficult to have a legitimate and philosophically rigorous complaint against your ancestors?
- **A** Because if they had done anything differently you would not exist

B Because you should be grateful for the sacrifices of previous generations

C Because it is good to respect your elders

D Because they didn't know better

7 What is the name of Rawls's form of intergenerational justice?

   A The difference principle

   B The just savings principle

   C The repugnant conclusion

   D The person-affecting claim

8 What is Rawls's claim about intergenerational justice?

   A That existing generations should be completely free to pursue their conception of the good

   B That resources should be distributed so as to maximize the position of the worst-off generation

   C That every generation should preserve sufficient resources for future generations to live worthwhile lives

   D All of the above

9 How can a liberal justify denying children the vote?

   A Children lack the necessary autonomy

   B Children are not yet rational

   C Children do not understand politics

   D All of the above

10 What is the strongest argument against the liberal claim in Question 9?

   A The same things can be said of many adults

   B Many children want to vote

   C Voting is not very important

   D Children should have a say in politics

Index

Answers

CHAPTER 1
1 D
2 B
3 C
4 A
5 C
6 D
7 A
8 C
9 A
10 D

CHAPTER 2
1 C
2 D
3 C
4 D
5 A
6 A
7 C
8 D
9 B
10 D

CHAPTER 3
1 A
2 B
3 D
4 C
5 B

6 D
7 A
8 D
9 B
10 D

CHAPTER 4
1 D
2 A
3 C
4 B
5 C
6 B
7 D
8 B
9 A
10 C

CHAPTER 5
1 C
2 A
3 B
4 A
5 C
6 B
7 A
8 B
9 D
10 A

CHAPTER 6
1 A
2 C
3 D
4 D
5 C
6 B
7 C
8 D
9 A
10 D

CHAPTER 7
1 C
2 D
3 B
4 D
5 A
6 D
7 A
8 D
9 A
10 C

CHAPTER 8
1 C
2 D
3 A
4 D
5 B

6 A
7 B
8 C
9 D
10 D

CHAPTER 9
1 C
2 B
3 A
4 C
5 B
6 D
7 D
8 A
9 C
10 A

CHAPTER 10
1 C
2 A
3 D
4 D
5 A
6 C
7 B
8 A
9 D
10 A

CHAPTER 11
1 A
2 B
3 C
4 B
5 A
6 D
7 A
8 D
9 C
10 B

CHAPTER 12
1 D
2 C
3 D
4 C
5 B
6 B
7 B
8 A?
9 D
10 D

CHAPTER 13
1 D
2 D

3 A
4 B
5 A
6 A
7 D
8 D
9 B
10 D

CHAPTER 14
1 D
2 A
3 B
4 A
5 C
6 A
7 B
8 D
9 A
10 D

CHAPTER 15
1 B
2 A
3 D
4 D
5 D

6 D
7 A
8 B
9 D
10 B

CHAPTER 16
1 B
2 D
3 A
4 C
5 A
6 A
7 C
8 C
9 C
10 B

CHAPTER 17
1 D
2 D
3 A
4 D
5 B
6 C
7 B
8 D

9 C
10 B

CHAPTER 18
1 C
2 B
3 D
4 A
5 C
6 A
7 D
8 B
9 A
10 C

CHAPTER 19
1 D
2 A
3 D
4 C
5 A
6 A
7 B
8 C
9 D
10 A